PAYBACK TIME!

AMERICA'S VETERANS UNITE TO CHALLENGE VA FOR OVERDUE BENEFITS

BY
EARL "DUSTY" TRIMMER

LIBERTY HILL
PUBLISHING

PAYBACK TIME!
America's Veterans Unite to Challenge VA for Overdue Benefits
by Earl "Dusty" Trimmer

Printed in the United States of America.

ISBN 9781498429764

www.LibertyHillPublishing.com

TABLE OF CONTENTS

PREFACE

ONCE UPON A TIME AND A LONG TIME AGO, IT WAS A COOL THING TO
BURN DRAFT CARDS AS WELL AS AMERICAN FLAGS OR TO RETREAT
TO CANADA TO AVOID CONSCRIPTION INTO THE ARMED FORCES. AT
THE SAME TIME, THERE WERE THREE MILLION AMERICAN PATRIOTS
WHO REMAINED LOYAL AND BRAVE TO ANSWER AMERICA'S CALL
TO CONTINUE THE FIGHT AGAINST COMMUNISM IN FAR-OFF PLACES
CALLED CAMBODIA, LAOS, THAILAND AND…VIETNAM. THIS WAS
A TIME WHEN IT WAS MORE POPULAR NOT TO GO…THEY WENT
ANYWAY! **GOD BLESS AMERICA'S VIETNAM WAR ERA VETERANS!**

As B.G. Burkett stated in his 1998 classic, *Stolen Valor*, "The men and women of
the Vietnam War deserved more than America was willing to give them." Almost
five decades later, the Vietnam War, which haunts many of its surviving warriors
to this day, still sets off passion within their close brotherhood and sisterhood.
The author of *Payback Time!* and *Condemned Property?*, his first book in 2013,
attempts to discredit the negative rumors and myths about the warriors of the
Vietnam War who have been horribly ravaged during and after the war by the
media. This author shows how the Vietnam War era's participants were some of
the most gallant and patriotic warriors America has ever produced, despite the
abysmal living conditions in a war that was in the twilight zone.

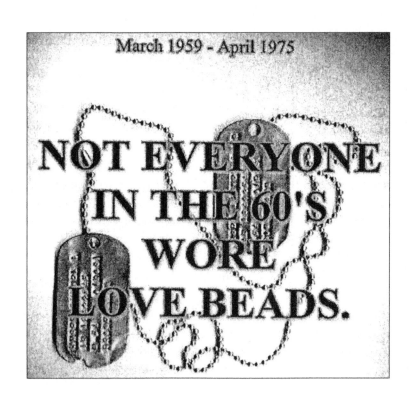

OPENING STATEMENT...
DEDICATION...

O n the cover of this book is a 1988 picture of six combat Vietnam War veterans. Four of them were wounded in Vietnam. Three of them are deceased or whereabouts unknown. I (author) fought side by side in-country with three of the men in this picture. The three of us who remain alive also remain best friends and brothers, united to keep the memory of our fallen war buddies living and...to stand up and challenge the Department of Veterans Affairs for the long overdue benefits they earned and deserve.

The primary reason for this book and my first book, *Condemned Property?*, is to bring awareness to America about our wounded in action (WIA), killed in action (KIA), missing in action (MIA), the plight of those veterans who are still living or those who have lost their battles to survive after coming home, and those veterans...still struggling to live another day.

In the Vietnam War, and maybe in our most recent wars, we never had time to grieve over our fallen war buddies. They were gone just like that, and the next day we had to greet the replacements and...welcome them to Nam! Then, we had to start all over with them—we had to. So today, we grieve every day for those guys...for the rest of our lives. The anger never goes away, not completely. The guilt continues (I made it—he didn't. Why?), and the feelings of betrayal continue on for us to our graves. Many of those who die prematurely take their untold stories with them, never to be told, and that is one of the worst tragedies of the Vietnam War's future legacy.

Over there, in Vietnam, Korea, Iraq or Afghanistan, we had to deal with things that were far beyond what an average person could cope with. Back here, many of these warriors are still dealing with their wounds from a war that lives on inside of them.

On the following page, you will read a news release about my first book, which released in December 2013. *Payback Time!* is a continuation of that book about the Vietnam War veterans' story, a story that has no foreseeable end. As I did in my first book, I have jumped around a bit mainly because I have tried to tie current happenings into the story, which may connect with something that did happen during the Vietnam War era or…did not happen, but should have.

One day, in a far-off land, very young warriors, mostly Americans, fought and died for reasons that were criminal. If we who participated and survived that war do not speak of it, others will (and they will) tell an untruthful story of that war's happenings and how they perceive it ended. This is cruel. And sometimes, after America sends its military off to fight for their country, they are forgotten by those who sent them and by those they were sent to risk their lives for. This is a painful feeling for the returning warriors that can inflict as much "permanent" psychological damage as the actual war itself.

In the Epilogue near the end of *Condemned Property?*, I made the following statement…**I would like to believe that this book will make a difference in someone's life, and that will be my "payback" to those who violated us during and after the Vietnam War.** The effect it has made has exceeded my wildest expectations, and this has provided the motivation and the reasons to write my second book.

Payback Time! is dedicated to every veteran of any war — those who fought and died in battle, those who found themselves in another war back home and died prematurely and those who still find themselves in a day-to-day seemingly never-ending battle to stay alive one more day, often without help.

Payback Time! is not a story of revenge or vengeance. Rather…it is sometimes a combination of short stories of actual happenings blended into a heartwarming story about America's war heroes, led by Vietnam Era veterans, who have begun to fight back with VA for long-overdue heath care benefits. However, the author does get some shots in, aimed point blank at those who have been the main culprits for turning many of America's warriors into…**endangered species.**

Even today, Vietnam War veterans suffer terribly, as our brave warriors from recent wars do, when their minds wander back to that war, thinking of those youthful, smiling faces of our war buddies and then suddenly…**THEY WERE IN BODY BAGS!**

America has a moral obligation to comfort those who experienced the unthinkable horrors of killing in combat, and that what they did in their war was necessary…and right.

One of the saddest things about the Vietnam War is…it continues to kill so many who have struggled to survive it after they came home!

- Author Unknown

Author – 1968

AMBUSH: On June 15, 1968, a Viet Cong sniper's perfectly aimed shot sent a bullet that tore through the frontal top of my helmet, blowing out through the back, slightly grazing my head on its fatally intended path and sent my helmet flying into the air...landing ten feet away.

THIS BOOK...

CONDEMNED PROPERTY? Challenges America's Conscience, Makes Vietnam Veterans Stand Proud, Sends an "In Your Face" Warning to VA to...SHAPE UP!

Released: December 2013

Written from the heart and experiences of "Dusty" Earl Trimmer, *Condemned Property?* takes a raw and blunt look at the Vietnam War, its veterans and how the nation has let them down. Readers and reviewers are shocked to learn that the war's biggest battle wasn't fought in South-East Asia but is currently being waged against the Department of Veterans Affairs on home soil. In fact, rumors that some VA officials deliberately stalled claims until the Veteran has died, making the phrase **"Deny, Delay Till We Die"** commonplace among those who fought in Vietnam. Trimmer embarked on his mission to expose the system's mistreatment of Vietnam Veterans in his new memoir.

Kudos and positive reviews for the book have been plentiful and continue, as follows:

-- (October 2, 2014) – *The VVA Veteran*/Vietnam Veterans of America's editor, Mark Leepson stated, "Trimmer wrote the book to honor our fallen warriors during and after the Vietnam War, along with living warriors of that war who are still fighting demons."
-- (September 2014) – **Military Writers Society of America** named Dusty Earl Trimmer "Author of the Month" for his book, *Condemned Property?* for August 2014, announced in the MWSA *Dispatches*.
-- (August 2014) – **American Legion Post #383** Commander Thomas Gretchko, a Vietnam veteran ranger, endorsed *Condemned Property?* with these comments, "This may be one of the last great books written by an actual Vietnam War combat veteran, giving a voice for millions of veterans from all wars."
-- (July 2014) – **Combat Infantry Association/Ohio**, Chris Callen, Commander, awarded Dusty Trimmer with a Certificate of Appreciation for outstanding support to the Combat Infantrymen's Association. Callen gave kudos to Trimmer for promoting the rights of Vietnam veterans with his book.

-- (June 2014) – **Togetherweserved.com**, Michael Christy, editor review on *Condemned Property?:* "Dusty Trimmer served combat infantry duty with the 25th Infantry Division. In his first book, he presents staggering descriptions that cut to the heart of the combat experience: the fear and belligerence, the quiet insights and raging madness, the lasting friendships and sudden deaths. It is an account of veterans long after leaving battle, as they struggle with physical and emotional damage. The book differs from most Vietnam War tomes; it bears witness to the things men do in war and the things war does to men."

Barnes & Noble gives *Condemned Property?* a five-star rating and Amazon gives the book a 4.8 star rating thus far. It is available at Ingram, **Amazon.com, barnesandnoble.com, condemnedpropertybook.com**

ABOUT THE AUTHOR

E arl "Dusty" Trimmer here. I was a combat infantry soldier in the most unpopular and most forgettable war America has ever fought on foreign soil. *Payback Time!* is just the second book that I have authored. My first book, *Condemned Property?*, which launched in late 2013 and early 2014, was also about the Vietnam War and the Americans who came home from that war, wounded or in caskets.

My books tell the reader that I remain one very angry combat Vietnam War veteran, grateful to be living and one who is willing to fight again…this time for my condemned war buddies, *not* for America's insensitive, ungrateful politicians who have abandoned us time and time again. My battle plan is directed at those villains.

Since coming home from Vietnam in 1969, after risking our lives on a daily basis during consecutive Tet Offensives, it has been a painful experience for us to witness countless Vietnam veterans continue to die prematurely after they survived those horror-filled experiences in hell. Those of us who are still breathing today continue our daily battle to remain above ground, but our adversary is no longer the Viet Cong.

Here we are in the 2010s, not 1968, and every day, Vietnam veterans are still dying from ambushes from many different directions…all from within our own country, the same country where Vietnam veterans were trained and brainwashed to fight for…America. I used to be one of those Vietnam veterans who had given up, considered other alternatives than living out my life, having to battle the aftermath of Vietnam. Fortunately, something woke me up, and I decided to resume the fight.

Condemned Property?, published by Dogear Publishing, not only sold well; it impacted people. It received numerous positive reviews and endorsements from highly reputable sources just within the first few months after its publication, including The Combat Infantry Association, The American Legion, TogetherWeServed.com, Kirkus Reviews, BookDaily.com, The Military Writers Society of America, the Vietnam Veterans Association magazine (*VVA Veterans*), and thousands of Vietnam War veterans and non-veterans alike.

In *Condemned Property?* I mentioned at the beginning that there was no moral to its story and that its end…is not the end as it has not happened yet. The same holds true for *Payback Time!* The Vietnam War is not over; it is as relevant today as it was 30-50 years ago. Believe it. I believe that this book's message is important to every American who cares at all about America and its future because what has happened to us Vietnam War veterans is happening again to the veterans of recent wars.

I was advised to divide my first book into two books. Quickly, I figured out that this would take another six months or longer and I decided to just eliminate half the images, plus one very controversial chapter that directed criminal accusations at the Department of Veterans Affairs and their inexcusable and unforgiveable treatment of our country's heroes since the end of the Vietnam War. Little did I know back then that the VA scandal would explode onto the scene shortly after *Condemned Property?* hit the public.

One of my favorite chapters in *Condemned Property?* was titled "DENY, DELAY…TIL YOU DIE! That chapter offered a strong indictment of the VA's wrongdoings to veterans going back many years. I received several notes from celebrities like Pat Sajak, a Vietnam veteran himself, as well as a dozen members of Congress. I kept them all, and they helped motivate me to write…*Payback Time!* I have definitely continued with that same overwhelming passion in *Payback Time! Payback Time!* is more than just a sequel to my first book. It is an extension of that book's story, a continuation, if you will, of…*Condemned Property?*

Anyone reading either of my two books does not have to possess a "magnificent grasp for the obvious" as you will soon figure out. I am not a timid Vietnam War veteran. I remain very motivated and sometimes very angry when I think about the damage that has been done to many of our war veterans by the VA, the American politicians and America's people. Sometimes, standing by and looking the other way can be considered just as criminal as those who actually committed the crime.

Please know this. I have said this before, and I am saying it again right here. Nothing will ever compensate Vietnam veterans for what happened to them and their families. Nothing. Neither of my books are attempts to substitute or replace any of the historical books about the war in Vietnam. What I want people to get out of my books is just to know what really happened to us over there, the cover-ups, the defamation of what we did and the ongoing attempts by our government, including the Veterans Administration that continues to this day. **Enough is enough!**

Payback Time - (Dictionary Definition): A time for revenge or retaliation or just an occasion for repayment in kind for an act or deed, well intended or not.

PROLOGUE

It Begins!

In the summer of 1967, I received my Induction Notice from the United States Government informing me that I was being drafted into the U.S. Army. At that time, I was taking a summer break away from attending college full-time, but had planned to resume in the fall. That summer, I played Class A sandlot baseball, and I was pretty good too. In fact, around the time my draft notice arrived, our baseball coach informed me that there would be scouts from several major league teams at one our games and that I was one of the players they would come to watch. I was the team's starting centerfielder and their "cleanup" hitter, batting fourth. None of these would matter as my college days were over and so was my lifelong dream to play professional baseball. I turned in my uniform and left the team to prepare myself for my new career, which would be one of America's warriors known as a…**Combat Infantryman in the Vietnam War.**

Changing from a baseball uniform to a military uniform was only the first step of the brainwashing procedure that Uncle Sam had planned for me and tens of thousands of other good, young American men. During the first sixty to ninety days of my new training, the U.S. Army would pay me $18.92 per week or $82.00 per month, which comes out to $984.00 per year.

I had just recently traded in my 1955 Chevrolet for a 1967 Ford Falcon. I would never make my first payment, not on a set monthly income from the U.S. government that would barely pay for a lobster and steak dinner at today's prices. So, my parents were stuck with the Falcon and had to figure out what to do with it. I was on my way to Nam.

Many 25th Infantry veterans of the Vietnam War remember this date for the Tropic Lightning's official beginning of a scaled-up Vietnam War. It happened on March 21, 1967 at 6:30 a.m. A battle began near the Soui Tre River near the Cambodian border of South Vietnam. This battle would last "just" four hours, fifteen minutes; however, it would be unlike any other battle of the Vietnam "conflict" up to this date. This was a fierce, in-your-face, intensely sustained battle between 450 Americans and South Vietnamese soldiers against a much larger, very determined force of 2,500 hardened professionals from the Viet Cong Army. As one of Soui Tre's survivors, Mario Salazar once stated, "As our unit, the 2nd 22nd Mechanized of the 25th Infantry Division reached the scene of the battle between the 3rd 22nd and the Viet Cong, the scene that we witnessed was worthy of an outrageous Hollywood set."

When the 2nd 22nd arrived, Bravo of the 3rd 22nd was virtually out of ammunition, and bayonets were being fixed to use. It was like the cavalry in a western movie, riding in to rescue a surrounded wagon train. So indeed, Oliver Stone's famous movie *Platoon* was based on a composite of this battle and a later battle of similar size, which Stone fought in, called Soui Cut, fought on January 2, 1968 by the 25th Infantry's same units.

When Soui Tre was over, just before midnight on March 21, 1967, the total casualty list of the Vietnam War's biggest single-day battle looked like this:

Viet Cong Casualties:	647 KIA	1,500 WIA
American Casualties:	31 KIA	187 WIA

One of Soui Tre's survivors said this in 2014, some forty-six years after Soui Tre was fought:

"Since that battle in Vietnam, March has always been a tough month for me to get through. Forty-six years ago, my life changed forever, just as it did for others who fought and survived that night at Soui Tre."

–Ted Rowley, Chaplain
Bravo 3rd 22nd 25th Infantry
U.S. Army, Vietnam (1967-1968)

Ted and I talked for a couple hours in July 2014, right at the time I started writing *Payback Time!* "My life changed forever," Rowley said. Now, the Vietnam "conflict" was starting to be viewed as a real war, as America was compelled to step up its participation, and troop levels would reach their peak level in the following year of 1968. More Soui Tre's would take place, as 1968 would be known as the Tet Offensive year, the bloodiest year of the Vietnam "War". In fact, the Tet Year of 1968 alone would suffer more total casualties than America's next several wars combined.

May 9, 1959 is the official beginning of when Ho Chi Minh invaded South Vietnam nearly a decade before the Battle of Soui Tre when he ordered a massive exodus of more than twenty thousand North Vietnamese Regulars (NVA) and military equipment and supplies to travel south to what was called the Truong Son Road, also known as the Ho Chi Minh Trail. The move on this date is considered to be the opening move by North Vietnam to begin their war for the conquest all of Indochina. Remember the Domino Theory? This invasion took place two years before U.S. President Kennedy sent a mere six hundred eighty-five advisers to South Vietnam. It happened three years before U.S. Marines were sent to Da Nang and at least five years before the Gulf of Tonkin incident. This war to come would not be fought with any rules, at least not by the communists. In the People's War, as it was named by North Vietnam, there would be no civilians. Everyone would be considered as recruited and trained as a combatant. Children from ages seven to eleven became lookouts, carried grenades and were armed with weapons if they were chosen to do so. In 1959, the South Vietnamese reported that there were over seven hundred kidnappings and over four hundred assassinations—and 1959 was just the beginning.

This is just a little early background on how America's longest war in history really started and why it started. I have covered this in greater detail in *Condemned Property?* So if you are not totally confused at this point, continue on, and I will have you straightened out or…absolutely confused.

On September 26, 1945 (yes 1945), the first American soldier was killed in Vietnam.

Lt. Col. Peter Dewey, a U.S. Army officer with the Office of Strategic Services (OSS) in Vietnam was shot and killed in Saigon. Dewey was the head of a seven-man team sent to Vietnam to search for missing American pilots and to gather information on the situation in the country after the surrender of the Japanese. According to the provisions of the Potsdam Conference, the British were assigned the responsibility of disarming Japanese soldiers south of the 16th parallel. However, with the surrender of the Japanese, Ho Chi Minh and the Viet Minh declared themselves the rightful government of Vietnam. This angered the French colonial officials and the remaining French soldiers who had been disarmed and imprisoned by the Japanese. They urged British Maj. Gen. Douglas D. Gracey to help them regain control. Gracey, not fond of the Viet Minh or their cause, rearmed 1,400 French soldiers to help his troops maintain order. The next day, these forces ousted the Viet Minh from the offices that they had only recently occupied. Dewey's sympathies lay with the Viet Minh, many of whom were nationalists who did not want a return to French colonial rule. The American officer was an outspoken man who soon angered Gracey, eventually resulting in the British general ordering him to leave Indochina. On the way to the airport, accompanied by another OSS officer, Capt. Henry Bluechel, Dewey refused to stop at a roadblock manned by three Viet Minh soldiers. He yelled back at them in French and they opened fire, killing Dewey instantly. Bluechel was unhurt and escaped on foot. It was later determined that the Viet Minh had fired on Dewey thinking he was French. He would prove to be the first of nearly 59,000 Americans killed in Vietnam.

(Source: www.history.com)

War is hell. Every battle is a bad one for the one who is in it. But Vietnam was very different from America's past wars. This was an in-your-face war where the combatants relentlessly sought out each other every day and night. The mind-boggling effect that such an ordeal would put on the Americans was never attempted to be understood by the psychiatric community until the latter 2000s. The Vietnam War was a...twilight zone.

The Soui Tre's continued for at least three more years. They just had different names such as...Soui Cut, Hue, Kham Duc, Khe Sahn, Lang Ve, Hoc Mon, Duc Hoa, Nui Ba Den, Dai Do, Dau Tieng, Tay Ninh, Hamburger Hill, Ap Cho...and the list went on. Most were clear-cut American victories like Soui Tre, but the enemy kept coming seemingly in greater numbers and armed with better weapons, compliments of our friends in China and the Soviet Union. How long would this go on? WHY are we continuing to fight an enemy that seems to choose when and where we were going to fight? WHY did they keep coming when we defeated them so soundly almost every time? WHY...we who fought in these meaningless battles, was what we were asking ourselves...**WHY?**

Who could have known that these questions would rattle between the ears of combat Vietnam War veterans...for the rest of our lives? Who could have predicted that the men who fought in such horrific battles and were forced to live in unimaginable, abysmal conditions would be forsaken, abandoned and betrayed by their own government after they came home? However, it happened, and it has not ended yet. Worse yet, it happened in supposedly the greatest country in the world—the United States of America.

This book is a continuation of America's unfinished wars. It is about America's conscience and those wars. It is about preserving an **Endangered Species**... Vietnam's veterans as well as veterans from other wars who could become prematurely endangered as well if Americans stand by and do nothing.

Unlike my first book, which was one hundred percent devoted to the Vietnam War and its participants from both sides, this book will meander back to that war in just the early chapters. It will then jump right into situations that have ensued since the end of the war and continue today.

So many of us have been quiet about that war for oh, so long. We who have survived are old now. We are in our mid-sixties to early seventies...those of us who are still alive. We were young when we were soldiers in that hellhole called South Vietnam. Being soldiers changed most of our lives forever. Most of us loved our country when we were young soldiers, and most of us still love our country. We did our job in a brave manner even though we were scared stiff and even though we didn't know it. We were obligated to go to Vietnam and obey our orders once we were there...regardless of the consequences.

CAUTION: Continue at your own risk. This author pulls no punches and tells his story with passion and sometimes, overwhelming emotion. *Payback Time!* will move you.

VFW National Helpline: 1-800-VFW (839)-1899

CHAPTER 1

FLASHBACKS!

A flashback is a common psychological happening where an individual has a very sudden and sometimes vividly powerful memory of a previous experience or event from the past. Flashbacks can be happy and exciting as well as sad and frightening. Combat veterans who experience flashbacks and are suffering from posttraumatic stress disorder have been known to have flashbacks from a war experience that can seriously disrupt their day-to-day lives.

Flashbacks can also be humorous. Sometimes, the examples of the flashbacks I have experienced (there have been hundreds) can seem very real. In this book, I have shared a few of those with you. If you are one who is experiencing flashbacks, please consider receiving professional consultation with a qualified psychologist. Flashback number one follows.

I guess it may seem odd to start my book off with a **Flashback** as the first chapter. But it came to my mind out of nowhere as flashbacks do. It was late April, about forty-seven years ago. I was twenty-three years old then. I remember this day in April 1968 as though it just happened yesterday. Today, as I write this story, I have recently left behind my sixties and have become a seventy year old...a seventy-year-old soldier and I hope to always be a soldier.

The day before a sizeable enemy force of several hundred North Vietnamese Army regulars (NVA) overran a local outpost that was defended by thirty soldiers from the Army of the Republic of Vietnam (ARVN). The North Vietnamese Army had little respect for the South Vietnamese Army, and this was made perfectly clear as the entire ARVN force was left lifeless to rot in the spot they fell, to be eaten away by maggots and leeches. We could smell the stench several clicks away as the tropical breezes carried the scents of death to us. The ARVNs actually fought well, inflicting massive casualties onto the determined NVA. About half of the NVA force was killed or wounded, and Bravo Company of the 3rd 22nd 25th Infantry was next on their menu. The remaining NVAs were still a formidable force of a few hundred.

The 1st Platoon had just finished reinforcing our bunkers with more sandbags, actually filled with jungle dirt (mud) when an order came down…"Saddle up; 1st Platoon's first squad is going out on ambush patrol tonight." It was our turn and it was not a warm and fuzzy feeling we had, knowing about the ARVN slaughter the day before.

Even though Bravo Company had been on an all-day search and destroy mission, a three to four click sweep through thick, steamy forest and swamp terrain, infested with leeches, poisonous spiders, snakes, etc., the 1st Platoon's first squad would not get any sleep this night. We were going out to find and engage, if necessary, the rest of that NVA battalion, which still numbered about two hundred war-hardened and well-armed professionals. Our squad was at full strength at the time, at about thirteen men. We were scared stiff and none of us thought this mission made any sense…OUTNUMBERED BY A FIFTEEN TO ONE RATIO and we were seeking them out? As we would learn, this would be expected of us over and over. After all, we were…combat infantry grunts who believed we were as good as any.

We started out just before dark, humping for half an hour or so until we found our spot in a thick tree line. This would be our home for this night and part of the next day as well. None of us would ever forget this night in the bush! We reached our designated ambush sight (all thirteen of us), made ourselves comfortable, set up who would pull watch first, second, third, etc., talked about putting our claymores out and twelve of us would then lay our heads down on the ground to get some sleep while guard duty was being pulled by the first guy.

All of a sudden, we heard a commotion, thrashing along a wood line about fifty yards away. We heard talking, laughing. OMG, their line seemed endless, as surely there were a couple hundred of them. This was the remains of that NVA battalion, and we knew they had a bad attitude. So what? We were sent out for an ambush mission regardless of the circumstances or consequences. This was a common scenario for combat Vietnam soldiers during the "blood bath" years of 1967-1969 and into 1970. We were sacrificial lambs, and we began to know this. No matter, we carried out our missions—we were soldiers, right?

Okay, we are set up and ready to launch our death ambush onto that enemy force that destroyed the ARVN outpost the night before. We can do it, right? We were trained (brainwashed) to do it from basic training to advanced infantry training. We were turned into nasty, lean machines, ready to shoot on sight again and again…until the enemy was dead. Our problem this night was…there were too fricking many of them, and our supposedly good position to pull off an ambush was no longer such. The chattering NVA chose to make camp close to us, still just fifty yards away. It was impossible to call in artillery on them and not hit our own positions. What a crock of shit this was as we wanted to pull off an ambush, but this one would be suicidal.

Guess what? Everyone—all thirteen guys pulled guard duty that night as no one even wanted to fall asleep. Some guys did doze off from time to time and we woke them up ASAP. Some guys snored and we stopped them ASAP. One guy almost sneezed…we grabbed his nose and mouth, muffling him…and that is how the entire night went on. We had to tolerate the mosquitoes, the red ants, rats and any other critters that found us that night. We had to remain quiet or our complete destruction would be the result. Good grief, I can remember them (NVAs), laughing and singing that night while we laid there sweating, terrified, getting eaten alive by mosquitoes and we couldn't even swat them (too much noise)… just lay there…say nothing…don't move…wait for daylight and pray they will saddle up and move out.

Each minute seemed like an hour that night. I don't think any of us had ever wanted to see the sunrise the next day as badly as we did that night. One of the newer guys dozed off, which was okay, as there were still a dozen pair of eyes wide open, looking in every direction even though we could not see anything more than twenty feet away. I remember this horrible thought—we never set up our claymore mines; we did not have the opportunity. If the NVA discovered us, it would have been close in fighting with every advantage to the NVA. All of a sudden, the new guy released a snore sound. He never got to finish it as we covered his face with towels to shut him up and wake him up. I guess his lone snore sounded more like a grunt from a pig as the NVA camp remained silent. But we went on to another level of alertness, terrified that the enemy could be on top of us at any second.

Rats! The rats were a potential problem that night as they were unusually active and several of them scurried over our legs and feet in the early hours of that night. All we could do was lie there and not bother them, hoping not to get bitten, which would surely cause a holler, not to mention the probability of rabies.

We had other visitors that night…snakes! One of them might have been a member of the cobra family, but it was difficult to tell at night. Cobras look like most non-poisonous snakes at first, as their infamous hood doesn't show itself unless the snake sets up into a strike position. Fortunately, another potential disaster went away quite smoothly as the very long serpent meandered away from us. For as long as it took that snake to disappear, I think our imaginations now have it to be twenty feet long although it was probably just ten feet…*just?* Sure glad it was not hungry enough to strike at any of the very large rats in the area. That would have generated enough commotion to bring the NVAs over for an investigation, for sure.

Obviously, our radio was turned off for that night. After the snake episode was over, I quietly rolled over, face up to the sky. There were some stars, enough of them to cause me to gaze and think about the world back home. I wondered why the thirteen of us were here in this place called Vietnam, and why we were in the predicament we found ourselves in on this particular night. Would tomorrow ever come? Would the NVA leave or would they remain where they were, just one hundred and fifty feet away? If they packed up and moved on, which was likely as they were always on the move, which direction would they take? What if they marched right into our position? Would I die that night from a bayonet fight? Would they take us as POWs or just slaughter us all and leave our bodies for the leeches and maggots? What if a tiger decided to pay us a visit? It was possible. Oh God, what a horrible night, just lying there helpless.

Those twelve or fourteen hours were the longest and the darkest hours of our lives. *Oh God, please make this night go faster.* We all prayed this to ourselves over and over again. I wonder what our pulse rates were that night. What if one of us died from a heart attack, as we were surely scared enough? Why didn't our instructors at Fort Polk's advanced infantry training have a class to prepare us for something like this? Come to think of it, they did offer some advice to us about getting lost in the jungles of Vietnam. I think they told us something like this, "Soldier, if you ever get separated from your unit in the Nam, that would be a good time for you to renew your vows with…God!"

Lost? Separated from our unit? OMG, that was precisely the situation we were in. Would our guys pull out before we could attempt to make contact with them? That was a strong possibility. Would they come looking for us in the morning? They had our coordinates. Or would they presume we had been captured or killed since we could not contact each other by radio?

Hey, here was an idea. Maybe one or two of us could make it back to camp and the rest of Bravo could come to our rescue this night. Bad idea as they would have to crawl all the way back, and the terrain was not crawl friendly. Bad idea as Bravo just might walk into an ambush by the NVA, and we had no way to warn them. Bad idea, so we decided to suck it up and wait.

Holy water buffalo! The NVAs were suddenly making a lot of noise over there. Did they spot us? Were they preparing for an attack? Would we ever see another morning sunrise? Wait, there it was—there was a sign of color in the sky. Daybreak was minutes away, so we thought to ourselves…*get out of here you bad NVAs; beat it!* We were in luck, or should we say we were blessed because all two hundred plus of them were in fact packing up and would hopefully be heading to a wood line in another direction from us! They did that.

Again, we thought about calling in an artillery strike, but our unanimous vote was NO WAY. Let's just "didi mau" or get the hell out of Dodge and rejoin our Bravo war buddies. Those NVAs and we would meet again sooner or later and hopefully, the odds would not be fifteen to one at night.

After the NVAs were long gone, presumably on their march back to Cambodia, we made radio contact with the rest of Bravo. Not sure who was happiest, them or us. When we made it back to the base camp perimeter, the other guys greeted us like a bunch of lost puppies, and we couldn't wait to tell our story of how close we came to being completely annihilated without anyone even firing a shot.

I sat down and wrote a letter, to whom I don't remember, but it had to be a short one as our orders called for a combat assault into what was called the Duc Hoa District west of Bien Hoa and Saigon. Bien Hoa had been hit by a fierce and determined Viet Cong unit last night, and we were going to make sure their plans for another counter-attack on our guys in the Bien Hoa area was a bad idea. Then again, the VC could have easily escaped through their elaborate tunnel system, which went right into Cambodia. Geez, this war sucked. So, another exciting day in III Corp War Zone C was about to begin. I ate some crap from my c-rations, and the Huey choppers arrived to take us where the action was going on. I remember thinking about last night as the Huey's M-60 gunner suddenly broke my thought. There were a few VC running frantically below. After another pass, I think we killed them all. We did not make a stop to find out, as we had bigger fish to fry in Duc Hoa. Last night was history, and for what lied ahead for us, last night was just another night in Nam.

Most of the squad who were out there the previous night and who are still living today have not forgotten that very traumatic experience. In fact, it was such a distressing experience that some of the guys were just never the same afterwards, not to this day, but there was no way to get out of it. We couldn't just quit. Of course, there was another way to escape the horrors of Nam…get wounded or killed or…suicide…or become a deserter. All of those thoughts crossed our minds more than once.

One night and one day at a time. That is the only way we could deal with this mind game war. Make no mistake; each night was like another day's routine. A twenty-four-hour day in the Nam could seem like a week. I was beginning to feel like the rest of this one year could last a lifetime or it might last just another second!

Flashback...Remembering Messmer

This one hit me while I was sleeping one day in December 2014. Maybe it should be called a nightmare, whatever. I had been rescued from the insanity of searching for the enemy in their backyard, under their terms, crawling around in the jungle and all that good stuff. I was into my second month of my new assignment in Cu Chi, working for the 25th Division's Adjutant General (AG), mostly driving him around. So, I was really like a medieval chauffer and bodyguard. My new buddy, Messmer from Montana, did a similar duty for the Inspector General (IG), so we had pretty good jobs now.

We were lying on top of Messmer's personal bunker, enjoying some not-so-cold beers (Blatz, I think), and Messmer was smoking marijuana along with sipping the suds. We had every intention of getting wasted that night; actually, we did that most nights in Cu Chi. The stars were plentiful on this clear night, and it wasn't too uncomfortable heat-wise. Like we cared anyway? We had most of the "base camp warriors" leery of us. Some were terrified of us as the stories we told them about the Viet Cong and NVA (which were the unexaggerated truth) caused these clerks and mechanics to lose an awful lot of sleep on many nights. We had them actually believing that the Viet Cong were capable and willing to sneak into a "so called" secure base camp like Cu Chi in the night, sneak into selected hooches, cut their throats, and escape undetected by the guys pulling guard. Truthfully, this rarely ever happened, but it did on occasion. On the other hand, our own allies from the Republic of Korea, known as ROKS, were documented to perform these killing tactics on the Viet Cong several times.

BOOM...BOOM...BOOM! Mortars, major proportions, landing fairly close to us as Messmer and I continued to drink our beers and talk as if nothing else was going on. Guys were running to bunkers, yelling, stumbling, falling down, and bumping into things, yelling as if the end of the world was here. Still, Messmer and I remained on top of his bunker, sipping, talking, sipping and just having a blast. I shit you not. But I doubt very much that I would have been game for this without Messmer's audacious but humorous decision to defy the threats that night.

As usual, the mortar barrage did not last long. Probably another ploy to draw out return fire from our big guns which would of course, hit and kill a lot of innocent South Vietnamese villagers—because our attackers were firing from there. This happened precisely at the moment together...as Messmer was taking a huge gulp from his beer, one or more of the VC mortars hit a nearby hooch, annihilating it, and Messmer and I, without any exchange of words, hightailed it into his luxurious bunker. From there, we continued with one beer after another, with his lavish stereo system in the background. So, it was another night in the twilight zone…the Nam.

The next day, Messmer and I reported to our AG and IG to escort them wherever their hearts (orders) desired us to take them. After we dropped them off (somewhere where the hooch maids were), Messmer and I headed to the Cu Chi PX for a few more beers (cold this time). It was there where we heard of the casualty report from last night's bout with the Viet Cong's mortar attack. **Five wounded Americans to receive Purple Hearts!**

All wounded in action for that night did receive their Purple Heart medals as all of them got bruised, scratched, bumped or nicked on the previous night while running, stumbling, falling down or bumping into something…on their way to safety. Nuff said?

As I look back to that evening, I think those guys faced one of the most life-threatening evenings of their lives and no doubt to this day, those who are still living, remember that night, dream about it, and have nightmares about it. I understand that now. But for Messmer and me, two hard core combat troops who had seen indescribable horror night after night…this one evening was like sitting at a drive-in movie. **Dear God…why did you allow those bastards to send us to hell…while we are still living?**

Messmer and I were granted our R&Rs—at the end of January of 1969. We opted to spend it in the "land down under" in Sydney, Australia. Man, oh man, did we wreak havoc during that very short vacation. It was almost unfair, living in hell for nine months, surviving it, and then sent to a heaven-like land for six and a half days and then…returned to hell. What a year!

After Australia, Messmer went home. I had another month or so left in the Nam. He and I swore we would stay in touch, but we never did, and I have no idea what may have happened to him…I hope that I will see him again someday.

Flashback…Nam and Now

My earliest memory of anything related to Vietnam goes back to around 1961 or so, when I saw the iconic Life *magazine cover photograph of a Buddhist monk immolating himself in protest of the Diem regime's treatment of Buddhists. I was just starting sixth or seventh grade. For the rest of my junior and high school years, Vietnam would be ever present in the news as our country escalated our involvement in that little country so far away. Somehow, I always knew I would end up going there.*

My parents were hardworking and underpaid but nevertheless provided a good home for my sister and two brothers. As our school years progressed, several of my older brother's friends were either drafted or enlisted in the military, went and came back from Vietnam. By the time I was ready to graduate high school in 1968, I expected to be drafted also. The Tet offensive of earlier that year had me convinced I would be called. I was willing to serve and believed it would be an honor to do so. I grew up on the stories of our WWII military victories and was certain our country could and would be victorious in Vietnam.

I did get drafted, thanks to the new lottery system, along with my twin brother Tim in June of 1970. I have no proof, but I suspect that earlier, the local draft board gave us a break due to the fact that my father died when I was in the eleventh grade and were being benevolent towards us with respect to our mother being a widow. Maybe true and maybe not. My mother then also died in late 1969 and within months, we were drafted, just after the Kent State shootings.

We went together to Fort Campbell, Kentucky and took our basic training there. Tim got orders for communications training at Fort Hood, Texas, and I got orders to report to Fort Polk, Louisiana for infantry training. Anyone who went to Fort Polk knew where the next stop would be, so when they asked us what our preferred choices of next duty station we wanted, I listed Vietnam, Vietnam, Vietnam. In December of 1970, I landed at Bien Hoa airbase and began my tour of duty with the 25th Infantry, patrolling the jungles of the Iron Triangle.

My first firefight came on my thirteenth day in the bush. This was when I saw my first person killed by gunfire. I still remember what he looked like, a young sixteen- or seventeen-year-old Viet Cong boy who was shot after his AK47 jammed. During the next four months, our unit had several contacts with the enemy, although nothing like our troops experienced in previous years. I recall one particular firefight that started at 8:00 and lasted till 16:00 hours. We walked straight into the middle of a bunker complex. This was when our medic earned a Silver Star for rescuing a man in the line of fire.

The mood of the average troop at this point in the war was to just survive and come home. President Nixon had initiated the Vietnamization program, and everyone knew the U.S. was not going to stay in Vietnam for long. Drug abuse and alcoholism were prevalent, and disregard for military discipline was very evident. I feared for my safety as line troops were compromising our positions in the field and becoming lackadaisical.

In April of 1971, the 25th Infantry stood down, and I was sent north to Chu Lai to serve with the 23rd Infantry Division. It was there that the 75th Infantry Rangers were recruiting for volunteers to join them. Several of us signed up. These guys were the epitome of a professional soldier, and that inspired us to join. Recondo School would be an intensive three-week ranger school culminating in an actual live mission in the boonies where each candidate would be evaluated. It was one of the hardest things I ever did, but I graduated and was assigned to Co G/2 Ranger Co. in Da Nang. For the next five months, our unit performed recon and ambush missions in the various areas surrounding Da Nang. The Rangers of that era were extremely professional. I have good memories of that time I served with them. We fought hard, and we played hard. I abruptly rotated back to the U.S. in September 1971 when the Rangers stood down.

Returning to the U.S. was something we always dreamed about, yet I missed and thought about the guys who are still there. I was ashamed that our country let the South Vietnamese down by reneging on our promise to support them. I remember when Da Nang fell in 1975 and thought about what probably happened to the Vietnamese friends I knew. For several years, all I could think about was Vietnam, Vietnam, Vietnam. I turned into a regular stumblebum for a couple of years.

Over the next few years, I slowly began to adjust to life as a civilian. My soul found healing as I came to accept Jesus Christ as my savior and Lord. I began to see the world and its system in a different light. I accepted the things that I could and could not change and began to rely on the God who is there for comfort and guidance. Stress from war experiences, though still remembered, can be relieved through prayer and the knowledge that I know and am known by God. The Lord is a very present help and comforter. Set pride aside and seek Him, and you will be found.

As a consequence of my war experience, I have developed a continuing interest in the political direction of our country. I love and respect the founders and framers of this great republic and have concerns that the foundations of our nation are being destroyed. Corruption within our government, wars on many fronts, the U.S. as the world's policeman and the use of our youth as so much cannon fodder cannot continue without it having a detrimental effect on all of us. If we, as a people, allow our God-given rights to be taken from us, then we will indeed be a nation in bondage again.

I was proud to serve my country as a soldier in Vietnam. I was proud to have served with men, many of who gave their all. I was proud to have, in my small way, tried to obtain peace for the good people of South Vietnam. We did our duty. May the God of peace comfort you my brothers and sisters who are burdened today with the effects of your time in Vietnam.

- Thomas Gretchko

Sergeant, U.S. Army, Republic of Vietnam 1970-1971

23rd Inf. Div., Co G/2 (Ranger) 75th Inf., Da Nang, and 25th Inf. Div., 3/22 Regulars

Flashback...Protecting Ours!

Dealing with flashbacks can be easier said than done, especially since they rarely make an appointment with the person. However, if you fear or absolutely feel like you cannot handle it, here are a few tips that have been passed on to me:

- Sniff something strong.
- Bite into something sour like a lemon.
- Turn on loud music.
- Hug someone or your pet.
- Take a brisk walk.
- Grab a piece of ice.

That is the best I can do, but of course, seeking help or the company of others who are aware of your problem is a great flashback stopper.

Flashback - War Veterans Storm Barricades Amid Obama's Government Shutdown. These were some of the news headlines on this day. Many more just like it would follow for a full week. One news source, Washington *AFP* began their editorial coverage of this day like this:

Compared to defeating Nazi Germany and the Japanese empire, storming the National World War II memorial was a piece of cake for a hardy column of octogenarian U.S. military veterans. With help from a congressional delegation, mostly Republicans, two hundred-strong overran a barricade to savor the grandeur of the nation's premiere memorial to the 1939-1945 war.

The memorial to the sixteen million Americans who fought in World War II and to the more than 400,000 who died, was among the iconic tourist landmarks up and down the National Mall closed to the public by Obama's shutdown.

October 2, 2013 – The U.S. government shutdown could not stop veterans from passing through barricades to visit their war memorials in Washington Tuesday. The veterans, many of whom fought their way to victory over Nazi Germany and Imperial Japan during World War II, came from Mississippi and Iowa and were not going to be denied access to federal landmarks built in their honor.

Traveling with the group from Iowa was past American Legion Auxiliary Department of Iowa president Ann Rehbein – wife of Past National Commander Dave Rehbein - and their daughter, Jennifer a Navy veteran. They went with 150 veterans of World War II, the Korean War and the Vietnam War through the Story County (Iowa) Freedom Flight program which gives those who served during wartime an opportunity to visit national memorials and monuments that recognize their sacrifices.

When the Iowa group arrived and found the World War II Memorial barricaded due to the government shutdown which closed National Park Service sites around the country, one of the Story County volunteers "removed the barricade and said, 'We're going in,'" Ann Rehbein said. "They (park police) just stood to the side, folded their arms and let us go."

By late afternoon, the veterans were moving on to the Korean War and Vietnam War Memorials. An Air Force veteran of Operation Enduring Freedom who had been furloughed from his Department of Defense civilian job for the day was impressed by the older veterans who weren't going to let the government shutdown stand in their way. "World War II vets shouldn't have to break into their own memorial," said Rob Joswiak, who had ridden a bicycle to the memorial to support the older veterans on the National Mall. "This is one of my favorite places," he said. "I run down here a lot and it's always inspiring."

The place had been much livelier earlier in the day when veterans crossed the barricades to see their memorials. Some of the veterans had been escorted by Sen. Tom Harkin of Iowa and Reps. Bill Huizenga of Michigan, Louie Gohmert of Texas, Steve King of Iowa and Steven Palazzo of Mississippi. The lawmakers had met the vets upon their arrival at Reagan National Airport earlier in the day and

led them to the National Mall. Park officers on the scene offered no resistance to what one congressman called "a peaceful act of civil disobedience."
(Source: http://www.legion.org)

Flashback... Veterans Removed at Vietnam Memorial
Posted at 2:31 p.m. on October 5, 2013 by Jazz Shaw

When I first saw this story, I assumed that it almost had to be a hoax. After the previous incidents with veterans and the added expenditures involved in closing open spaces to keep veterans from paying their respects to the Honored Dead, one would assume that even a novice politician would move to staunch the bleeding. Instead, it seems that the White House is doubling down as reported at The Weekly Standard.

Via William Jacobson, NBC's affiliate in Washington D.C. reports that police ordered tourists and Vietnam War veterans who were visiting the Vietnam Veterans Memorial Wall to leave the memorial at one point on Friday. After one group of veterans went around the barricade, "the park ranger told them the wall was closed," NBC's Mark Seagraves reported. "Later another group of vets showed up and moved the barricades. At that point, the memorial filled with vets and tourists. That's when the police came and moved everyone out."

As usual, it sounds like our veterans accounted themselves in a professional dignified manner, but were not going to put up with any nonsense. Seagraves described the exchange as pleasant and respectful. The veterans then moved the barricade and walked down the wall to pay their respects. But a flood of tourists followed even though the memorial is closed to the general public. "The consensus among the group of Vietnam veterans was we're going to go anyway. We'll go through the barricade," North Carolina resident Reid Mendenhall said. U.S. Park Police arrived at the scene, asked everyone to leave and put the barricade back into place.

Conflict over the closure of D.C.'s war memorial has drawn a lot of controversy this week. Yes...a lot of controversy is putting it mildly. The President can pick all the battles with congressional Republicans that he likes and probably not draw too much political fire from the middle. But if you wanted to conduct a poll of who is least likely to be blamed for anything in this country by the general public, veterans visiting war memorials would have to come in somewhere near the bottom of the list, behind possibly only puppies.

Flashback...Veterans "Arrested" at Vietnam Memorial

This shameful incident was avoided, ignored or covered up. Take your choice, by every major news media even though it happened in our country's largest city...NYC. Here is what one lone newspaper reported on this strange happening:

Veterans of the Vietnam War were arrested earlier tonight at the New York City memorial after staying on the premises past the curfew of 10:00 PM. As Vietnam War veterans continued to honor their fallen comrades by reading off their names, police began loading them into a paddy wagon.
(Source: *The Atlantic*, October 8, 2013)

Okay, so why was there a 10:00 p.m. curfew? I know that veterans and non-veterans visit war memorials in Washington D.C. at various hours. My war buddies and I have done it. Memorials are supposed to be freely accessible public places and...doesn't NYC claim to be the city that stays open all night?

I remember in 2012 around Memorial Day weekend when hundreds of veterans were turned away from carrying out their annual ritual of honoring their fallen war buddies. Again, they were mostly Vietnam veterans, attempting to visit The Vietnam War Veterans Memorial, The Wall. The reason? President Obama's security ordered to have the area around The Wall cleared so that he—Obama could spend a "few minutes" to visit The Wall. Retired U.S. Army Lieutenant General John Sylvester was there as he too was turned away. He talked about this incident on Fox News as he said this, "It's about those 58,000 plus soldiers, airmen and marines that are represented on that wall. That wall is America's wall. It is not Obama's wall." As it was also reported by several media and verified by retired Lt. General Sylvester, Obama spent about fifteen or sixteen minutes at The Wall around 9:00 a.m.; however...**The Wall remained closed until 3:00 p.m.?**

My take on these all-but-forgotten and disgusting incidents was that the American veteran can only be pushed so far, regardless of his or her age. If these shameful acts by our government had continued for much longer in 2013, I know for a fact that Washington D.C. would have received visits from many more thousands of veterans—veterans still very loyal to their country but willing to stand up for their rights as well.

One of the saddest things about the Vietnam War is...it continues to kill so many who have struggled to survive it after they came home!

- Author Unknown

CHAPTER 2

KOREAN WAR – VIETNAM WAR...SAME, SAME?

Same, same is probably the official slogan of Vietnam, Cambodia, Laos, and Thailand people for that matter. It refers to the sameness of everything. Someone could write an entire book about the differences and/or similarities between the Korean and Vietnam Wars. Someone probably has. I just have not seen it. The differences versus the similarities are evenly balanced, but who cares except the most avid war historians, and they would already have that information deeply embedded in their amazing memories of data. I am not reaching out to PhD military war historians with this chapter or this book, although I most certainly welcome the readership of *Payback Time!* from all who have an interest and are able to read it. I am one who cares. Why else would I be undertaking another painful experience of trying to write a book about the Vietnam War's damage to its victims? The last time I did this, after completing *Condemned Property?*, I suffered two ischemic strokes. Okay, enough on that because I am committed to *Payback Time!*

Here is a short Korea – Vietnam test for readers. Grade yourselves, but don't complain to me if you flunk this test.

1. Which war was referred to as a "police action"?
2. Which war was referred to as a "conflict"?
3. Which war had its roots in the Truman Doctrine **and** the Domino Theory?
4. Which country (Korea or Vietnam) was split into Communist North and Democratic South?
5. Which of the two was considered a cold war between the Democratic West and the Communists?
6. Which "conflict" never received an official Declaration of War?

7. Which "conflict" had an armistice or peace treaty signed, establishing a Demilitarized Zone (DMZ), which was supposed to prevent further hostilities from both sides?
8. Which war has often been referred to as the…forgotten war?

Eight easy questions, right? Trouble is, the answer could go either way — to the Korean War or the Vietnam War. All eight questions could be answered correctly as follows…"BOTH WARS!" And that *is* the correct answer…in my opinion.

While we can discuss for hours and years the differences between these two wars, one was just an extension of the other, and Vietnam was planned by the communist duo of China and the Soviet Union. The Vietnam War could have been called Korean War II, except it was fought across the South China Sea in the tropical environment of Indo China's Vietnam.

When the earliest rumblings were quietly going on in South Vietnam, most Americans were trying to put Korea out of their minds, rightfully so as WWI, WWII, and then Korea had made us tired and sick of war. However, as the Korean War was winding down and the tide had turned in our favor, China saw that a clear-cut victory in Korea was not possible. China was cutting back from Korea, and at the same time, they had already been sending massive military equipment and financial aid to the country called North Vietnam, a communist regime just as North Korea was. North Vietnam held similar goals as North Korea, to take over and conquer South Vietnam and…every neighboring country they could overpower.

Their only obstacle would be the United States as France was soundly defeated by the Chinese and Soviet backed North Vietnamese Army (Viet Minh at that time) at the infamous battle of Dien Ben Phu. Over ninety percent of the French force was destroyed in that battle. The Korean War ended…Vietnam War was to begin, and it would last for a long, long time.

Most people who have studied the Vietnam War are aware of the massive financial and personnel contributions that China and the Soviet Union put forth. Most would also be aware that South Korea sent several hundred thousand of their military to fight alongside South Vietnam and its main supporters, the United States, Australia, Thailand, the Philippines and even Canada. It is a well-kept secret that North Korea sent war supplies and manpower to their fellow communist allies during the Vietnam War, but South Korea sent a much larger ground force to fight alongside its democratic allies. In reality, Korea and Vietnam combined were "almost" World War III. They were both a far cry from just a "police action" or a "conflict".

It is also a little known fact that South Korea was willing and anxious to start sending military personnel to Vietnam way back in 1954, shortly after its war with North Korea and China came to a stalemate. However, the United States did not accept or even consider South Korea's proposal. It seemed that they knew what was to come, and America did not or just refused to believe what was to come.

What was to come had already been in the making…the Korean War simply continued for another twenty-plus years under a different name. That "Domino Theory" thing could have been the foundation of both wars, but few realized it at the time. Korea and Vietnam's wars were meant to be "policing actions", meant to contain the advancement of communism into other far eastern countries.

The veterans of Korea and Vietnam should have developed a closer bond, not that many haven't done so, but not the way WWII veterans stuck together or the way Vietnam veterans formed their brotherhood. Many Korean War troops were also veterans of WWII, and that might be the main reason that they kept Vietnam veterans at a distance. In *Condemned Property?* I dedicated a chapter related to this uncomfortable scenario. I called it "Where Was Our Iwo Jima?"

In the Vietnam War, there was no Iwo Jima, no Okinawa, no Bunker Hill or Yorktown, no Gettysburg or Bull Run, no Normandy, no D-Day or Chosin Reservoir, but we did have the infamous Tet Offensive, which shocked the world back in 1968.

Many Vietnam veterans, if not most, will agree that we were not embraced by the WWII and Korean War veterans when we came home. In fact, the so-called "greatest generation" degraded us with painful insults about our war being nothing compared to theirs. They even tried to keep Vietnam War veterans from becoming members of the main service clubs such American Legion, Veterans of Foreign Wars (VFW), etc. Hard to believe? Try…SHOCKING! People still wonder why most of us never talked about our war until now. No one should keep something like fighting in a war for his or her country bottled up inside him or her forever.

It seems to me that the single most fundamental difference about the Korean and Vietnam Wars was reflected in the outcome. The United States and its allies continued to protect South Korea from communist takeover attempts and any encroachment across the Korean DMZ. I repeat…we continued to defend South Korea to ensure their sovereignty as a free nation.

After the Paris Peace Treaty was signed, the United States government completely abandoned the government of South Vietnam, allowing North Vietnam to roll over the south, riding on their tanks and armored personnel carriers, compliments of our friends, the Soviet Union. I repeat…the men and women who fought as bravely as any American military before them had ever fought, were abandoned. Here is a breakdown of the allied casualties from the ten-year Vietnam War:

VIETNAM WAR
ALLIED CASUALTIES

South Vietnam (ARVN)	1,393,511
United States	362,924
South Korea (ROK)	21,467
Australia / New Zealand	3,767
Thailand	1,709
Canada	N/A
Philippines	N/A

(Source: cybersarges.tripod.com)

Nearly two million allied casualties? For what? Abandoned. Betrayed. Forgotten. By the people who sent them into harm's way.

Today, in the 2010s, Vietnam and the United States carry on normal diplomatic relations. South Korea and Vietnam do likewise. In fact, the Republic of Korea (ROK, also known as South Korea), not North Korea, has been looked at as a very good example for Vietnam to follow as a participant in world trade. This is in spite of the pain that the ROK inflicted onto the Vietnamese civilians during the Vietnam War. Actually, the ROK has issued their apologies to the Vietnamese government for its alleged war atrocities in the Vietnam War. Apparently, the apology has been accepted, as the two countries seemed to have formed a workable partnership.

Maybe now, today, there is no longer a Domino Theory threat to Southeast Asia. Then again, maybe we can ask China for that answer…time will tell as China has quietly built the world's largest military force while the United States and most western countries have reduced their military forces to pre-World War II numbers.

While Korean War veterans did not return home to any major welcome home parades, they managed to blend into society because Americans accepted them. (Remember, many fought in WWII.) It is no secret to any American who is still breathing how the Vietnam War veterans were treated as they returned home after their war. That non-welcome-home treatment remains one of the most tragic disgraces in the history of the United States. I have been touched by several Korean War veterans during the last ten years or so, reaching out to me with heartfelt words of understanding and even sympathy for how we were treated when we came home. **THANK YOU KOREAN WAR VETERANS! Much of America still owes Vietnam War veterans an apology.**

According to a November 2000 Gallup Poll prompted by President Clinton's visit to Vietnam, sixty-nine percent of American people still believed that sending troops to Vietnam was a mistake; however, only thirty-four percent of the same Americans surveyed thought sending troops to Korea was a mistake. This ignorance factor has seemingly gone without putting the blame where it belongs. An invasion by communist forces of a free land of free people was blatantly carried out. There was no difference between the primary reason of both wars…none.

The significance of both wars is profound. The difference between both wars is miniscule in some respects but vastly not alike in others. The fact remains that both wars could have turned into…World War III.

The Vietnam War Begins

The facts to follow will interest you, intrigue you and shock you, whether you are a Vietnam War vet or not. Here it is, the end of 2014 and I am still wondering… why were our adversaries in the Vietnam War so persistent, so determined, so ruthless and…so brave? When did that morally corrupt war really begin—surely before we entered the scene? Yeah, I said elsewhere in this book that the Vietnam War was just an extension of the Korean War, and I believe that. But there just had to be some things going on that should have tipped our deaf and dumb leaders off in Washington well before the Tet Offensive in 1968.

With the Korean War long over, as I mentioned earlier, China had already begun its buildup for the next war by arming and training the conquerors of the French…the Army of North Vietnam. Long before most Americans had ever heard of it, the Ho Chi Minh Trail was being used for the invasion of South Vietnam—two years before the USA President at that time, John F. Kennedy had sent our country's first resemblance of military personnel to South Vietnam. This was five and a half years before the Gulf of Tonkin Resolution and five years before the U.S. Marines placed their feet on the ground in Da Nang Province.

It is now known that on May 19, 1959, the communists in North Vietnam secretly authorized the transport of twenty thousand North Vietnam troops accompanied by supplies and weapons generously provided by China to traverse southward on the Truong Son Trail, to be infamously known as the Ho Chi Minh Trail. Inside the borders of Laos and Cambodia, North Vietnam had set up its support bases from where they would begin their war against the South Vietnam regime and all others who would dare to oppose them. This move by North Vietnam and

China was a must for them if they were to have any chance of achieving their future goal, which was…take control of Indochina—all of it.

One of the most well-kept secrets by the American media, and it is public knowledge today—for anyone interested—is that the South Vietnamese government under Ngo Dinh Diem's lead had all but eliminated most of the upcoming Viet Cong organization, at least in the major cities before the 1960s arrived. The Viet Cong structure managed to hang on and maintain a not-very-influential presence in the outlying hamlets. The massive infiltration into Laos and Cambodia would serve as training camps for rebuilding the Viet Cong as a worthy foe of the South Vietnamese government, which had a horrific reputation of corruption in its own right. But they were the enemy and the blocking force for the advancement of communism and the USA would have no choice but to come to their rescue as it did for the South Koreans.

North Vietnam was calling out for a massive uprising in South Vietnam as their newly trained guerrillas were advancing and positioning their so-called patriotic forces and calling their campaign the "people's war."

Why and How…The North Vietnamese Were So Brave, Persistent and Viciously Ruthless!

Maybe our American bureaucrats should have done a better job of researching the history of the North Vietnamese. So should the French; then maybe the once-proud French military would not have suffered its most humiliating defeat in their long history of wars and revolutions. It is old news. The Viet Minh (North Vietnamese) annihilated a thirty-thousand-man force at Dien Ben Phu in 1954.

Genghis Khan himself might have had something to do with the French having their asses handed to them in that shocking battle. Genghis Khan…Viet Minh…North Vietnamese…was there a connection? You betcha, by golly there was. Guess what, my dear Americans, history shows that the people of northern-most North Vietnam are descendants of the Mongols. Remember reading about these guys in your history books, a group of harmless nomads who became known as…the Mongol Hordes? In just a few years, Genghis Khan (Temujin) almost destroyed half of the world's known population at the time. It all took place from 1206 to 1227, just twenty-one years.

Hey, Nam vets, we were not fighting the junior varsity team in our war. We fought the descendants of an army that punctuated its victories with this term…"rape, pillage, plunder." So, how and why did the arrogant U.S. bureaucrats assume an easy victory was a given? What were these people smoking back then?

In Chapter Two of *Condemned Property?*, I refer to the North Vietnamese Army (NVA) as "they", and I give them the credit they deserved. They earned it on the battlefield. We were fighting a brainwashed, professional, well-armed army of warriors who would not back down from all of America's military might, and the last thing they were afraid of was…a U.S. general with bright shiny stars on his uniform.

Arrogance? This is an illness that I assign meaning to such as this: being overly proud to a level of acting contemptuous of an opponent's inabilities—in other words, underestimating or giving too little credit to them for being accomplished or worthy.

One of today's examples of this elite type of arrogance would undoubtedly be…America's President Obama and how he looks down at the Islamic state forces that were still wreaking havoc in Iraq and nearby areas at the time of this writing. The "JV team" as Obama labeled the Islamic terrorists of 2014, may have done their homework by studying the Mongolian descendants in North Vietnam. After all, Genghis Khan also conquered most of Persia, India, China and parts of Russia. What other reason would the Iraqi military and local population lay their arms down and just give up their cities to the advancing ISIS forces? They had to have begun their systematic process of infiltrating into the cities when the first Americans were being pulled out of Iraq by Obama. My, my—caught sleeping again, just like Vietnam all over again. When are these pompous bastards going to study their history?

In *Comrades in Arms* by Roger Canfield, PhD., there are a few paragraphs offering up a profound description of what America's innocent, apple-pie-loving warriors comprised of teenage boys, were being trained and brainwashed to engage in face-to-face combat for an entire year or two (or less) of their lives. Women and children and all cooperative villagers (who had not been beheaded) were forced into the "people's war" against the South Vietnamese Army and their allies, mainly us, the Americans.

North Vietnam's fearless and devoted General V.O Nguyen Giap was credited with motivating and establishing a battle frenzied mindset like this:

- Every citizen will be an enemy killing combatant.
- Every house is to become a combat cell.
- Every village, hamlet and factory will be a fortress.
- There will be no such thing as a non-combatant civilian.
- There will be no civilians. Women will be recruited and trained to join main force troops in the "people's war."
- Children aged ten years or older will be armed.

- Children aged seven years or older would serve as lookouts and they would toss grenades and prepare booby traps to kill Americans.
- Giap ordered...we will not differentiate between those dressed in military uniforms and civilian clothing; they are all targets.

(Decades later, nearly the same words were told to ABC News in an interview with Osama bin Laden.) These orders or guidelines set by Giap (and probably initiated by his ancestor, Genghis Khan) were meant to force Americans to kill women and children in self-defense. Giap knew the value of this and ways in which he could use it against the American military with the American people themselves. A seven or eight year old throws a grenade—killing Americans—Americans fire back. Then the American media portrays us as..."baby killers." And the American public bought into this. Taking on the shame, they actually were lead to believe that we were war criminals, not war heroes.

In North Vietnam, the rules of the Geneva Convention meant nothing. It had no jurisdiction there, so they actually believed they were not committing any war crimes. Today, the same tactics are used in the Middle East, most notably against the Israeli military when they retaliate against terrorist attacks against Israel's citizens. Lo and behold, fifty-some years later, some of America's media, mostly the liberal sources, are still portraying Israel as the criminal when they counter-attack, not to seek vengeance, but to prevent continued attacks on their innocent population.

Accuracy or lack of accuracy in America's media continues today, and it does not always shed a bright light on the "good guys", those who risk their lives so that everyone can enjoy freedom. I can't decide which has done more damage to our country, its military and their families—America's sickening arrogance in the White House or the lying American media. Both have killed Americans in battle. I'll let this chapter end on that note...nuff said.

One of the saddest things about the Vietnam War is...it continues to kill so many who have struggled to survive it after they came home!

- Author Unknown

CHAPTER 3

1968—ONE HELL OF A YEAR!

S ome have said things like this to us after we came home, and some say it to this day:

> *You were only there for one year. Can't you block just one year out of your life?*

> *That war ended over thirty or forty years ago...just get over it!*

GET OVER IT? Oliver Stone wrote in his book version of his famous movie, *Platoon*, "one battle alone called Soui Cut impacted his mind for the rest of his life." Getting over Nam just ain't going to happen, not ever. And for some of its participants who experienced the unspeakable, unforgettable horrors that wars like the Vietnam War generated, their memory bank will receive unwanted, uninvited interruptions or *flashbacks* for as long as they are still breathing. This, I believe is a result of intense combat with massive casualties, and the Vietnam War was every bit of that for about ten percent of all who served there.

I have tried very hard to write *Payback Time!* without being redundant with stories from my first book *Condemned Property?*, and I believe I have accomplished that. While some of the statements or descriptions of some events and reflections may seem repetitive to those who read it and they may be similar...everything in this book is different or supplemental to what was written in *Condemned Property?* Then again, the Vietnam War is not over. It remains a war without an ending in the minds of those who survived it.

1968! One of the most dreadful and dramatic years in U.S. history. There were so many impactful happenings in this one year that the world would be changed... like it or not. Just my opinion. Not only did a U.S. President withdraw with a new one elected, two emblematic figures were assassinated and the Vietnam War hit a new high or low, depending on how we look at it.

The year 1968 stunned the world when it began, and it remained stunning throughout the year. When the initial Tet Offensive was launched and soon repulsed, the American media (Tom Brokaw, *Life* Magazine, etc.) referred to the North Vietnamese/Viet Cong assault like this:

"Late on January 30, 1968, the communist Tet Offensive began, ultimately involving more than eighty thousand communist troops in a successful and coordinated assault on more than one hundred South Vietnamese towns and cities. The news was reported back to the U.S. as though the Vietnam War was over *now*!"

In my opinion, as well as others with high credentials, it is short of a miracle that our warriors not only stood ground in Vietnam during the Tet Offensive year... they often pursued after the enemy into their own domain. The result was a decimated enemy. But...those who were sitting comfortably back at home sweet home were rarely shared with such information that American warriors had in fact won another victory. Damn, this is extremely difficult to swallow, but hey, my brothers— it happened.

Heart Broken...Still Loyal to America!

At this point in my life, it has become quite evident that it will take an act of Congress to rectify the damage done to the Vietnam War veterans who are still living. Yeah, sure, pressure is finally being put onto the corrupt VA system, but will the pressure continue? I pray it will continue. The VA criminals who have gone unpunished deserve to be pressured to the point that they cannot stand it—I MEAN IT! When and if the current VA scandals are straightened out and I truly pray they are, think about this:

- What if we dug deeply into the records of how many Vietnam War veterans have died so prematurely over the last...40 years? Americans wouldn't be able to handle it.

Most likely, the majority of those politicians and high-ranking VA bureaucrats in charge back then are no longer around. But if they are, regardless of how old they are (and that should not matter), what they did to us deserves to be dug up, examined thoroughly and acted upon. Don't worry, you scumbags this pertains to, it won't happen, so crawl back into your hole and wither away.

One does not have to be a certified historian to recognize that 1968 was one of the most controversial, dangerous, heart-pounding, unpredictable and challenging years in U.S. history. A self-proclaimed weekend history buff, even I know about that incredible year. Vietnam veterans who were lucky enough to have been in

South Vietnam in 1968 were in for the adventure of their lifetime. It was a year that would impact most military troops, their families and close friends...for the rest of their lives.

On January 1, 1968 in the bayous of southern Louisiana at the U.S. Army base, Fort Polk, I had begun my Advanced Infantry Training (AIT) at North Fort Polk, also known as "Tiger Land" or "Little Vietnam." Our AIT was not to be taken lightly as the longevity of our lives as upcoming combat infantry soldiers in the Vietnam War would depend on how well we trained at "Tiger Land."

I remember finishing second overall in our class, having run one mile in uniform and combat boots in a nifty four minutes and fifty-eight seconds. I remember the one guy who beat me in that final race. He ran the mile in four minutes and fifty-four seconds, well ahead of everyone else. He was a kid from North Carolina named Mangrum. I was quite pleased with my performance in the finals. I felt as though I was in the best shape of my life, weighing one hundred seventy pounds with a twenty-nine- to thirty-inch waist. Often, I thought that if I was back in high school at Twinsburg-Chamberlin High in this kind of shape, I could have contributed to our sports teams much greater than I actually did. Like many overly active athletes back then, we tried to participate in every sport available to us. I managed to earn the Varsity "T" letter in football, basketball, baseball, wrestling, soccer, cross-country and track-and-field. I excelled in only one of them—baseball.

While we were being trained to become killers in Vietnam by some of the scariest guys I had ever seen up to that time in my life—Green Berets, Army Airborne Rangers and the like, something was brewing across the Pacific in our next destination...the Army of North Vietnam and their communist partners, the Viet Cong forces launched a coordinated attack against America and our allied forces in South Vietnam.

As most Americans living today who were old enough to remember 1968, the end of January 1968 was the lunar New Year (Tet) holiday. America and its allies were caught completely off guard by the succession of "human wave" attacks on every major city in South Vietnam. The fighting was a vicious, in-your-face style and despite the surprise of these attacks, the communists were soundly defeated by a very well-trained American military. Ho Chi Minh and the other leaders of North Vietnam were shocked at the tenacity of the Americans. They had anticipated easy victories...there were none.

Casualties were staggering for both sides. And Americans back home were suddenly awakened as they watched some of the combat operations right in their living rooms, courtesy of the American media.

Back at "Tiger Land", we who were training to come to the aid of our war buddies to be, immediately erased any silly notions of taking it easy during the rest of our AIT presence at Fort Polk. If anything, I thought our last few weeks went too quickly as I think back now…it is like "Tiger Land" ended and "Good Morning Vietnam" came the very next day. There wasn't much time to prepare mentally anymore. It was time to put up or shut up, walk the walk instead of talking the talk as cocky trainees just setting foot on the shores of Cam Ranh Bay, South Vietnam.

Our group from Fort Polk would miss the first phase of Tet in January and February 1968. Not to worry, Ho Chi Minh hard-core professionals were just getting warmed up as we would soon find out in March and April 1968. Up until January 1, 1968, our U.S. losses had totaled 19,975 from 1961-1967 or about 3,329 for each year on average. When December 31, 1968 closed its doors, the Vietnam War's bloodiest year revealed these devastating and shocking results for the American and South Vietnamese forces…in just one year!

TET YEAR 1968 CASUALTIES*		
U.S. Military	16,899	KIA
	87,388	WIA
	104,287	**Total Casualties**
South Vietnam Military	27,915	KIA
	172,512	WIA
	200,427	**Total Casualties**

* United States DOD (2012)

1968 TET YEAR CASUALTIES VS. RECENT WARS

War (Years)	Total KIA / WIA Casualties*
Vietnam War (1968 Only)	**104,287**
Gulf War (1990 - 1991)	1,231
Afghanistan (2001 – Present)	12,135
Iraq War (2003 – 2011)	36,395
	49,761

*United States DOD (2012)

In one week of February 11-17, 1968, American casualties alone totaled 3,090! Remember, U.S. casualties had averaged just over 3,000 per year up until 1967 and all of a sudden, that total was recorded in **one week** of 1968.

More of the same was in the cards. When Phase I of the Tet Offensive had ended, the communist forces merely regrouped and replaced their casualties with more live bodies, mostly from the North Vietnamese Army. My new foxhole, bunker buddies and I arrived in March-April 1968, which was just in time for Phase II of the Tet Offensive, which ran through May-June. In fact, the month of May 1968 would prove to be the bloodiest year for U.S. casualties of the entire war. This was a distinction that everyone who survived one attack and one counter-ambush could have done without, and we would not have minded. We had been led to believe that this war was going to wind down soon, that we were inflicting such heavy casualties onto the enemy that any day now, we could expect them to surrender. That day never arrived.

Hold your shorts! After a so-called lull in July 1968, our worthy and very determined adversary launched Phase III of the Tet Offensive, and it lasted into October, which is how long I lasted in the field as a U.S. Army combat infantry pointman. Due to some pretty bad infections from cuts, scrapes, wounds, including a serious case of cellulitis, I spent a couple weeks in Tay Ninh Province Hospital and was transferred to the 25th Infantry Division's Headquarters at Cu Chi. Note, Cu Chi was discovered to be the headquarters for the Viet Cong Army underground. (You should read *Condemned Property?* for more about Cu Chi.)

Condemned Property? also describes our daily itinerary during our search and destroy missions by day and night during those Tet Phases I, II and III. It will move you whether you are a combat veteran or not. Especially if you are not.

The Viet Cong or National Liberation Front had received the worst battering in 1968. Some sources say the VC could never be a viable military source again. No matter. For every VC we took out of action, they were replaced by two or three North Vietnamese Army (NVA) regulars. How would that affect your motivation for the days ahead of you?

1968...1968...1968! It deserves mentioning three times. IF you were a real thrill-seeking, dare-devil type and IF you thought you were game enough for the ultimate adventure, the supreme life-risking challenge, look no further than to your U.S. government's recruiting station...IF you were a real dare devil? Vietnam wasn't the only event on TV every night during 1968. It was just the most horrifying real-life history making entertainment in the flesh at that time. Here are some other interesting happenings in that unforgettable year of 1968, including some that were Vietnam War related:

MEMORABLE EVENTS OF 1968

January 1   Evil Knievel's attempt to jump Caesar's Palace Fountain fails.

Netherlands gets color TV.

January 2   Vietnam War's second largest one-day battle takes place at Soui Cut. Oliver Stone fights in this battle; total casualties…1,700.

January 5   Dr. Benjamin Spock indicted for conspiring to dodge the draft law.

January 6   Dr. Shumway successfully performs first U.S. adult cardiac transplant.

January 8   Jacques Cousteau's famous underwater specials begin on TV.

January 15   Earthquake in Sicily with over 1,400 casualties.

January 21   Vietnam War Khe Sanh battle begins, lasting until April 8, 1968.

January 23   North Korea seizes USS Pueblo.

January 29-30   Vietnam War Tet Offensive begins.

U.S. Embassy in Saigon attacked.

Battle of Hue begins.

January 31   Viet Cong shocks America as the First Battle of Saigon continues.

Viet Cong officer executed on public TV around the world; shot in head.

February 1   Vince Lombardi retires as Green Bay Packers head coach.

February 6   Former war hero, President Eisenhower shoots a hole-in-one in golf.

February 8   Three protesting students are killed by police in South Carolina.

February 11   Madison Square Garden in New York City opens at its current location.

February 11-18   One week record for U.S. casualties is 543 KIA and 2,547 WIA.

February 24	Tet Offensive is halted; Hue is recaptured from NVA.
March 4	Martin Luther King announces Poor Peoples campaign.
March 7	Battle for Saigon ends.
March 16	My Lai Massacre takes place in Vietnam; not publicized until November 1969.
March 21	Israel enters Jordan to attack PLO forces.
March 23	Afrocentrism, Black Power students at Howard University sign new era of militant student activism.
March 26	Country singer Kenny Chesney is born.
March 29	Student protestors seize buildings at Bowie State College.
March 30	Canadian singer Celine Dion is born.
March 31	Lyndon Johnson announces he will not seek re-election.
April 3	North Vietnam once again agrees to meet U.S. for preliminary peace talks.
April 4	Martin Luther King shot dead in Memphis.
April 5	Khe Sanh, South Vietnam Marine base is approached by NVA.
April 8	Bureau of Drugs and Narcotics is created.
April 8 - May 31	Vietnam War's largest search and destroy mission to date, Operation Toan Thang I, a counter reaction to communist Tet Offensive.
April 11	Lyndon Johnson signs Civil Rights Act of 1968.
April 13	Battle of Good Friday takes place in Vietnam War.
April 18	Bell Telephone employees strike nationally.
April 19	American actress Ashley Judd is born.
April 20	Trudeau is sworn in as Canadian Prime Minister.
April 23	United Methodist Church is formed.
April 24	Leftist students riot, take over Columbia University in New York City.
April 26	Students riot at Ohio State University, take over administration building.

April 29	*Hair* opens at Biltmore Theater.
May 2	Gold reaches record high of $39.35 per ounce.
May 5	Mini Tet Offensive begins in Vietnam War. May will be the bloodiest month of entire war.
May 6	Over one thousand injured in Paris as students riot in streets.
May 10	Vietnam peace talks resume as Tet Offensive Phase II continues.
May 10-12	U.S. Special Forces overrun at Khan Duc in Quang Ten Province.
May 12	Australian task force begins significant series of actions outside Saigon.
May 13	Over 1,000,000 demonstrators in France.
May 21	Nuclear powered sub Scorpion sinks, entire crew found dead.
May 24	Mick Jagger and Marianne Faithful arrested for drug possession.
May 25	Gateway Arch dedicated in St. Louis.
May 27	Thailand announces to dispatch five thousand more troops to Vietnam War.
May 29	Truth in Lending Act is signed.
May 30	President De Gaulle disbands French Parliament.
June 1	Helen Keller dies.
June 3	Poor People's march in Washington.
June 4	Dodgers' Don Drysdale pitches sixth straight shutout en route to record fifty-eight scoreless innings.
June 8	The Standard & Poor's 500 Index closes above 100 for first time.
June 17	The Malayan Communist Party launches insurgency and state of emergency is imposed in Malaysia.
June 21	Supreme Court Chief Justice Earl Warren resigns.
June 23	In Buenos Aires, football stampede leaves hundreds dead and injured.

June 25	Bobby Bonds hits grand slam in his first major league game.
June 28	Daniel Ellsberg indicted for leaking Pentagon papers.
July 1	Central Intelligence Agency (CIA) is formed.
July	General Abrams takes over MACV forces from Westmoreland in Vietnam.
July 3	Cleveland Ohio records lowest temperature on record for July at 41 degrees.
July 4	Cleveland Indians' Luis Tiant strikes out nineteen Minnesota Twins.
July 5	Wilt Chamberlin traded from Philadelphia 76ers to Lakers.
July 7	The Yippie movement formed by Abbie Hoffman, Jerry Rubin and Paul Krassner, begins with displays of disorder, disrupting New York Stock Exchange to destruction of property at Grand Central Station.
July 14	Hank Aaron hits five hundredth home run.
July 15	Soap opera, *One Life to Live* premieres on ABC.
July 17	Saddam Hussein becomes Vice Chairman of the Revolutionary Council in Iraq after coup d'état.
	Beatles' film, *Yellow Submarine* premieres.
July 18	Semiconductor Intel is founded.
July 20	First international Special Olympics is held.
July 23	Race riot in Cleveland leaves three police dead.
July 24	PLO hijacks an El Al plane.
July 24	Hoyt Wilhelm breaks record for pitching appearances at 907.
July 26	South Vietnam leader, Truong Dinh Dzu sentenced to five years hard labor.
July 26-29	Anti-Vietnam War riots in Chicago disrupt Democratic Party Conference.
August 1	Cleveland Zoo opens.
August 5-8	Richard Nixon is nominated for President by Republicans.
August 10	Race riots in Chicago, Miami and Little Rock.

August 20-21	The Prague Spring ends as 750,000 Warsaw Pact troops, 6,500 tanks and 800 plans invade Czechoslovakia, the biggest operation in Europe since WWII.
August 21	The Medal of Honor is post-humously awarded to James Anderson, Jr., the first black U.S. Marine to receive the award.
August 22-30	Chicago riots as anti-war protestors clash with police during the 1968 Democratic Convention.
August 24	France explodes its first hydrogen bomb.
August 25	Arthur Ashe becomes first black to win U.S. tennis title.
August 29	U.S. Ambassador to Guatemala is assassinated on the streets of Guatemala City.
September 6	Swaziland becomes independent.
September 13	U.S. Army Major General Keith L. Ware, Medal of Honor recipient in WWII is killed in Vietnam.
September 14	Nigerian troops conquer Biafra.
	Detroit Tiger Denny McLain wins 30 games and remains the last to do it.
September 15	WUAB TV Channel 43 begins in Cleveland.
September 20	*Hawaii 5-0* debuts on CBS, becomes longest running crime show in television history until Law & Order.
	New York Yankees Mickey Mantle hits final homerun #536.
September 23	Vietnam War's Tet Offensive ends.
September 24	*60 Minutes* debuts on CBS and is still running in 2014.
September 28	Beatles' "Hey Jude" goes #1 for nine weeks.
September 30	Boeing rolls out its new 747.
October 2	Student protests in Tlatelolco, Mexico end in blood bath of 500 killed.
October 11	Apollo 7, the first manned Apollo mission.
	A military coup d'état in Panama over throws the democrat elected regime.

October 12	Equatorial Guinea declares independence from Spain.
	Summer Olympics open in Mexico City; boycotted by 32 African nations protesting South Africa's presence.
October 20	Jacqueline Kennedy marries Aristotle Onassis.
October 22	Gun Control Act enacted.
October 31	President Johnson halts U.S. bombing in North Vietnam.
November 1	Operation Rolling Thunder comes to an end after three and a half years.
November 4	Jordan's army battles Al Fatah forces.
November 5	Election Day. Nixon receives 31,770,000 votes — Humphrey 31,270,000 votes.
November 11	Yale University admits women for first time.
November 14	National Turn In Your Draft Card Day prompts rallies and protests across America.
November 18	Military coup in Mali.
November 26	U.S. Air Force First Lieutenant helicopter pilot James P. Fleming rescues an Army Special Forces unit from a large enemy attack, earns Medal of Honor.
	South Vietnam agrees to join Paris peace talks.
November 27-30	First National Women's Liberation Conference.
December 1	Unemployment rate at 3.3%, is the lowest in fifteen years.
December 3	Elvis Presley's 1968 Comeback Special
December 10	A 300 million yen robbery occurs in Tokyo, Japan.
December 20	Famous American writer John Steinbeck dies.
December 22	Dwight D. Eisenhower's grandson marries daughter of President Richard Nixon.

Christmas 1968 at a Real Resort

On December 23, 1968, I was given an unexpected surprise, compliments of the Adjutant General's office in Cu Chi. I remember the words that came from one of my hooch mates who worked with coordinating Rest and Recuperation Leaves (R&Rs) to places most combat troops in Vietnam could only dream of, but rarely live to enjoy. These words that were shouted on a heat-draining day—there was no shade in Cu Chi…"Trimmer, pack your shit. You are going to Australia… tomorrow!" Oh my gosh, I stopped in my tracks. My first thought might have been…"round-eyed women?" Second thought, "frolicking on a beach?"

Then, my heart stopped beating at faster than humming bird speed as the next words out of the AJ clerk's mouth were…"just kidding." "Bad joke," I said. "You know how I have dreamed about spending my R&R on one of the famous beaches of the land down under." "Hold your horses, Trimmer. Yes, I was kidding but you do have a long weekend for Vung Tau if you are interested."

Christmas on the beaches of the South China Sea, basking in the sun—in a bathing suit, oh my! Of course, I was interested and I started packing some "civy" clothes. I had to buy a bathing suit at the Cu Chi PX (if they had one).

Turns out, as the clerk told me, the opening for this weekend furlough came about because some other unlucky warrior in the field was killed in action (KIA) and I was saddened to know that was the reason I was getting this 3 ½ day retreat in Vung Tau. When I was out in the bush for all those months, we often heard stories from other troops who made it to Vung Tau. I never actually met another soldier who made it to Australia as most of the base camp warriors grabbed those slots. Unfair as that was, I never dwelled on it. I felt like, heck everyone in this hellhole deserves to get out of here for a break.

Vung Tau was well known for the fact that there were "round-eyed" women there. Most were a mixture of French Chinese or French Vietnamese. I was not disappointed when I arrived in Vung Tau. I spent every day on the beach, sleeping most of the time. I never realized how tired I was from enduring the last 9 ½ months with little or no sleep day after day after day. The evenings are a blur to me—lots of rum and cokes. I do remember chumming around with several fun-loving and rowdy Australians who were stationed in Phuoc Tuy Province, which held Vung Tau. Little did I know that I would be in Aussie-land the next month.

Lots of silvery pristine beach sand, very big lobsters and…no Viet Cong, But I still had a hard time letting my guard down for the entire 3 ½ days. Three of the Aussies constantly told me about Sydney and places like…The Kings Cross, Bondi Beach and Manly Beach and the largest great white sharks in the world and…the friendliest women in the world. I hoped I would get there someday but first priority was to make it though the rest of my couple of months left in South Vietnam. Those 3 ½ days in Vung Tau flew by at jet speed, and all of a sudden, I was back in dusty (dry season) and muddy (monsoon season) Cu Chi. Back to reality.

Hey GI, lookee here! Just for old time's sake, I looked up hotel deals for 2015 in Vung Tau and I think some of you might be half tempted to consider investigating what the amenities include. The prices aren't bad…here's a peek just for kicks.

Muong Thanh Vung	2 rooms left	$56 per night
Ky Koa Hotel	5 rooms left	$37 per night
Vung Tau P & T	2 rooms left	$35 per night
Thanh Thuy	2 rooms left	$27 per night
Green Vung	5 rooms left	$25 per night
Seika	2 rooms left	$21 per night
Loc An Xanh	3 rooms left	$13 per night
Hoa Bae	2 rooms left	$10 per night
	Average Room Rate:	$28 per night

If any of you guys react to this news and give it a shot, please write to me about your experience. You can thank me later.

OTHER NOTABLE EVENTS OF 1968

- Rowan and Martin's *Laugh-In* premieres.
- Battle of Hue in Vietnam War.
- N. Scott Momaday, a Kiowia Indian, wins a Pulitzer Prize for House Made of Dawn.
- Battle of Kham Duc, devastating defeat for U.S. as hundreds of troops and civilians were killed or left behind.
- Chief, the last U.S. Army Cavalry horse dies.
- President Johnson amends Civil Rights Act by signing the Indian Bill of Rights.
- Redwood National Bank is established.
- Battle of LangVei, NVA force with Soviet tanks overrun Special Forces camp, inflicting massive casualties.
- Ambush at Ben Cui, NVA force ambushes entire column of 1st BN 5th Infantry mechanized unit outside of 25th Infantry's Dau Tieng outpost, destroying half the column in minutes.
- Clint Eastwood and Eli Wallach star in *The Good, the Bad and the Ugly*.
- Battle of Buell, NVA and Chinese forces overrun some 25th Infantry positions, but Americans counter attack successfully…paying a huge price.
- Ohio State beats O.J. Simpson's led USC team in the Rose Bowl and is named college football national champions.
  (Source: www.brainyhistory.com)

As you can see, the year of 1968 was a happening year and not just because of the Vietnam War's infamous Tet Offensive. However, as 1968 closed its chapter, the U.S. command in Saigon released figures showing that more Americans died during the first six months of 1968 than in all of the years of the war combined up till then. **Good riddance to 1968…one very nasty year!**

1968's Bloodiest Months of the Vietnam War

More Vietnam stuff—because it is a preamble to what follows in this book. Believe it or not, there were occasional lulls during the Vietnam War. There just was not ever a lull in the threat of something happening, not ever, for pure combat troops. One of those lulls took place at the end of 1967. It did not last long as the war was quickly taken to another level in January 1968.

Make no mistake. Overall, the Vietnam War was extremely active in 1966, 1967 and 1969, especially with battles like Soui Tre that took place, as mentioned previously. But the year mentioned in Chapter 3 would prove to be THE bloodiest year of the entire Vietnam War, as more than 100,000 Americans would end up as a casualty in 1968. That unthinkable number of Americans killed and wounded was more than double the total of American casualties incurred in the Gulf War, Afghanistan War, Iraq War and throw in the Spanish-American War...combined. So, when one hears of a troop doing multiple tours in one of America's recent wars, please, with all respect, put it in the proper perspective in comparison to the Vietnam War...which was unquestionably America's most horror-stricken combat experience in history for American combat troops.

Many of our battles with the Viet Cong, North Vietnamese or a mixture of both (and throw in a few Chinese Army regulars) were fought within twenty to thirty yards of either side. Easily, we could see each other's facial expressions. Our enemy in the Vietnam War was stubborn, persistent and unbelievably courageous. At least, in my mind, they left that impression on me and most of the men I fought side by side with for the eternity we were there (those who made it) have echoed the same feelings.

Those Damn NVA's

The North Vietnamese Army (NVA) emerged as a fighting force to be reckoned with at the battle of Dien Bien Phu where they shocked the French in a decisive victory in 1954. In a memo from Robert McNamara to Johnson on November 3, 1965, he told the President there were only 7,500 NVA troops in South Vietnam that year, that the main enemy would be the primitive and untrained 25,000 Viet Cong force.

McNamara was partially correct but mostly wrong. The part he missed was simply too difficult to accept or he did not want to accept it—that the NVA force had an endless supply of men to keep their 500,000 main force at that level. During 1968 and the following post-Tet years of the war, North Vietnam was drafting well over 100,000 men at a draft age of seventeen every year, so the NVA manpower reserves were always more than adequate. Oh, by the way, the Viet Cong army was 150,000 strong. McNamara was not too far off with his estimation of 32,500 enemy troops for Americans to engage. He missed the other...617,500. Still, American forces clearly defeated the combined VA – NVA armies before the Tet Offensive, during Tet, when fighting reached its peak in intensity and casualties on both sides, and we defeated them on the battlefield in the post-Tet years.

The North Vietnamese Army, without counting several hundred thousand "advisors" from China, North Korea, Cuba and the Soviet Union, became a one million strong army by the peak of the Vietnam War. It did not matter how many tens of thousands (hundreds of thousands) of them we killed. Those who replaced their fallen NVA comrades fought just as ferociously and this became a horrible nightmare for America's combat troops. Still…we did defeat them, but our history books haven't told that story, not yet and we who survived Vietnam's nightmare have had to endure the untruths told about how we were defeated?

America had won a clear-cut victory, not a stalemate — a resounding victory. The NVA admitted to this. Their top military guy, General Vo Nguyen Giap, knew it, and he understood why America's politicians gave up on their own American military. Giap published these facts in his memoirs. They are available for everyone to read.

There was one area of the Vietnam War in particular in 1968 and 1969 that was literally a disgusting bloody cesspool. It was called War Zone C, located in III Corp. Our Marine brothers up in I Corp would of course, disagree and state that I Corp was the hottest area throughout the war…the records prove they would be wrong. In late 1967 and thereafter, the Vietnam War had become a PROTECT SAIGON AT ALL COSTS mission. If the enemy could succeed with a highly successful blow (killing as many as possible) in Saigon or surrounding areas such as Cholon, Hoc Mon, Bien Hoa, etc., it would be such a psychological victory that would overwhelm Americans back home, that calls to end the war would be heard around the world. Unfortunately, it happened.

I served with the U.S. Army's 3rd 22nd 25th Infantry Division in War Zone C as a combat infantry pointman for nine and a half months. The average life span for my counterparts and me was about two weeks. While my documentation of things in this book is limited or curtailed (as it was in *Condemned Property?*), please understand that it has been extremely difficult to convince other combat Vietnam War veterans to contribute their stories and help substantiate my statements by sharing their experiences. It has been this way since the day the Vietnam War ended, and unfortunately, many Vietnam veterans have taken their untold stories to their graves. This is very unfortunate because the liberal educators have distorted the accounts of the Vietnam War to their intended targets, their students, future American leaders…**I can't stand it!** So, I sit down and painfully write books in an effort to do what I can, regardless of the effect it might have on the few who are offended…sin loi minoi.

I hope to remain above ground for some time to come, regardless of the many attempts by incompetent VA employees to put me underground prematurely. It has almost happened, but they just don't know how strong my will to survive is—compliments of the Vietnam War and the brave men that I fought next to over there.

Actually, I have personally fought the VA tooth and nail over several things, and I have occasionally ended up as a victor over that 1,200-pound gorilla. I hope to chalk up more victories over the next several years or as long as I am still breathing.

- Yes, War Zone C incurred the most total casualties in the short period of time (December 1967-May 1968), more than any other six-month period in the war.

- I repeat myself here (sorry)…1968 in the Vietnam War ended up with the most casualties of any year during the war, and more Agent Orange was sprayed in 1968 in War Zone C than at any other time or any other area during the war.

To all of you who know "real" combat veterans who participated in that war… they deserve a handshake, a hug, a THANK YOU from the non-Vietnam veterans. An apology from our government. If your Vietnam War relatives or friends served in combat during the 1967-1969 time frame, they deserve considerably more than what America has begrudgingly given them.

Most times when I am into deep and private thoughts with no interruptions, Vietnam is usually one of my subjects of concentration. Sorry America, I just can't help it—I deal with it. Our beloved God knows we who went to that forsaken hellhole did not go there of our own accord. Therefore…IF…I end up in heaven after I finish my stay on the planet Earth, I hope to be reunited with all those good men who died in Vietnam and who have continued dying very prematurely since coming home.

In the 2007 book, *Days of Valor*, author Robert L. Tonsetic provides his inside account of the bloodiest six months of the entire Vietnam War, from December 1967 to May 1968. Tonsetic was one hundred percent right on. This time period included the infamous Tet Offensives in early 1968 into April and the May "mini" Tet, which was by no means a miniature anything. The month of May actually registered the largest casualty losses for U.S. forces than any month of the entire Vietnam War. This was the time period that my brave war buddies and I fought side by side. I never dreamed that I would be writing about that time in our lives nearly half a century later and actually visualizing many things that happened in 1968…TODAY!

Tonsetic's combat unit was the 199th Light Infantry Brigade, which operated heavily in War Zone D outside the northern areas of Saigon. In the end, one of the ultimate targets for the communist forces was Saigon. So, the 199th LIB had to remain close enough to Saigon to defend it when the city was threatened. Next door in War Zone C, where my war buddies and I spent our tour in Vietnam, was northwest of War Zone D. It was our job to block, deter, and eliminate enemy advancement from invading War Zone D. The 25th Infantry and the 199th LIB depended heavily on each other's success in order to make it home alive.

SINCE 'WE' CAME HOME FROM VIETNAM, THE AMERICAN GOVERNMENT HAS KILLED MORE AMERICANS SOLDIERS THAN "THEY" DID !!!

War Zone C

The term "War Zone C" was used by the United States Army to describe a region near the Cambodian border in III Corp where the Viet Cong activity was exceptionally strong. Reportedly, the general location of the headquarters for communist military and political activities in South Vietnam was in this area, underground in the Tay Ninh province near the Cambodian border. War Zone C included Tay Ninh, Binh Long, and Binh Duong provinces, which were three of the most heavily sprayed areas of Agent Orange during the war.

- *Over half of the Agent Orange sprayed during the Vietnam War (about twenty million gallons) was dumped into War Zone C (over ten million gallons) to the level that some areas such as The Iron Triangle would eventually become completely uninhabitable.*

Iron Triangle (War Zone C)

The Iron Triangle was a National Liberation Front (NLF) stronghold twenty miles northwest of Saigon, which had been built by the Vietminh twenty years before in the war against French colonialism. It served as a supply depot and staging area with an immense underground complex including command head- quarters, dining halls, hospital rooms, munitions factories, and living quarters. Comprising of about one hundred twenty-five square miles, it was never cleared by the French nor was it neutralized by the United States or ARVN, Army of the Republic of Vietnam until the war was nearly over. It was by and large bounded by the Saigon River, the Song (river) Thi Thinh north of Bien Hoa, and the Than Dien Forest in Binh Duong Province. The area was thickly forested, consisting of jungle and rubber plantations and containing a few small villages and hamlets.

In January 1967, the United States and ARVN mounted the war's first major com- bined operation and the first U.S. corps-size operation. Operation Cedar Falls deployed 32,000 troops into the Triangle. Its "search and destroy" objective was not to evade the enemy but to engage and eliminate enemy forces, destroy base camps and supplies, remove all noncombatants along with possessions and live- stock to strategic hamlets, and completely destroy four principal villages. Vast underground complexes were found, and large quantities of supplies and papers were captured. This was just the beginning of what was ahead for America's military. The complete arsenal was utilized—intensive bombing, flamethrowers, chemical warfare (defoliants and the first authorized major use of CS, or tear gas), and land-clearing Rome plows. Units participating in Cedar Falls included the 173rd Airborne Brigade, the 196th and 199th Infantry brigades, elements of the 1st and 25th Infantry divisions, the 11th Armored Cavalry Regiment, and the ARVN 5th Ranger Group.

The enemy fled in masses to sanctuaries in Cambodia until the operation was finished. However, the destruction, chronicled in Jonathan Schell's The Village of Ben Suc, *was considerable. About seven thousand refugees were created and the region was made almost uninhabitable to anyone other than NLF-NVA forces. The operation's magnitude increased NLF utilization of Cambodian sanctuaries; however, they did return to rebuild camps, which became springboards for the assault on Saigon during the Tet Offensive, 1968. Ensuing operations against the Iron Triangle included Uniontown, Atlas Wedge and Toan Thang.*
(Sources: Vietnamwar.net and 25thInfantry.org)

Needless to say, War Zone C's combat participants did not have the luxury of knowing what their life expectancy might be. I say that anyone who was a real combat troop in War Zone C during the years of 1967 through 1969…and is still living today is here purely by the graces of the highest power. Thank you, dear God; I am happy and appreciative to be one of those as of this writing.

In Ronald H. Spector's 1993 book, *After Tet, The Bloodiest Year in Vietnam*, he dedicates a nice chapter to mostly those warriors who fought in 1968. "You Don't Know How Lucky We Are To Have Soldiers Like This" was the title of one of his chapters. Spector himself is considered by many qualified sources as one of America's leading military historians. I like how he builds up America's soldiers, marines, aviators, and sailors who fought in the 1968 Tet Offensives to be in many respects, the finest military force the United States had ever sent overseas. Our grandfathers in World War I were often sent to battle only half-trained. Whose fault was that? In World War II, Americans had suffered devastating defeats in Bataan and at Kasserine Pass. In the Korean War, many of the first Americans to fight against the North Koreans abandoned their equipment and fled in panic. In the Vietnam War, combat troops met combined forces of Viet Cong and North Vietnamese Army—supported by China and the Soviet Union, and not only held their ground but also counterattacked the numerically superior communists over and over, earning victory after victory in most major battles…FOR WHAT?

Why then, were these warriors who fought as bravely and as ferociously as any Americans did before them being regarded as "society's" losers, suckers who risked their lives in a wrong war? Vietnam's warriors did everything their fathers and grandfathers did. They did everything asked of them, even died for their country. They fought with everything they had, rarely complaining and never did they give in to the enemy. All they wanted when they came home was…a little respect, maybe an apple pie, a hug, some appreciation. That is all we wanted. Didn't happen like that. **Shame on Americans for that.**

They Bring Their Wars Home Too!

We Vietnam War veterans saw this coming, and we tried to warn America. The following headline was featured in the *San Antonio Express News* on November 8, 2014:

As Iraq, Afghanistan faded, veterans of both conflicts began to fight a new war at home!

Those headlines appeared repeatedly, loud and clear in American newspapers from the 1990s until the present, except they featured veterans of a war that rampaged decades earlier, the Vietnam War, of course. Bringing one's war back with him or her is no small matter. It means there is the threat of a mental health disorder, which is far more dangerous and life threatening than a shrapnel wound to the leg or arm, and longer lasting. It had been no different for war-returning warriors from Operation Enduring Freedom (OEF) and Operation Iraqi Freedom (OIF) than it was for us after Vietnam ended. High combat stress and trauma would linger on for many for the rest of their lives. At least our country offered these newer returning veterans a small, short-term health-care package that looked like this:

- Eligible for two years of free military service-related health care through the Department of Veterans Affairs (VA) health-care system. Still, even at this time, so little was known about the burden and clinical circumstances of mental health diagnoses among these most recent wars, let alone those from the Vietnam and Korean wars.
- Soon, the veterans from the Afghanistan War that began on September 30, 2001 were included, and they also were found to be suffering from psychological problems from their highly stressful combat exposure. And they would be taken care of, jumping in to the long line, pushing Vietnam War veterans further back towards the end of the growing line of America's wounded veterans that were in need of timely mental health care.

Unfortunately, as I write this part, it is no longer a secret to most of America that Vietnam's veterans have been ignored for too long, and their premature death count has surpassed what anyone could have imagined when they came marching home to their non-welcome-home parades. I know very few of my Vietnam War buddies who harbor any resentment towards our war veterans from the Gulf Wars. To the contrary, we have stepped up and have been their biggest supporters. They know this to be a fact. What has become so very obvious is that we have a common adversary and that adversary's initials are...**VA!**

To the credit of the VA, they were able to detect mental health illnesses caused by battle horror a lot earlier and why not—we had entered the 2000s. The Vietnam War era seemed so far back that those who fought in that war must have fought with rocks and slingshots—they did, didn't they?

The conscription program (draft) during the Vietnam War force-fed quick and profound choices for those who chose not to go just as it did for those who went away to serve Uncle Sam. Lives would be changed for entire families. Unfortunately, in too many cases, these changes would have an effect on the rest of their lives. If the draft did anything positive, it led to our present all-volunteer and very professional military force.

In Vietnam's war, helicopters took battles to a whole new dimension as a weapon and as a life-saving machine. Many analysts have estimated that helicopters may have been responsible for saving 50,000 to 100,000 Americans who had incurred life-threatening wounds that would have terminated them where they lay with Vietnam's war-ravaged swamps and jungles as their last memory. To this day, in the gulf conflicts, the helicopters are saving lives from physical wounds as the flying ambulances come to the rescue. Whenever I hear a helicopter today, forty-seven years after the Tet Offensive, I look up and search the sky instantly. Sometimes, I just stand there and watch it until it flies out of sight or far, far away from my fading hearing senses. I may get hit with an instant flashback, which has a ninety percent chance of not being a good one.

When Vietnam War veterans came home—about three million of them—many of them were angry, shocked, and depressed with feelings of hopelessness, thinking...**What just happened to us this past year?** On the other hand, many Vietnam War veterans came home with the intent of resuming their lives, changed, but vastly matured, attempting to get on with their lives, returning to a job or college and hopefully leaving Vietnam behind them. This worked for some. It did not work for others as memories resurfaced over and over again, tormenting them, forcing them to seek help. This is where most Vietnam War veterans that I know, are today...accepting help.

The lasting legacy of homelessness or suicide has not spared today's returning veterans. Although most homeless veterans are survivors (or victims) of the Vietnam War stigma, they are dying off—obviously—and being replaced by their children and grandchildren and for many (not all) of the same reasons. They too have been cursed with...**bringing their wars home.**

In *Condemned Property?*, I attempted to volunteer a gentle and soft warning to the readers. That warning was...expect history to repeat itself again and again. Damn it! The VA claims that the younger veterans from the OEF/OIF and Afghanistan are at greater risk for PTSD problems and need to be taken care of with a higher priority than the older veterans are. What? So, a Vietnam War veteran who fathered an OEF/OIF or Afghanistan veteran and experienced as much, probably more combat trauma...is a lower priority for extending their lives?

Now that they have brought their wars home, they need to be taken care of far better than we were, than we are being taken care of today. I seriously mean this. If you want to help our country's veterans, you need to do it by **shaming the VA.**

Vietnam Veterans Deserve a Better Place in History... They Earned It

No event in American history is more misunderstood than the Vietnam War. It was misreported then and it is misremembered now.

- Richard Nixon

I chose to start this book with a few chapters relating to the Vietnam War. I guess I was extending my story from *Condemned Property?* Honestly, there will never be enough of the truth shared with Americans about that place in which my war buddies fought their hearts out. I am simply trying to give my best shot with my meager ad budget to bestow honor to the warriors of a war that fought against a very sinister, evil and merciless enemy, **the communists.**

My hope is that my brothers and sisters will unite to participate in the correct re-education process of today's generation and generations ahead by joining me in sharing their stories of what was done to us. So, as in my first book, I sought out some of my brothers who read *Condemned Property?*, and I asked them to participate. Only in *Payback Time!* I have used alias names as some of their stories are too personal to divulge their identity. Sorry—that is the way I had to do it out of respect and love for them and what they have been through...and are still going through.

There have been loads of Vietnam War movies. Some became award winning. Many of them had anti-war viewpoints. My books attempt to convey the TRUTH in no uncertain terms, so if you are looking for fictional stories to stimulate your imagination...might as well stop here. But thanks for buying my book and reading this far. Really, I thank you for that...IF you stop here.

Still with me? Hold on to your hats because we are going to fast forward away from that dark era of the Vietnam War and address things as they are today for all veterans. However, I reserve the right to interject an experience or two from a Vietnam War veteran. They deserve the exposure…they earned the respect.

Please don't let the titles of my books (so far) fool you. Sure, the anger is displayed, but I do want to sell some books. I hope to be entertaining in that you will want to stay glued to my book as so many told me they were with *Condemned Property?* These so-called marketing experts have warned me that I must detach myself emotionally and not view book sales as a referendum on my writing ability or talent. **What the hell does that mean?** I am a Vietnam War veteran. I have baggage. I have PTSD. I have Diabetes Type II. I have suffered ischemic strokes, etc. I have watched my dear buddies die and die prematurely after the Vietnam War—right? So, how do I…detach myself emotionally?

Now Americans are listening to us. They are making noises to their congressmen and they aren't leaving it there. They are following up on their letters and emails and asking for explanations…FACT, my buddies. On the following pages are a few abbreviated responses that our congressmen have sent back to me, responding to letters (lots of them) I have sent…sometimes over and over, certified, signature required or whatever. One could say that I overwhelmed them with an actual 'human wave of letters' barrage. I came to the conclusion after receiving so many responses that I must have hit a severe lull period in their lives. "Make no never mind." Remember that one?

In 2014 and 2015, Vietnam War veterans continue to be "veterans under siege" from being deceived and dishonored by our own government's VA system. I have seen and felt the attitude of a VA official in three Compensation & Pension exams. The antagonism I felt from these people (non-veterans, of course) made my skin cringe. Only now, we Nam vets have company as our brothers and sisters from all of the more recent wars are routinely being denied timely benefits and health care that they are entitled to and sometimes die waiting for.

Since *Condemned Property?* was launched in 2013, the whole planet Earth has become privy to the VA problems, and they stay tuned in to what happens next. There have been monumental happenings during the entire year of 2014 after *Condemned Property?* made its appearance. *Payback Time!* will address these revolutionary changes—most improvements and that is a good thing.

From this point, I will leave the Vietnam War Era and fast-forward to the post years of the Vietnam War and then to what was going on as 2014 came to an end. But first, I have assembled several nostalgic news headlines and images from those *unforgettable* years from the earliest years when it was just a conflict to the shocking Tet Year of 1968 and beyond, when a conflict turned into a

CHAPTER 4

IMAGES OF VIETNAM—THAT WON'T BE FORGOTTEN

O n the following pages, you will find images which represent memories of my visit to the twilight zone called South Vietnam. I tried not to duplicate too many pictures that I used in *Condemned Property?*, but a few of them just had to be shown again.

Memories? What is their value if they bring sadness or even horror and cause flashbacks and hallucinations, which I continue to experience? My thinking is that no matter how painful those times were, you never want to let go (I don't) of the only images you have left of your war buddies who are gone.

These photos on the following pages may be a bit old fashioned, as they did not originate from a "smart phone." How about a 110-instamatic camera with black and white film? They are good enough to capture moments in time that are gone forever. The most unique thing about our memories is that they belong to the owners, lock, stock and barrel. No one can take them away from you or invade them unless you allow them to. Now, please don't let this confuse you. Sometimes, our memories can be about something that surely happened, and yet…it has not completed its happening yet. Ponder that one for a few. "I still go back to Vietnam every day." Those were the words from a combat Marine veteran who read my first book and called me in the middle of his first reading of it. This Marine fought at and survived the battle at Khe Sanh. He earned three justifiable Purple Hearts, and when he came home in 1969, he shut up about everything that happened to him over there. No one was interested or cared.

I also visit Vietnam each and every day and some nights as well, although those visits aren't as pleasant as the daytime visits or…day mares. I will continue to visit Vietnam, and there is neither therapy existing today nor medication powerful enough to block memories. Anyway, to follow are a few images to keep my memories alive. They do not require captions as they speak for themselves. Some of them may have appeared in my first book and were important enough to share again.

Viet Cong Mortars Hit School Yard
Eight Small Children Are Wounded

CU CHI – For the children of Duc Hue, 14 miles southwest of Cu Chi, the morning had been one of running around the school yard much as children everywhere on summer vacation. A meeting had been called by the district chief to discuss the formation of a civilian defense group to protect the hamlet from the Viet Cong. But for the children, the war was far away as they played while their parents met in the schoolhouse.

Hi Love! Chris Noel here.

I once told a reporter that I was "just a girl who's trying to make the men she loves happy. You see, I'm in love with half a million men... all our American troops in Vietnam."

That was in 1965. Fifty years later, I'm STILL in love with our troops... and I hope YOU are too!

If you'd like to make a donation to help shelter homeless American veterans at Chris Noel's Cease Fire House, please call or e-mail us today. We need the money desperately!

God bless you.
Thank you, love!

Chris Noel

Chris Noel's
CEASE FIRE HOUSE
291 NE 19th Avenue
Boynton Beach, FL 33435
Phone: (561) 736-4325
E-mail: vetsville@aol.com

The only ones qualified to talk about

Vietnam

are those who lived it!

Alvin Warner Robertson

Private First Class
A CO, 3RD BN, 60TH INFANTRY, 9TH INF DIV, USARV
Army of the United States
Twinsburg, Ohio
June 07, 1948 to December 28, 1968
ALVIN W ROBERTSON is on the Wall at Panel 36W Line 087
See the full profile for Alvin Robertson

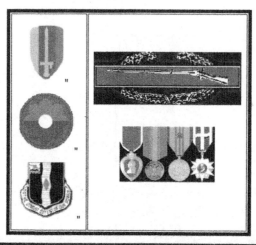

John William Viktoryn, Jr

Private First Class
1ST PLT, B CO, 3RD BN, 506TH INFANTRY, 101ST ABN DIV, USARV
Army of the United States
Cleveland, Ohio
April 27, 1947 to May 08, 1968
JOHN W VIKTORYN Jr is on the Wall at Panel 57E Line 011
See the full profile for John Viktoryn

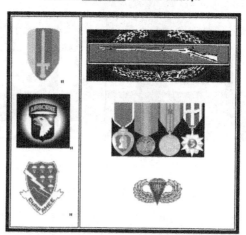

Vietnam generation fading as death rate rises for vets

CHAPTER 5

PTSD...BEYOND REPAIR?

It was a nice fall day in November 2014 when this happened. I responded to another Vietnam veteran's "reach out" to meet with me...on the very day he called. I did not know this veteran, but hey, if he was a "real" Vietnam veteran, I had to accommodate his request to meet on that day. He also stated that he had heard of my first book, *Condemned Property?* and he wanted to buy a signed edition. The meeting was confirmed and we both showed up.

We exchanged some family stories and shared some pictures of our families, our dogs (he had his dog in his vehicle) and our Nam family brothers. He was badly wounded in Nam, lost a leg and had other nasty looking scars, which looked like shrapnel damage. His family situation was quite tragic as many combat Vietnam veterans' families do not often include ...*happily ever after* endings.

He had three daughters, but two of them had unfortunately died very prematurely. One was killed by a hit-and-run driver, which this Nam vet had attempted to find—don't blame him for that. He searched for his daughter's killer for years, planning to hunt him down and end his life. His goal was never fulfilled, not at this point, that is. He talked about it as though he was still on that mission. I wondered somewhat how he would perform the act if he was successful in finding this murderous criminal, being so physically challenged. I did not ask him that question—did not need to as he would show me how and with what, at the end of our meeting that day.

His wife was still with him, but he admitted not understanding why. They had been married for thirty-four years (his second marriage), but they slept in different rooms because of his nightmares, which could include some aggressive reactions to an imagined enemy in his sleep. I could totally relate with this, although I believe he would never hurt his wife intentionally as I would not hurt my lovely wife. And I do experience similar nightmares and vivid hallucinations, which are covered in more detail in *Condemned Property?*

Our first hour and a half of the meeting went as well as I had hoped—it is never a given that a meeting between two combat veterans with intense and grotesque memories of combat deaths will even begin well, let alone end well. But we are usually okay when we meet for the first time and this meeting went well.

I have met a few other Nam veterans or those who were trying to come off as "real". Nam veterans and I have been able to smell their phoniness as many of their details just didn't match up. In two cases, I challenged the imposters' stories and just excused myself from the conversation.

This Nam vet was not an imposter. I knew the places he had been. There is no way anyone could have described the details as he did without having been there. The names of people, places, battles, scenes, the smells he described, his people descriptions—it was all appropriate. And he couldn't have gained such knowledge out of a book or from the internet. However, as the conversation went into its third hour (We were drinking just coffee.), I began to get very concerned for this new Nam brother. He wasn't telling me anything that he did not believe he did or that he did not believe was done to him. I'm not a certified "shrink" by any means, but my amateur diagnosis of him was..."extreme" PTSD, almost to the brink of a disaster happening with him and others around him—of which I was now one.

I know combat Vietnam War veterans who served with elite units: Green Berets, Rangers, Recon, Long Range Recon Patrol (LRP), Tunnel Rats, Snipers and Seals. I have great respect for all of them, and they generally have the same respect for what I did over there as a combat infantry point man for the United States Army.

Some of the combat veterans I know have been awarded or have earned boatloads of decorations for their heroic actions. I totally respect their honors, and I am proud to know them. And they have mutual respect for my decorations and what I did to earn them. However, on this date, I must have met America's super soldier of the entire Vietnam War. I will just refer to him as "Jake" in this story. Oh, he did not claim to be a super soldier, but he truly believed everything that he told me in that final hour, as follows:

- He was recommended for three (3) Silver Stars, but...he claimed to have turned them down as he did with a recommendation for the Bronze Star – Valor.
- He served with an elite infantry recon unit where he was the #1 sniper, not only with his unit, but also in the entire U.S. Army or Marines for that matter.

- He was the only survivor after his platoon was ambushed by a combined force of Viet Cong and North Vietnamese Army near Cambodia. He was left behind in the bush for several days, having to eat off the land and tend to his many wounds on his own—remarkably.
- He earned the rank of First Sergeant…in a very short time. I let him think that.
- He told me how he accidentally shot an American helicopter down with a .50 cal machine gun, and there was a Major inside it. (I did not get the details of that one from him.)
- Oh, and there was his pet "Baboon" who was a killer and guarded him until he took a round from a Viet Cong…pet "Baboon"?
- In one battle, he told me that he was shot and wounded…38 times. Now our meeting was beginning to get uneasy for me.

I had to stop him at this time as I remembered his dog was in his van for the past three hours and I had to get home to walk my own dog. I made my exit gracefully, showing him as much respect and sympathy (more of the latter) as I could muster. On the way, Jake insisted I come over and meet his dog, Max. Being an animal lover, I went over to his van. Sure enough, there he was, a beautiful German shepherd, but he may have had some mix in him like an Australian Dingo. Regardless, he was a good-looking dog. My attempt to depart was delayed again as Jake pleaded to show me the array of handguns (all loaded except the first chamber) that would have made Wyatt Earp, Doc Holiday and Billy the Kid envious. I am guessing his 45 cal., 9mm and 44 magnum guns were not for dealing with road-rage loonies. These were in his van "just in case" he stumbled on to the killer of his daughter. **And who could blame him?**

Whew! After I arrived safe and sound at our warm and friendly condo, walked and romped with my frisky 176 pound Newfoundland—Bella Lu, I settled down and called three of my Vietnam War buddies…Jack Bellemy, Bob Best and Dennis Amily. I needed to have conversations of reality that evening so that I could attempt to have a sound sleep. But for the rest of the evening and the next day, I could not get this lost soul out of my mind.

When my lovely wife, Ginny came home, I described my evening to her. She wondered how I was going to handle the situation. I said that Jake is getting psychiatric consultation at the VA. I told her that is a good thing for him and all around him. My plan is to just be there for him so that he has another Nam vet friend to talk to. Sometimes that is all the PTSD victims of this degree really need. I did not challenge his stories, just nodded a couple times and offered my friendship from there on out. Can't help loving the guy—he is my brother.

My personal experience with VA hospitals in the States did not begin until the 2000s and then again in the 2010s, compliments of Agent Orange exposure in Vietnam nearly half a century ago. Those experiences were positive for me in every respect.

I did spend eight to ten days in Tay Ninh Hospital in 1968 and of course, I had a few short visits to VA clinics throughout the war, and I don't recall too many bad experiences. Then again, a chance to get out of the boonies and into a bed with a real mattress and a real pillow as well as warm meals? Come on, are you kidding me? What could one find to complain about? The rats, roaches, snakes, centipedes, spiders, lizards, etc. that were everywhere—hell, we ate some of those out in the bush. They didn't bother me—I just swiped them away...get away bad thing!

Forty-plus years ago, the big news in America was Woodstock. Over half a million Americans were fighting in one of the most brutal wars in the history of the world under the worst conditions imaginable of any war and...nobody back home cared. We stood alone back then. But hey, when we would come home (those of us who did come home in one piece or in fragmented pieces physically and mentally), we had these waiting for us:

- Professional counseling.
- Special adoption to society programs.
- Disability checks for the disabled and wounded from physical wounds, PTSD or Agent Orange.
- Traumatic Brain Injury treatment (we were hit by rockets and mortars too).
- Homelessness / poverty relief.
- A job placement program.
- Free medical care.

Surely, all of my Vietnam War buddies remember receiving all of those "bennies" when we came home to indifference, scorn, ignorance, hate, betrayal and that list went on. Actually, all of the "bennies" listed here (and more) are what our government is providing for today's veterans. Great! We fought a long battle to make this happen for them.

Yeah, Woodstock rocked while we were being rocketed...wow! Guess what, my fellow Americans—who attended Woodstock? Rich kids, the kind whose families got them into the National Guard or Reserve units to which middle class or poor kids had little or no access. Throughout the war, hundreds of thousands of wounded and very sick Vietnam War veterans came home. What most people don't know and will *never* know is how many of them died in VA hospitals from their unattended wounds, which of course were vulnerable to bacterial infections.

My fellow patriots, there have been dozens of professional studies conducted since the end of the Vietnam War, which have substantiated that most Vietnam War veterans who had PTSD a decade or so after the war ended have shown little improvement, and a large percentage have died very prematurely.

The term PTSD was not put on the map as a signature mental injury of the Vietnam War until this historic study—the *National Vietnam Veterans Readjustment Study* finished in 1992. My math tells us that those who fought in the bloodiest years from 1967 to 1969, also the peak years for Agent Orange usage, were not even thought about as having PTSD until well over twenty years after they had already returned home. Is there any wonder why Vietnam veterans suffer from their PTSD problems for most of or all of their lives? Still, the VA compensation and pension examiners continue to place more doubt on a Vietnam veteran's claim than for a younger returning warrior who is receiving his or her treatment almost immediately upon returning home, not twenty to forty years later. It has taken Vietnam War veterans several decades to receive their just due recognition of illnesses from their combat horrors, which have been accelerated by the poisons that infect many of their brains and bodies today. There can be no comparison between a returning veteran just home from a Middle East war being diagnosed *now* for PTSD and being treated *now* versus a Vietnam War veteran who had been fighting off his demons and poisons all alone for decades... no comparison.

Lately, scientists and policy makers (who rarely or never fought in combat) are debating or doubting that trauma actually does exist in some veterans longer than in others. Some of them have gone so far as to suggest that a veteran who is receiving service connected disability benefits is likely not to get better, that there is more incentive to remain sick? Those researchers and policy makers might be missing something when they make such statements about a particular veteran's present condition, such as:

- How old was he or she when treatment was initiated?
- What illnesses have set in since the veteran returned home and was first treated for PTSD and/or illnesses associated with PTSD such as...hypertension/high blood pressure, ischemic heart conditions, ischemic strokes, diabetes type II and related problems, etc.?

The sixty-five-year-old veteran who has had to battle one or more of the life-threatening illnesses and diseases associated with Agent Orange Dioxin is more likely to suffer from the trauma and stresses of those problems.

My PTSD problems were obvious back in the 1970s and 1980s. It is just that no one in the VA or the private medical community knew it. Remember, PTSD was not even declared until 1992. So then...**Who was going to help us?**

I have often sought professional counsel from the VA mental health department once I became aware that it was available. I started ten years ago...thirty-five years after I had returned home from Vietnam. To compound matters, as I have mentioned elsewhere in both of my books, I was diagnosed with diabetes type II in 2010, for which I am still being carefully treated. I suffered from an ischemic stroke, presumed to be associated with my diabetes type II, which is presumed to be caused by my Agent Orange exposure. The result of the ischemic stroke...elevated hypertension/blood pressure, permanent vision damage on one eye, suspected brain damage affecting a number of my mental functions. Add this all up:

- Combat horrors – one full year
- Agent Orange exposure – one full year
- Post-traumatic stress from above
- Hypertension from above
- Diabetes type II – Agent Orange
- Increased stress and hypertension
- Ischemic stroke – Diabetes – Agent Orange
- Increased hypertension and PTSD from above
- Permanent loss of vision in one eye from stroke
- Suspected brain damage from stroke
- More increased hypertension and PTSD from above

Where does it end...when I die as a million plus of our Vietnam War buddies already have, as will many more? **Don't send us to Vietnam – no PTSD or hypertension! Don't spray us with poisonous Agent Orange – no diabetes or hypertension!**

America paid us a couple thousand dollars for our year in Vietnam. We came home much less than what we were before we left. The scientists and policy makers can debate and doubt all they want, but there is no survey or research study ever made that can provide you with factual data of how much pain we were put through over there and back here. The total cost of fighting in a war continues for as long as the veterans are living. Veterans keep paying the price until they die. America can *never* do enough for the Vietnam War veterans.

Let's move over to eyewitness/hands-on veterans or victims who bore witness to the following nightmares at various hospitals as told to me by Robert "Smokey"

Ryan (deceased), Curtis Daniels (deceased), Gary Tetting (deceased), and Bobby Best (hanging on):

"The unbelievable filth of the VA hospitals we were in was nauseating and I will remember this for my entire life."

- Bobby Best

"Dusty, I still get sick thinking about seeing amputees stored in hallways and basements in VA hospitals and the filth that was disgusting, to say the least."

- Curtis Daniels
(Deceased)

"I always dreaded just walking into a VA hospital, but I had to in order to receive my care."

- Robert "Smokey" Ryan
(Deceased)

"A lot of my buddies who took early outs to attend college ended up in prison because the GI Bill was not adequately supporting their financial requirements to finish it out."

- Gary "Tets" Tetting
(Deceased)

Even more disheartening, as I covered in *Condemned Property?*...the meager GI bill for Vietnam War veterans was gutted, and our WWII vets influenced this as they did in denying Vietnam veterans from gaining membership in most veteran service organizations. I am not attempting to pick on or rub salt into the wounds of our WWII heroes...just trying to do my part in correcting what will be the legacy for my war brothers and sisters of the Vietnam War.

Some of you who have stayed with me to this point are probably sweating and feeling a lot of guilt right now, and if you are, ask yourself *why*? The policy to handle or deal with Vietnam War veterans was, if nothing else, consistently disgraceful. Why should anyone care? The future combatants knew what was ahead. They asked for it, didn't they? Oh, sure we did. This was concealed back then by the media—but why? Vietnam's "real" combat veterans (messed up badly in so many ways), were a dominant part of the population of prison mates, homeless shelters, local or county jails, etc. Oh shit, I have a very tough time continuing on with this part...come on. It sucks, but it happened.

PTSD? It cracks me up as to why the VA brain doctors find it so difficult to believe that a "real" combat victim of a war that took place way back in the 1960s could still be affected by it today. **Maybe the answer is...they (the so-called experts) don't know shit.**

Continuing on with the direction I seem to be heading, and I have no problem with it—what few, if any Americans realize or are prepared to acknowledge is... many of us "real" combat Vietnam War veterans actually suffered from malnutrition on a massive scale. Many times, not even stale and decrepit c-rations were readily available to nourish us. Can you believe this?

PTSD...beyond healing? Why is PTSD so difficult or impossible to cure or control with so many veterans of the Vietnam War?

- The war itself was unlike any other war in America's history as I have described in my books, *Condemned Property?* and now *Payback Time!*
- The type of combat required as described in both books.
- The perception of a war of losers—same as above.
- The cold, cruel, un-welcome home—same as above.
- Agent Orange after-effects, a lifelong battle, also described in both books.
- Little or no immediate after-war treatment, and that which became available to us came way too late, as described fully in both books.

Vietnam War veterans do not have to search for or fabricate reasons as to why so many of them remain very ill and/or...die very prematurely. It is all around us. We still live that war every day; and I personally cannot see how any discussion group, psychological counseling, medication or therapy will ever be able to cure the mental pain, let alone the physical illnesses caused to us from the mere six items I have listed above.

Who is giving up? Writing my books, attempting to reach out to my war buddies and to every other patriotic American is the best therapy that I can contribute to everyone who has been affected by that war, and yes, the recent wars as well. I know this because the readers have told me so, and they continue to encourage me to write my very passionate and truthful stories. Stories that may irritate some senior bureaucrats at the VA, but many Congressional members have encouraged me to continue. I plan on doing just that for as long as I can afford it and for as long as I am physically and mentally capable.

The Vietnam War and the Vietnam veteran are both embedded into my heart and engrained into my injured brain. And the VA will never be able to medicate me enough to make me forget or get over those memories...memories that we risked our lives for over and over again. But it appears that many of the scientists, researchers and policy makers just don't get that.

Is the case of my friend's PTSD mentioned at the beginning of this chapter beyond healing? Is it not curable? Scientists and policy makers will tell you that it absolutely is if those of us like my new special friend are not in denial of their obvious illness; they can control it with one of the many therapies available and many of us do just that. Is it completely curable? Not yet.

In closing this chapter, I would comment on a statement that I have heard many times in different forms from different types of people, but each time, it has the same meaning. It goes something like this—they think that PTSD victims refrain from association with other veterans who are afflicted with PTSD. In other words, make new and different friends. This has been suggested to me several times. My response has always been the same. It remains the same today and can be summed up simply...BULLSHIT!

One of the saddest things about the Vietnam War is...it continues to kill so many who have struggled to survive it after they came home!

- Author Unknown

CHAPTER 6

DENY, DELAY...UNTIL FORCED TO APPROVE?

I n *Condemned Property?*, Chapter Thirteen titled **"Deny, Delay...Till You Die!"** and subtitled 'Our Government's Ongoing War Against Vietnam Veterans' (Pages 259-274), I mentioned that I was given my first physical ever in the Cleveland VA Medical Center's Agent Orange Clinic. The date was December 5, 2005. It was an extensive and complete physical—chest x-rays, EKG, urination analysis and various blood tests. I did fast for this, although the VA's Neanderthal record keeping at that time is unable to confirm that I fasted. Why wouldn't they have me fast? It was supposed to be a *complete physical* in their Agent Orange Clinic.

The results of the blood tests recorded a glucose reading of 151, which was twenty-five points above the danger level of being a diabetic, which was 126 back then. However, it was not until 2010 that the VA officially diagnosed me with Diabetes Type II, and my lifestyle was forced to change dramatically from that point. Okay, that's life. Sometimes, everyone has to make sacrifices, so I've tried to do that and tried to move on.

Who knows what will be discovered someday about the health of our brothers and sisters who served multiple tours in Afghanistan and Iraq. But first, there is older business that deserves to be taken care of. Vietnam veterans from that war are still being neglected. Proof of this can be easily viewed by anyone as the VA's own records show that more than thirty-five percent of all backlogged claims for service-connected disability are Vietnam War veterans. MORE THAN 35% IN 2014?!

I have seen nothing in recent years that would indicate much as changed with that linear mindset. In fact, there might be a better term to accurately label the VA compensation and pension examiners' examinations and final decisions with many American veterans. How about this one: **DENY, DELAY...UNLESS FORCED TO APPROVE!**

If you are like me, you are sick and tired of the unearthing of tragedies that have been taking place at VA hospitals around the country and yet, it didn't seem like enough was being done about it other than a few headlines in the media. These events have shaken America, probably destroyed whatever trust remained in the VA system that has been wallowing in a culture of corruption, lies, greed and arrogance that defies description. The depths of VA crimes have been breathtaking, and I am not sure if a massive hanging would be enough to punish the guilty. Never mind revenge and vengeance. Let's do better than that. Let's fight back. Let's give them some...**PAYBACK!**

Come on, my brothers and sisters, you have plenty of time on your hands—certainly enough of it to write a letter or make a telephone call or both to the VA or Congress. Let them know you are still out there...still have some fight in you like we had in us over "there" when the VC and NVA came knocking on our door. This time, we do the door knocking on VA's door. It is overdue.

If you are a Vietnam vet and aren't feeling well, take a deep breath, get up the gumption, get mad again for what the VA has been doing to us (or has *not* been doing for us). If nothing else, let's go down together fighting like we were trained to do. If you are reading this book and if you are not a Vietnam vet or a vet from any war, please feel free to join in and help us give the corrupt and murderous VA something to remember us by some good old-fashioned...**PAYBACK!**

I have received (and saved) over forty letters from government representatives who responded personally to one or more (most times more) of my letters with fact supported grievances...and in each one of them, I expressed my views with as much passion as I could muster. I never imagined such a level of response, and I became extremely motivated by it. I have displayed examples of Congress and Senate's responses to my letters in a later chapter.

If every Vietnam War, Gulf War, Afghanistan War, Iraq War and Korean War veteran wrote just one letter or one email or one fax or made just one phone call expressing his or her unhappiness with how the VA has gotten away with so much for so long...**and people have died** because of this, a profound statement would be made, heard and a response would follow.

I read the headlines every day, and when they read like the following, I just could not sit still. I had to convey my thoughts and share my concerns to people—I had to. Headlines such as these motivated me to fight on for our benefits:

"Number of veterans who die waiting for benefits claims skyrockets."

Veterans Reporter (December 20, 2012)

"53 vets die each day waiting on their veterans' disability claims."
Kerry Patton, War Novelist (February 13, 2013)

"Obama administration violates another court order and more veterans will die."
John De Mayo, Freedom Outpost (December 17, 2013)

"Long appeals leave Vietnam vets without benefits for years."
*USA Today (*May 26, 2014)

"Vets died. VA lied. Heads must roll."
Fox News (May 29, 2014)

"VA horror stories keep coming!"
The Daily Progress (June 25, 2014)

"VA manipulated vets' appointment date, audit finds."
USA Today (July 30, 2014)

"VA audit: Philadelphia staffers told to falsify."
Philly.com (August 1, 2014)

"VA misled on number of deaths tied to care delays, Congressman charges."
CNN (August 5, 2014)

"VA blames confusion for misstatements about deaths."
CNN (August 8, 2014)

"Georgia VA hospital closes, stranding vets without medical care."
The Washington Times (August 12, 2014)

"VA dodges questions on veterans' deaths and destroyed records."
The Furnace (August 18, 2014)

"New VA secretary apologizes for stunning lack of clarity over preventable deaths."
Mark Flatten (August 18, 2014)

"A fatal level of trust in Veterans Affairs care."
The Examiner (August 19, 2014)

"Alabama VA director, chief of staff placed on leave."

CDT (August 22, 2014)

"No proof of deaths caused by delay in VA care, says Inspector General."

Army Times (August 25, 2014)

"VA 'Oscar the Grouch' training guide trashes veterans."

The Inquirer (August 27, 2014)

"What does it take to get fired by the VA?"

Montgomery Advisor (August 30, 2014

"Veterans Forum Calls for Resignation of VA Management."

KCBY News (August 31, 2014)

"VA retaliation lawsuits near final phase."

Military News (September 1, 2014)

"Father of SEAL Team 6 Hero: Obama administration lied to us."

Courtney Coren and Bill Hoffman
Newsmax TV (September 3, 2014)

I realize that when *Payback Time!* publishes, these news headlines will be old news, and I certainly hope that they don't repeat down the road, a repetition of such in 2015, and I dread what the response would be like from veterans — maybe, just a tad more than a tough letter or passionate book from some frustrated Nam vet like me. I think a profound, passionate action would be inevitable...and who could blame the vets? As we Vietnam veterans say...**Never again shall one generation of veterans abandon another generation of veterans!**

How Did We Get From There...To Here?

To all of my war buddies who survived one of the most evil wars in U.S. history: Remember when television crews were sent to the battlefields and most Americans were shocked to see the gruesome violence of that war? Remember that the Vietnam War became known as the "living room" war?

When Vietnam was divided into two countries in 1954, once again, just like the Korean War, the major communist countries lined up in support of communist North Vietnam and many free world countries joined with the United States, supporting democratic South Vietnam. China and the Soviet Union were pouring billions in aid, weapons and military advisors to North Vietnam for one purpose… to take control of South Vietnam. The cause to come to South Vietnam's rescue seemed like a just one, but Americans were still recovering from the Korean War and World War II. Our country was divided on fighting another war that seemed necessary to keep communism checked in Southeast Asia. Other neighboring countries also feared the threat of communism and that their countries would eventually become targets if South Vietnam fell to the communists. The Philippines, South Korea, Thailand and Australia joined the United States and so…our country's longest war in history was on.

In 1965, President Johnson sent approximately sixteen thousand troops to South Vietnam. They were referred to as "advisors" to help the South Vietnamese military in its threat from a communist-backed rebel force called the Viet Cong. Unexpectedly, what was being called "conflict" would become another global-type war…even larger than the Korean War. In fact, when the Vietnam War had officially ended, America had suffered more casualties than any war America had ever fought in except WWII.

Then, from 1967 to 1969, our country's military force in South Vietnam had reached an unexpected level of 544,000. When the Vietnam War had ended for the free world countries that supported South Vietnam, over 2.8 million Americans had served in this ugly war. Another 750,000 would participate in the war as support troops from Thailand, Guam or U.S. aircraft carriers. Of that total of 3.5 million troops, less than ten percent or approximately 240,000 would actually be in the field in face-to-face battle situations. They would incur most of the casualties that Americans would suffer during the Vietnam War. Nearly fifty percent of America's 362,924 Vietnam War casualties were absorbed by the field combat marines and U.S. army soldiers.

Few who fought in the Vietnam War had previous battle experience other than a tussle with a sibling or friend back home. Most arrived in Vietnam with innocence that would soon be lost by most…forever for many. As a field combat troop, you witness firsthand the atrocities that the communist forces of the Viet Cong and the North Vietnamese Army inflict onto the helpless South Vietnamese civilians, which include women and children. You are asked to protect the innocent villagers who are being maimed, killed or abducted. Who else is able to help them? So you begin to think that your presence in this war is justified and necessary in order for another democratic country to live in freedom. Soon, you encounter another shocking fact. Your platoon conducts a successful ambush one night against a Viet Cong unit that was apparently setting up their own ambush on an unsuspecting American unit. As you are checking the dead and badly wounded from your unit's successful ambush, shocking reality hits you like a round of C-4 exploding in your face. What the ??? is going on here as you discover that two of the dead Viet Cong are in fact from the village you and your war buddies had been attempting to protect...from the raids by the Viet Cong! Now, you are really confused, but you get over it, thinking they were just a couple of bad apples in the barrel. You move on—you have to because now, you aren't sure who the enemy is or where they will pop up next. You feel more threatened than ever.

That same day, you hear your buddies talking, saying some things about Americans protesting against the Vietnam War. Maybe they were protesting against you and your war buddies. You become more confused, but you have to deal with it because the only mission that matters to you right now in this moment is...**surviving another day with your family of war buddies.**

Our minds would wander off, thinking about that day (*if* it comes) when that great big Freedom Bird picks you and your war buddies up and takes you home. But you snap out of that day dream as you realize that you still have over three hundred days left in this god forsaken, Agent Orange scorched, bomb-battered land called Vietnam. **How did we get from there to here?**

It was a war that divided a country more than any war since the Civil War. I might have mentioned this already. I will probably say it again. This war would have no highly recognizable heroes, no Pattons, no MacArthurs, no Eisenhowers, just "perceived" losers like Westmoreland. Men like Oliver North, David Hackworth, Colin Powell, John Schwarzwalder, and all Vietnam War hero types would rarely be linked to that war. It just wasn't fashionable nor was it necessary for the American public to identify any of these heroes with that war...the ugly Vietnam War.

How Do We Get From Here to There?

The Bush administration (the one that used to get blamed for everything), the next Bush administration (the one that took the blame for things away from the previous one) the Clinton administration, the Obama administration and all of Congress were receiving constant warnings from veterans' groups and veterans as well about the horrors that had been going on at VA facilities across the country.

In March 2014, the Veterans of Foreign Wars (VFW) sent another "wake-up" warning to the House of Veterans Affairs committee about the continuing problems that veterans were experiencing in receiving their health care and benefits from the VA. Well before the VFW March 2014 report, I launched *Condemned Property?* in December 2013, and those who read it were *shocked* at my descriptions of how so many Vietnam veterans have died so prematurely while waiting and waiting for years or in some cases, decades to receive proper health care or disability benefits for serious service-connected injuries and illnesses. To this day, no one and no organization can provide an accurate number of how many Vietnam War veterans have perished prematurely since they came home from that war. Various resources have estimated that out of the 2.8 to 3.1 million Americans who served in-country during the active years of the war, approximately one million have perished. Some estimates have put the death toll as high as 1.5 million, which would mean half of us are no longer breathing.

How many of those 1 to 1.5 million post-Vietnam War casualties died while waiting for badly needed benefits from VA will undoubtedly remain a mystery forever. Only another act from Congress could scrape up the answers and that would cost America another small fortune. That seems to be one of the secrets about a war most people wish would go away that will not be solved anytime soon. And where would we begin? Who was the first Vietnam veteran to die prematurely after coming home? Who was the first Vietnam veteran to die prematurely because of exposure to the deadly dioxins proven to be in…Agent Orange? Who was the first Vietnam War veteran who died because of PTSD or suicide?

Most of us have heard the ghastly horror stories about the abysmal conditions that existed in the VA hospitals during the pre-Vietnam War era as well as the early post-war years. Those stories are what kept many veterans away from seeking health care from a VA facility. As mentioned elsewhere in this book, I did not enter the VA system until 2005, more than thirty years after separating from the U.S. Army.

In my searches for historical data, I found that the VFW, along with some other veterans' organizations, had been warning Congress about the dangerous problems at VA since 2002—thirteen years ago, but nearly thirty years after the Vietnam War.

Several of my war buddies and I know all too well how important timely health-care access can be critical to our living awhile longer or not living any longer. I like the way it was put in a 2013 report from the *Independent Budget* (IB):

Timely access is crucial to the Veterans Health Administration (VA) health-care system's capacity to provide health care quickly after a need is recognized and is crucial to the quality of care delivered. Significant and recurring delays for appointments result in patient dissatisfaction, avoidable waster of finite resources, and possible…adverse clinical consequences.
(Source: www.independentbudget.org/2013)

No surprise to most veterans, especially Vietnam era veterans, one of the most disturbing facts unveiled after the VA scandal of 2014 is the attitude of VA patient advocates...**apathetic**.

The VA Patient Advocate division of the VA was nonexistent until 1990. It was created to serve as the liaison between veterans receiving health care at a VA facility and the hospitals' staff of administrators and service supervisors responsible for coordinating that care. I have personally gone to a patient advocate for advice on how to deal with the apathy and ineffectiveness I have often been faced with in trying to communicate with some of the VA administrators. I have been very satisfied with how I was treated by the Cleveland, Ohio Patients Advocate, and I highly recommend any of my military buddies to go to them with your complaints and grievances toward any particular VA deadbeat who does not show you the respect you deserve. You can file a lawsuit or Tort Claim against the VA through the Patients Advocate. I have come close to taking this action, but I cannot do it while my claims are pending for a decision. If and when I receive that decision on one or more claims, I may then proceed with the Tort Claim through the VA's Veterans Advocate's office in Cleveland. Hopefully, I will know my status on things before *Payback Time!* unleashes itself.

PROBLEM. We will never "get there" until the broken VA system and their apathetic or pathetic attitude towards their patients is cured. I think this can happen, and I believe in Secretary Bob McDonald to get it done. I pray that he can because we who have fought in and have been wounded in wars must depend on the VA's medical services. VA is an absolute must for millions of veterans. So, the VA health-care system must remain intact, must be capable of managing and delivering better quality of care for us. Civilian health-care facilities do not have the capacity to fulfill the needs of the millions of veterans that are under the care of VA right now. Our injuries and our illnesses can be very different from the non-veteran world. Some of our health-care problems can only be addressed by and rehabbed by the VA such as:

- Combat-related mental health (PTSD)
- Combat-inflicted brain damage
- Blast or explosion injuries
- Toxins exposure – Agent Orange
- Prosthetics for loss of limbs in battle

I would be dead if Cleveland's VA had not found a blockage in my carotid arteries in December 2013 and performed successful emergency surgery.

I have recorded and sent off many compliments to VA about several VA facilities that have treated me very well. Unfortunately, the wrong things, the acts of negligence, apathy, and acts of just not doing their jobs have over-shadowed the good acts and they have cost me dearly in terms of health loss and financial loss.

Cheers. There is one small VA Outpatient Clinic in Portage County's quaint town of Ravenna, Ohio that I refer to in this affectionate manner—I call it…The Cheers Bar where everybody knows your name…and they do. Again, mentioning *Condemned Property?* I dedicated a well-deserved 'atta-boy' to Ravenna VA's terribly friendly and conscientious staff…in every department from the lab to the mental. THANK YOU, Ravenna Ohio Outpatient Clinic. Ravenna VA deserves greater mention than a couple brief paragraphs and if I live long enough, I will probably make an attempt at writing a book about the place I will always refer to as…The Cheers Bar of VA.

Hurry up and…wait. Every active military troop and every veteran knows of this old cliché all too well. Unfortunately, it still applies to just about anything that pertains to the VA. But Secretary Bob will simply wave the magic wand handed to him by President/Commander in Chief/King/Emperor Barack Hussein Obama, and everything will get up to speed. Right.

Seriously, I can see improvements already. I really can. Proof of this was revealed in a recent study conducted and completed in September 2014 by none other than the VFW. In this recent study, for the first time in a long time or forever, this study showed that VA compliments almost matched the number of complaints. That is progress. Here are the results of that survey, state by state, so you can see how yours is doing. You may consider moving…

VFW Report of the State of VA's Health Care
September 2014

State	Positive	Negative	Total
Alabama	2	17	19
Alaska	2	5	7
Arizona	49	53	102
Arkansas	3	17	20
California	41	46	87
Colorado	7	21	28
Connecticut	4	3	7

Delaware	2	3	5
District of Columbia	10	5	15
Florida	24	56	80
Georgia	2	23	25
Hawaii	2	2	4
Idaho	6	8	14
Illinois	8	22	30
Indiana	9	8	17
Iowa	7	5	12
Kansas	22	16	38
Kentucky	6	13	19
Louisiana	3	14	17
Maine	4	3	7
Maryland	8	31	39
Massachusetts	8	7	15
Michigan	110	35	145
Minnesota	15	13	28
Mississippi	4	6	10
Missouri	21	28	49
Montana	1	5	6
Nebraska	9	3	12
Nevada	3	14	17
New Hampshire	4	2	6
New Jersey	4	9	13
New Mexico	1	11	12
New York	22	27	49
North Carolina	14	35	49
North Dakota	3	1	4
Ohio	12	19	31
Oklahoma	24	11	35

Oregon	11	23	34
Pennsylvania	20	28	48
Philippines	4	3	7
Puerto Rico	0	1	1
Rhode Island	1	0	1
South Carolina	1	13	14
South Dakota	5	4	9
Tennessee	2	15	17
Texas	29	81	110
Utah	5	3	8
Vermont	4	3	7
Virginia	11	17	28
Washington	23	36	59
West Virginia	10	13	23
Wisconsin	11	7	18
Wyoming	2	5	7
No State	71	120	191
Total	**686**	**969**	**1655**

Connecticut, District of Columbia, Indiana, Iowa, Kansas, Maine, Massachusetts, Michigan, Minnesota, Nebraska, New Hampshire, North Dakota, Oklahoma, Philippines, Rhode Island, South Dakota, Utah, Vermont and Wisconsin—only seventeen states (DC and the Philippines excluded) reported more positive comments over negative comments or thirty-four percent.

We are not there yet. Looking at this report, the great state of Michigan stands out like a shining star with a good to bad ratio of 75.8%. Wonder what their secret is. Just a few miles to the southwest lies the great state of Illinois with a good to bad rating of 26.6%. The national average is 41.4%.

Secretary Bob…get on over to Michigan with a staff of consultants and find out their secret. Please, do it. If the majority of the other states can pull it together like Michigan, that might be one of the clues to…**HOW DO WE GET FROM HERE TO THERE?**

Until we get there, the situation remains…**Delay, Deny, Delay—Till Forced to Approve.**

While Secretary Bob and his new staff in progress are formulating their game plans and implementing them on the run, so to speak, it is up to the rest of us, not just veterans—but the responsibility or obligation belongs on the shoulders of every American citizen who appreciates their freedom…TO KEEP THE HEAT ON VA by communicating to your respective Congress Representatives and Senators. Please…do it.

Vietnam Changed the Course of History

One night, my lovely wife Ginny and I were discussing how our society has changed so drastically since the 1950s and early 1960s. Our music changed, people's attitudes and morals changed, and the change continued in the wrong direction. In the early 1960s, no one in America had the slightest inclination of what was brewing in South East Asia…no one.

Our music in the 1950s and early 1960s was fun music. Sock hops at our high schools, dancing, dancing, dancing to the happiest music ever created. What an era! My mind drifts back there often, and I wonder when it changed, when it came to a screeching unannounced halt. When?

Folks, as I see it, the Vietnam War is what changed the world's mindset. It was a gloomy, senseless, meaningless and brutal war that was pretty much kept a secret to the world until…**The Tet Offensive** began in 1968. It shocked the world. It traumatized every family back in America, and they became glued to their TVs every evening as the "living room war" was being showcased by the media… falsely in most instances. Americans were being brainwashed into a biased condition with a biased and hate-filled attitude towards most or all Vietnam War veterans. What a shame. What a disgrace. And so…I write my books…*Condemned Property?* and *Payback Time!* and next? Who knows, but I suspect that I have one more book left in me, at least one. I think I owe it to my war buddies. If God allows it…I will continue because I love those guys I fought with side by side. They were incredible human beings of the likes who match up with my generation.

Why Old Soldiers Die…Waiting!

The VA's secret policy has been for decades: do not award a veteran any service-connected disability compensation until the link between their service assignment and their illness to be is irrefutable—as clear as a 50-caliber machine gun severing a human torso. If "they" could not actually see it happen, then "they" could claim that we did not have sufficient proof, and tens or hundreds of

118

thousands of deserving veterans were cheated out of their justified compensation. And the veterans would most likely live the rest of their lives "cheated".

What level of criminality is this? Murder of the lowest scum-sucking degree. And some of the readers of *Condemned Property?* questioned the degree of anger I expressed in that book? Really? What is wrong with this mind-set? "They" put the troops there, so "they" are obligated to take care of us for our damages. Right? Oh, I apologize. Some people who did not enjoy the opportunity to experience the horrors of Vietnam-style combat might think we are looking for a *handout*.

Every veteran who has had dealings with the Department of Veterans Affairs (and the Veterans Administration before that) knows there will be delays and lost files, then more delays and more lost files, and this goes on and on very conveniently for the VA's position. To the modern war veterans this ghastly process is infuriating to them, just as it was to young Vietnam Era veterans in the 1970s and 1980s. But Vietnam Era veterans are older veterans now, and we are far more concerned about outliving our appeals with the VA. What a way to live after putting one's life on the line…mind-boggling.

I wanted to stay away from making this book a disgustingly sad list of VA horror stories from veterans because one book could never do the justice these tragedies deserve. But here is a brief recap of one Vietnam veteran's horror story, and keep in mind that this story is an example of what has been going on for almost…forever:

The case of Belie Bowman—a Vietnam War veteran from North Carolina was a near perfect example of how bureaucratic delays will dishonor veterans. Like many, Bowman had gone to war as a healthy young man, and when he returned, he was dishonored. Some sources called him skittish, very easily angered, uneasy in crowds, etc. He applied twice for what appeared to be service-related benefits because of his nervous condition and was DENIED in 1971 and again in 1995. He retained an attorney and filed papers showing that he suffered from PTSD. This case endured six grueling rulings without a definitive resolve. After he contracted pancreatic cancer, the VA Board of Veterans Appeals agreed on June 16, 2004 that he had proved his case, which was pretty much the same one he had filed several years earlier. By then, his cancer had taken a drastic downward turn and for whatever reasons, his treatment had been stopped. On June 21, 1995, Bowman's attorney had been talking to VA officials every hour or so. The next day, the attorney was informed that a check for $53,784 could be issued. All they needed were a couple more signatures. It was in the computer system, the attorney was told. That night, Bowman died and the VA never cut his check. **Case closed.**

America…these stories are more common than you ever care to believe. Until 2014, there has never been any outrage—no passionately directed fury at those who have gone unnoticed and untouched at the VA's administrative level…not until 2014. So another old soldier died…while waiting.

In 2003, a VA secretary told major news agency reporters that he was stunned when he learned just a few years earlier how frequently veterans had been dying while their cases were still in the appeal process. That secretary of the VA stated, "This is not acceptable; we need to do something about it."

"We need to do something about it." Understand—this was 2003, not 2014. But similar stories exist from previous decades as well. It has been going on for seemingly forever. Note that in this case, the VA secretary had learned about the problems several years earlier, yet he had allowed nearly a decade to pass before he expressed how outraged he was. This is what is wrong in Washington and at the VA. We need to express our outrage. How else can I say it…WE NEED TO EXPRESS OUR **OUTRAGE!**

Actually, I for one, have an ounce of sympathy in my heart for the VA compensation and pension examiners' monumental task of separating the exaggerators and fabricators from the real victims. Here is what I mean at the risk of offending some rear echelon or base camp warriors who did what was asked of them, but…

> I read in a very credible source (glad to provide it if asked) that since the end of our war in Vietnam, nearly two million of the approximately 3.3 million men and women who served in the Vietnam theater (Thailand to Vietnam) of operations are reported to suffer from PTSD.

You bet, these figures are mind-boggling and pretty much unbelievable, so the VA compensation and pension examiners will naturally treat most of us as though we are imposters. Why is the two million so difficult to swallow? Simply because less than 300,000 of our 2.8 million military personnel who served IN Vietnam itself were ever in direct combat. I have explained this unfortunate scenario elsewhere in both books. Yes, of course military personnel in support units could conceivably suffer PTSD from the sounds of rocket or mortar attacks on their bases, and there was a slim chance of them being hit (quite slim); however, most large base camps were relatively free from the amount of extreme danger and horribly abysmal living conditions that combat units were forced to put up with daily.

Now, don't get bent out of shape on this if you were rear echelon. I know many Nam veterans who experienced little or no exposure to severe or continuous combat situations, and they are pretty messed up in the mind. Just being there in the Nam was traumatic, especially at night. It has been proven over and over again, and it should need no further research to prove that…military personnel who were exposed to high combat experiences will have a higher likelihood of suffering from PTSD and other post-war psychological problems than those personnel who were located in the rear. The likelihood is significant.

Here is one of the problems that the VA is running into—how do they differentiate those who served in secure base camps from those who were in combat on a relatively routine basis from those who were subjected to severe combat conditions on a continuous basis? They were all in the Vietnam War. They were all faced with some degree of danger from time to time. They all served in a "combat zone." There is just NO WAY that a VA compensation and pension examiner can know the difference between a records clerk in Saigon and an airborne ranger in Tay Ninh. They just can't figure it out, nor do they care to. So quite often, we both get...**DENIED!** Then again and worse yet, the freaked out and severely damaged combat vet gets denied and the base camp warrior receives an OK for service connected PTSD. Sad picture—I have seen it—and unfortunately, I have been victimized by this. Oh well...I just keep on fighting as I am doing by writing these passionate books.

No doubt, this section will raise the blood pressure of some, but they should get over it. In the meantime, our brothers continue dying from PTSD and Agent Orange associated illnesses, and whether you were a rear echelon support troop or a grunt-like Neanderthal...we can help each other better by working together against VA as a team again. Do it, please.

Strength in Numbers

For more than thirty years, America's warriors from the Vietnam War have stood alone, one by one, in their frustrating battle with VA to receive their healthcare benefits. Korean War veterans were pretty much in the same precarious position that we were—but not quite. WWII vets? Our fathers and uncles—come on—their attitude toward Vietnam War veterans was—*You boys didn't even fight in a real war, so get your benefits on your own.*

Vietnam War vets went to Washington when his highness and Commander in Chief, President Obama closed down veterans' memorials. They went there and stood up for WWII vets and Korean War vets. Vietnam War vets have never shunned the warriors coming home from any of the Gulf wars, and those warriors know that.

Today, as I write this section, there are welcome-home parades going on silently across America for Vietnam War veterans, but they are not being held on Main Street in any town or city anyone knows. They are happening on military bases. We are being recognized by today's active duty service members and current veterans. I take this in the most positive way. I see a "teaming up" trend here like I have never seen before. Why not? VA has been treating the returnees from Afghanistan and Iraq almost as badly as we were treated. Team up, brothers and sisters…let's **team up!**

Veterans Earn Hiring Preference

This payback shouldn't have received resentment from some Americans but it did, especially those who are seeking federal employment. Haven't those who put their life and their future in harm's way so that others can benefit, earned enough respect from their countrymen that they would be more understanding when a veteran wins the coin flip on an employment opportunity? Of course, they have.

Those federal workers or applicants for federal jobs might be better off if they did not challenge the preference towards veterans hiring practices by the U.S. government. If present American Legion Commander Michael Helm has much influence on such preferences, the practice may gain more support, not less, from Americans. Helm said in October 2014 that, "Helping those who have served in uniform, especially disabled veterans to get hired is a policy that must remain in place." Well stated, Commander.

Even though the complaints from the disgruntled received substantial media attention (no surprise there), only 6.5 percent of workers surveyed for a report by the Merit Systems Protection Board on veterans hiring practices felt that the system has unfairly benefited veterans. I think that hiring preference to qualified veterans is a clear-cut right thing to do. Especially because of the sacrifices most veterans have made most willingly, such as the following:

- Service-connected injuries, illnesses, disabilities to veterans warrant special hiring preferences to "qualified" vets.
- While certain military training is beneficial for a veteran when entering the civilian workplace, many veterans may take a step backwards in a career they may seek due to the lost time while serving their country.

Commander Helm offered this advice to the non-veterans who have a problem with the veterans hiring preference. He simply said, "Become a veteran." Kudos to Legion Commander Helm for stepping up and for speaking up…stick together vets. **Cover each other's back.**

Hey VA…By the Way

We know that VA was mired in the scandal from 2014, but they continue to struggle with another very old responsibility—paying compensation to veterans who were wounded or injured or who grew ill from their military service. While the VA claimed to reduce a huge backlog in veterans' claims in 2013, the appeals to the VA's denials continued to grow rapidly in 2014. Then again, it is common knowledge now that those VA reports of so-called success in reducing pending claims were inflated to save some people's asses.

Compensation for service-connected injuries or wounds is one of the most costly programs within the VA, in the $75 billion range for 2014 alone. And THEY ARE WORTH IT! Because of the generation of warriors coming home from the Middle East or Gulf conflicts who seem to have greater and quicker access to compensation benefits for PTSD, TBI, etc., the backlog of total compensation requests soared in 2014, and it punished the older claims, which were largely… Vietnam War veterans. Is this déjà vu again or what? Vietnam War veterans getting the short end again or should I say *still*? But hey, we never gave up over there in the Nam, so of course, we can deal with repeated neglect by the VA. Certainly.

Characteristics of the Pending Compensation Inventory

VA tracks claims that make up the pending Compensation Inventory by a Veteran's era of service. From the most recent VA report, claims from Veterans of the following eras make up VA's inventory (total number of claims) and backlog (claims pending for more than 125 days):

- Post 9/11 (Iraq and Afghanistan conflicts) claims make up 23% of the total inventory and 24% of the backlog.
- Gulf War claims make up 24% of the total inventory and 23% of the backlog.
- Peacetime (period between end of Vietnam and Gulf War) claims make up 11% of the total inventory and 12% of the backlog.
- Vietnam claims make up 35% of the total inventory and 36% of the backlog.
- Korean War claims make up 3% of the total inventory and 2% of the backlog.
- World War II claims make up 3% of the total inventory and 2% of the backlog.
- Other claims make up 1% of the total inventory and 1% of the backlog.
(Source: Department of Veterans Affairs, 04/05/2014)

VFW National Helpline: 1-800-VFW (839)-1899

CHAPTER 7

AGENT ORANGE AND GENOCIDE?

W as Vietnam veteran Luther King correct in labeling our own government by way of The Department of Veterans Affairs as being guilty of *genocide*? Think about it. *Genocide*—the term itself did not exist before 1944, so says a statement by the United States Holocaust Museum in Washington D.C. *Genocide* is defined at Dictionary.com as the systematic destruction of all or a significant part of a racial, ethnic, religious or national group. *Genocide* is defined by the *Free Merriam-Webster Dictionary* as the deliberate and systematic destruction of a racial, political or cultural group.

In 1944, Polish-Jewish lawyer, Raphael Lemkin searched out a word to describe the Nazi policies of systematic murder, including the destruction of European Jews. Lemkin formed the word *genocide* by combining *geno-*, the Greek word for race or tribe, with *-cide*, derived from the Latin word for killing. In 1945, the International Military Tribunal held at Nuremburg, Germany charged top Nazis with "crimes against humanity". The word *genocide* was included in the indictment but as a descriptive term, not a legal one. Thereafter, Lemkin continued tirelessly to create awareness of the *Holocaust*, and eventually in 1948, in the shadow of the *Holocaust,* the United Nations approved the Convention on the Prevention and Punishment of the Crime of Genocide. That convention established genocide as an international crime, defined as follows:

The Crime of Genocide

On December 9, 1948, in the shadow of the Holocaust and in no small part due to the tireless efforts of Professor Raphael Lemkin, the United Nations approved the Convention on the Prevention and Punishment of the Crime of Genocide. This convention establishes "genocide" as an international crime, which signatory nations "undertake to prevent and punish." It defines genocide as:

Genocide means any of the following acts committed with intent to destroy, in whole or in part, a national, ethical, racial or religious group, such as:

(a) Killing members of the group;
(b) Causing serious bodily or mental harm to members of the group;
(c) Deliberately inflicting on the group conditions of life calculated to bring about its physical destruction in whole or in part;
(d) Imposing measures intended to prevent births within the group;
(e) Forcibly transferring children of the group to another group.
(Source: United States Holocaust Memorial Museum)

I will bet the Vietnam veterans who are reading *Payback Time!* and have been violated by the criminal negligence of VA will have their eyes glued to this chapter.

I can see how (a) through (d) clearly fits the treatment (lack of treatment) by VA of Vietnam veterans for the last forty-plus years. I see it, don't you?

A. Have Vietnam War veterans been killed due to VA's *Deny, Delay Till We Die* policy?
B. Have any Vietnam War veterans suffered serious bodily or mental harm from our horribly incompetent treatment from VA?
C. Does anyone believe that VA's destruction of our lives was purely acci-dental, just a little old mistake...or was it a deliberate, systematic plan to kill us and therefore eliminate the cost to keep us alive? That would pre-clude the expense of treating us for the damages done to our bodies and minds from the poisons of Agent Orange and the trauma inflicted on us by a rotten war that *no one* wanted to win, let alone even be there. Little old accidents? There are several hundred thousands of premature dead American warriors in graves from coast to coast...not dozens or hundreds, hundreds of thousands!
D. Have our children and their children been afflicted by our exposure to the deadly Dioxins of Agent Orange? No question about it. How about this scenario—many Vietnam War veterans never fathered children or just never married because of the fear of birth deformed children.

This scenario that I am suggesting will most likely never amount to anything and I am just putting my personal suspicions into a book for others to read and let those who are interested decide for themselves. I remember reading this in a religious publication. I cannot remember which one, but I know for certain it was not the *Christian Science Monitor* because that rag turned me off a long, long time ago:

An individual's greatest enemy appears to be his or her own national government. A source has estimated that two hundred million people probably have been murdered by governments in the twentieth century.

If the Vietnam War veteran population becomes prematurely extinct, as opposed to being naturally erased from the face of the earth, who is to know the real killers outside of Agent Orange, PTSD, diabetes, cancers, etc.? I have provided substantial facts in this chapter, facts obtained from readily available resources today. However, when our Vietnam War buddies first started to file disability claims for alleged Agent-Orange-associated illnesses, the VA compensation and pension examiners would have had an easier time in denying them because the veterans were asked by the VA to produce information to substantiate their exposure to Agent Orange spraying…and that information did not exist yet.

I cannot imagine that the VA did not know there were no records available from the militaries or the Department of Defense that could verify a veteran's potential exposure to herbicides as no such records existed at that time. In 1980, the VA rescinded the requirement that veterans prove exposure when asking for information, assistance or treatment for what they believed to be Agent-Orange-related illnesses.

NEWSFLASH: Most governments do not publish or keep "findable" records for the number of their own citizens that they exterminate, at least not in America.

But of course, most of this book's readers already knew about the above. Well, I wonder if most of you (any of you) were aware of this…the democratic government of Uganda seriously considered a bill to legalize the judicial genocide of gays, lesbians and bisexuals who engage in same-sex sexual behavior. So that's how life is in other parts of the world.

Waiting for an Army to Die, The Tragedy of Agent Orange (1989) by Fred A Wilcox is one of my favorite and most frightening books about the Vietnam War. One cannot read it without coming away with a feeling of outrage. In chapter eleven, titled "Vietnam Veterans Are America's Future", it opens with a visit to the home of Vietnam veteran, Ronald Anderson who was a combat infantryman with the 101st Airborne Division. Ron Anderson was the perfect Vietnam War veteran to be interviewed for this chapter. Here is a brief description of Ron Anderson as he was in 1989:

> His once curly black hair had fallen out, attempting to come back in white broom-like patches here and there. His once young handsome face is covered with rashes, his cheeks are sunken and his eyes resemble those of a dying cat. Therefore, he avoids mirrors because he cannot stand what he sees. Unfortunately, there is more...he has chest pains, recurrent bouts of dizziness, his physical coordination is gone from a man who was able to hike several miles in thick jungles with sixty pounds of gear on this back and an M-16 rifle. Anderson's muscles are so weak that he is unable to open a jar of peanut butter for his kids. There are many days when he sits for hours waiting for suicidal depression to leave. Then of course, there are the nightmares of Vietnam. Anderson has other ailments that had doctors stymied back then because you see, the damages caused by the poisons of Agent Orange being "dumped" onto America's warriors in Vietnam was not fully understood yet.

Anderson mentioned new studies that were being funded to better understand the aftereffects of Agent Orange. Anderson read from his newspaper that VA was ordered by Congress to conduct much research on Agent Orange and complete them as soon as possible. VA was ordered to begin...three years ago, his newspaper stated. Tearing the article out of his newspaper in disgust, he reads that VA now projects that these studies will not be completed...for another five years. "Five years, five more years," Anderson said back then. "I think I've got it now. I think we've all got it now. They are just waiting. They are waiting for us all, every fucking one of us Vietnam War veterans to die."

At the time of Anderson's statements, his physical appearance was that of a very elderly man. In 1989, he was just thirty-six years old.

Fast forward. Of course, many research studies were eventually completed, and Vietnam War veterans are now receiving service-connected disability compensation for their exposure to Agent Orange. Unfortunately, no one is exactly sure just how many Vietnam War veterans died while those studies were in the holding stage or how many have died very prematurely while the studies were being methodically completed. Several sources state that at least one million warriors have perished prematurely since coming home from Vietnam. Some sources put the figure at 1.5 million and climbing.

I am one of those living Vietnam War veterans who is still fighting the fight to keep on living awhile longer. My service with my war buddies planted us smack dab into the heart of the most heavily sprayed areas of Agent Orange of the entire year. Here is a list of the most heavily sprayed areas:

Herbicidal Warfare in Vietnam War
August 10, 1961 – October 31, 1971
Top 15 Areas – Heaviest Spraying (Fixed Wing Only)

1)	Phouc Vinh	643,769 Gallons	III Corp
2)	Katum	558,815 Gallons	III Corp
3)	Cu Ch / Dau Tieng / Tran Bang	372,860 Gallons	III Corp
4)	Nha Be	247,650 Gallons	III Corp
5)	Nam Can	214,640 Gallons	IV Corp
6)	Ben Cat	190,955 Gallons	III Corp
7)	Nui Ba Den	188,620 Gallons	III Corp
8)	Firebase Rakkassan	166,580 Gallons	I Corp
9)	Bien Hoa / Hoc Mon	163,745 Gallons	III Corp
10)	L Z Sandra	156,830 Gallons	I Corp
11)	Plei Jerang	155,255 Gallons	II Corp
12)	An Loc	152,170 Gallons	III Corp
13)	Loc Ninh	152,170 Gallons	III Corp
14)	LZ Rock Pile	133,140 Gallons	I Corp
15)	Tan An	126,010 Gallons	IV Corp

III Corp, III Corp! Six of the seven most heavily and most continuously sprayed areas are where units of the 25th Infantry dug our foxholes, conducted our search and destroy missions, conducted our combat assaults. It's where we slept, where we ate our food, where we spent half of our lives in Agent Orange drenched swamps, rice paddies and jungles. Adding to this—if a Vietnam War veteran was lucky to spend his or her visit to Vietnam during the three peak years of Agent Orange spraying, 1967, 1968 or 1969, his or her chance of becoming Agent Orange poisoned was even greater. Chapter 6 shows how we divided up the poisoning of the South Vietnam environment by time period.

Clearly, those military personnel stationed in III Corp and the specific areas listed above were subjected to an astonishing amount of Agent Orange spray in comparison to all other areas in South Vietnam. Then, if you were really lucky enough to have been there in 1967, 1968 or 1969, you just increased your opportunity to breathe, drink, or eat Agent Orange, as 76.6% of the war's Agent Orange sprayed in South Vietnam from 1961 to 1971 happened between 1967 and 1969.

What do most people take for a headache? One, maybe two aspirin should be the remedy—right? What happens if someone takes thirty or forty grams of aspirin in one dose? Death is likely. Agent Orange dioxin is not known to be a short-term killer, but it can cause illness twenty to forty years later…and death! Just as repeated heavy exposure of the poisons in Agent Orange will most likely cause more death from heavy and continuous exposure than minimal exposure. Duh!

NEWSFLASH: VA medical professionals should be educated about these statistics. They are readily available all over the place. If a Vietnam War veteran was placed in these hot areas during the hot years, that Vietnam War veteran should be given extra attention in monitoring the possible illnesses and diseases that can be associated with Agent Orange exposure. That is what I think VA medical professionals ought to do…we'll see.

How Many Died From Agent Orange?

In the early days, the U.S. government just flat out denied everything, every claim for Vietnam veterans for physical problems that attempted to be linked to Agent Orange exposure. Just like our fathers and uncles who came home with their memories of Iwo Jima, Normandy, Tora Bora and Inchon, we brought memories from battles at Hue, Hamburger Hill, Saigon, Dak To, Soui Tre, Khe Sanh, etc. Today's heroes are also coming home with their nightmarish memories from Kuwait, Fallujah, Baghdad, etc. Their claims meet with more and faster approvals.

Those memories created an illness termed as…shell shock, battle fatigue, combat stress, traumatic stress and eventually…post-traumatic stress disorder. Fighting in war is stressful. That is a given. Fighting in continuous battles of war is even more stressful. Fighting in close quarters like the in-your-face type of battles of the Vietnam War has produced an unexpected and unprepared for overload of mental problems. As a result, the Department of Veterans Affairs failed terribly to deal with the masses of Vietnam War veterans who are seeking treatment for their PTSD problems.

Moving fast forward to the present. The true cost of today's wars will not be known for years to come. For every U.S. military man or woman killed in the Afghanistan and Iraq Wars, official reports document that another sixteen have been coming home injured. To provide you with a shocking dose of reality, here are some factual comparisons, facts from the Departments of Veterans Affairs (VA):

KIAs IN WARS vs. WOUNDED/INJURED

WWI & WWII	1 Single KIA	Wounded/Injured Average = 1.8
Korea	1 Single KIA	Wounded/Injured Average = 2.6
Vietnam	1 Single KIA	Wounded/Injured Average = 3.0
Afghanistan & Iraq	1 Single KIA	Wounded/Injured Average = 16.0

What this tells me, just my personal opinion, is that America has yet to realize the true cost of the recent wars as their combatants are still so young. If the VA was unable to handle the damaged veterans from Vietnam, how are they going to keep up with the expected volume down the road from the modern-day wars? Keep in mind that in Vietnam or Korea, many of the wounded just died, but the combat hospitals in Afghanistan and Iraq saved lives and sent them home with disabilities that may need attention for the rest of their lives. That will cost money!

The Killer of Vietnam Veterans Since Coming Home
Figuring the "Dosage Response Factor" of Agent Orange

For those of us who fought and suffered the horrors there, leaving Vietnam with just the memories was difficult enough, but the constant reminders of Vietnam have never ceased. The III Corp area in Vietnam, where the 25th Infantry Division served was one of the most heavily sprayed with all types of toxins…throughout the Vietnam War.

Determining the amount of Agent Orange exposure is extremely difficult and there does not appear to be much evidence that Veterans Administration has ever put forth much effort to make such determinations. In science, the degree of exposure is called **"the dose/response factor."** Degree of exposure should be investigated for each Vietnam veteran in order to estimate the potential long-term health effect of exposure to Agent Orange (some say critical) to be able to estimate how much exposure a person may have had in quantity, frequency and duration as well a means of exposure.

Dosage Response Factor
December 16, 2013

Dose Response Relationship describes how the likelihood and severity of adverse health effects (the responses) are related to the amount and condition of exposure to Agent Orange. Hypothetically, as the dose increases, the measured response also increases. At low doses, there may be no response. At some level of dose, the responses begin to occur in a small fraction of the study population or at a low probability rate. Both the dose at which a response begins to appear and the rate at which it increases given increasing dose can be variable between different pollutants, individuals, exposure routes, etc.

- **How can exposure be quantified with precision? "Exposure"**, in epidemiology, means the person had the "opportunity" for contact in some manner with the chemical. But what is contact? Does this mean direct contact, such as physically being sprayed with the products, or does it include more remote opportunities, such as contact through airborne particulates or contact through the food and water chain?
- **Effect:** Science looks for "cause and effect" in determining health outcomes. It is extremely difficult to accurately state that a behavior or exposure causes an outcome. For example, it is widely accepted that cigarette smoking may cause lung cancer, but this does not account for those who smoke for years and never get cancer or those who never smoked and get the disease.
- **Delay:** Many diseases, including cancer, have extremely long latency periods. It is possible, therefore, for a person to be exposed to a toxin and not have the effect of that exposure manifested for twenty years or more. During the years, however, a person may have been "insulated" with other additional exposures through the workplace or the environment. It becomes extremely difficult assessing and separating these "confounding" exposures when looking for the source of a disease.

Diabetes Type II is recognized as a potential result of exposure to Agent Orange, although it is not conclusively caused by Agent Orange. Type II diabetes involves the body producing high blood-sugar levels, when it cannot properly respond to the hormone, insulin.

Vietnam vets exposed to Agent Orange do not have to prove a connection between diabetes mellitus type II and our military service to receive a service connected VA disability compensation. The VA simply presumes a service-connected relationship exists and that diabetes mellitus type II is associated with exposure to the dreaded dioxins in Agent Orange.

Approximately 65% of people in America with diabetes also suffer from hypertension or high blood pressure. Most people with diabetes develop high blood pressure during their life. Hypertension can be a life threatening condition, and it should be treated immediately. Symptoms of high blood pressure often do not show until years after its initial appearance, giving it the nickname "The Silent Killer."

When your blood pressure is high, it puts extra pressure on the walls of your arteries. This added stress on your circulatory system can reduce blood flow and lead to a stroke or heart attack. An aneurism can also result from this extra pressure on your arteries. An aneurism occurs when a bulge forms in your artery and bursts, causing excessive bleeding.

Having diabetes makes high blood pressure and other heart or circulation problems more likely because diabetes damages arteries by making them targets for hardening (atherosclerosis). Atherosclerosis causes high blood pressure, which can lead to blood vessel damage, heart failure, heart attack, kidney failure or…STROKE!

- www.WebMD.com, 2013

Agent Orange exposure and Stroke: *Stroke was added to the growing list of possible health effects Vietnam War veterans may face long term after exposure to Agent Orange. In response to new evidence showing a statistically significant overall increase in stroke associated with exposure increase to chemicals in Agent Orange, a committee examining these health effects has moved stroke to the "limited and suggestive" evidence category.*

- Pauline Anderson,
December 10, 2013

The Development of PTSD from a Stroke

There are a number of different events that can be considered traumatic and place a person at risk for the development of posttraumatic stress disorder (PTSD). Experiencing life-threatening illnesses or medical conditions such as a stroke, is one such type of event.

A stroke is considered to be a sudden impairment in brain function. During a stroke, a person may experience an inability to speak or speak clearly. They may also have difficulties walking or moving a limb. This is because blood is no longer flowing to an area of the brain as a result of a blockage or the rupture of a blood vessel.

Strokes vary in the damage they can cause. Some strokes are associated with symptoms that resolve themselves on their own in less than 24 hours. These are generally referred to as ministrokes or transient ischemic attacks (or TIA). However, an ischemic stroke (when there is blockage of blood flow to an area of the brain) or hemorrhagic stroke (when a blood vessel ruptures) can lead to significant damage, including long-lasting neurological deficits.

As you can see, experiencing a stroke can be considered a traumatic event. The 4th edition of the Diagnostic and Statistical Manual of Mental Disorders *defines a traumatic event as a situation where both of the following occurred:*

- *The person experienced, witnessed or was confronted with an event where there was the threat of or actual death of serious injury. The event may also have involved a threat to the person's physical well-being or the physical well-being of another person.*
- *The person responded to the event with strong feelings of fear, helplessness or horror.*

Without a doubt, a stroke meets both of these criteria. It threatens a person's life and because it is unexpected, a person may feel completely helpless to do anything about a stroke. Given this, surviving a stroke may place an individual at risk for the development of PTSD.

- Matthew Tull, PhD
Updated May 22, 2013
Reviewed by a board-certified health professional

Facts to Ponder:

- *Diabetes Type II is associated with exposure to Agent Orange.*
- *Diabetes is associated with stroke. In fact, it has been well documented that diabetes confers a significantly increased risk of stroke as well as increased mortality following stroke.*
- *Diabetes IS associated with hypertension (high blood pressure). In fact, evidence suggests that some of the increased risk of stroke among diabetics is attributed to the increased prevalence of hypertension directly from diabetes.*

- Ellen L. Air, MD, PhD
Care.diabetesjournals.org

- *Agent Orange exposure can cause hypertension.*

- WashingtonPost.com

STATISTICAL SUMMARY OF THE
HERBICIDAL WARFARE
IN THE VIETNAM WAR – EACH YEAR
August 10, 1961 – October 31, 1971
(3,735 Days)

	OPERATIONS TRAIL DUST & RANCH/HANDS		
YEAR	TOTAL GALLONS USED	TOTAL ACRES EFFECTED	TOTAL SQ. MILES EFFECTED
1962	17,171	5,724	27
1963	74,760	24,920	117
1964	281,607	93,869	440
1965	664,657	221,552	1,039
1966	2,535,788	845,263	3,962
1967	5,123,353	1,707,784	8,005
1968	5,089,010	1,696,337	7,952
1969	4,558,817	1,519,606	7,123
1970	758,966	252,989	1,186
1971	10,039	3,346	16
Year Unknown	281,201	93,734	439
TOTAL:	**19,395,369**	**6,465,123**	**30,305**

The VA has been trying to discourage us from filing claims for benefits since we Vietnam vets came home. At this point in my life, when I can barely walk up one stair without tripping, I am convinced that the Department of Veterans Affairs has succeeded in keeping many of us discouraged.

Moving away from the **disabling, psychological damage** of PTSD and being disabled from physical wounds, it is no longer a secret to the public, from Australia to the U.S.A., that the use of "chemical warfare" in the Vietnam War has affected millions in every country that participated in that war...it is *still* affecting us. The name **Agent Orange** will live on infamously. It brings three things to mind—pain...suffering and...death to my war buddies and their families.

For those of you who are not very familiar with Vietnam or just never gave a rat's butt (like most politicians), Vietnam is a country of some hills and lowlands, heavily forested and very humid. Vietnam, especially the southern part where the Vietnam War's battles were most often fought as the war matured, was the perfect environment for dense vegetation to grow and grow and grow. Vietnam was not an ideal place to fight a decade-long war for the combatants sent there from other countries.

Southern Vietnam's dense, tropical setting was perfect for the Viet Cong and North Vietnam military but very hazardous for the U.S. troops. Even today, some American troops who served in and survived the Vietnam War may suffer from diseases caused by the tropical climate, which was perfect for several types of fungus to survive. Many Nam vets still have problems with this.

U.S. leaders made the decision to use defoliant chemicals to clear out the vegetation and the hiding places for the communist troops. Agent Orange, along with other *Rainbow Defoliants*, was used generously to deprive our enemy of its use of the jungle from which to launch surprise attacks. What most people did not know back then and choose not to be aware of today is:

> Agent Orange's chief ingredient, **Dioxin** had undergone military tests during World War II, and those tests concluded it to be a very deadly compound, so deadly that the U.S. Congress listed **Dioxin** as a potential Weapon of Mass Destruction (WMD). In fact, in the jungle battles in the South Pacific during World War II, the U.S. government decided not to use these herbicides to eliminate vegetation for enemy cover because of the health problems which might occur.

As the Vietnam War began to intensify in 1967 and 1968, it became obvious that our U.S. leaders had badly underestimated the capabilities of the Viet Cong and North Vietnam's military (supported generously by China and the Soviet Union). It seems now that Agent Orange was a desperate but unthinkable move by our country's leaders. Therefore, the potential for health problems from Agent Orange, which were likely to occur with human contact were seemingly...**overlooked in Vietnam!**

To some degree, Agent Orange was also used near the end of the Korean War, but southern Vietnam became almost a wasteland where there used to be thick forests and jungles. I don't have to source what I am saying here; it has become common knowledge for the public to see...if they are interested. So, why should anyone not understand why the veterans of the Vietnam and Korean Wars are so angry with the ongoing delays, denials and more delays? Our government did not hesitate for one minute about the decision to eliminate the South Vietnam vegetation with Agent Orange, knowing that all human life could be facing a lifetime of medical problems, and in many cases (way too many), these problems became…**death sentences.**

I am happy that the VA changed its rules several years ago so that all vets who were in Vietnam during the Agent Orange spraying period are presumed to have been exposed. (I do touch on this in other parts of this book.) This means they will be covered for service-related benefits if they develop symptoms for specific maladies to be presumptively caused by Agent Orange exposure. Nothing was done to address the exposure our military would face when we went into the jungles after Agent Orange spraying by planes and helicopters. And the wind currents were able to carry the chemicals for many miles past the target areas. If the VA compensation and pension examiners were to go into more case detail with each Vietnam War veteran they are evaluating for their alleged service connected illnesses, they would be *shocked* at what they find with certain Vietnam veterans who served in the Agent Orange "hot spots" during the "hot years" of Agent Orange. Come on now — if more of a good thing is better, as we often say… what is more of a bad, bad thing?

Obviously, no two veteran's claims are exactly alike. So many Vietnam War veterans have experienced many health issues over the years after participating in that disgusting war. We did not know that we were quite likely to be infected with diseases related to exposure to Agent Orange. We were also unaware that it had been discovered that much of the blood used in military facilities, especially in Vietnam…was **contaminated!**

On August 22, 2014, I visited a local VA to consult with a different psychiatrist about new problems I was experiencing. My blood pressure readings that day were scary looking…172/104 and 164/97. Reminder, I had suffered from two ischemic strokes in December 2013, requiring a four-day hospital stay and emergency surgery on my right carotid artery. When the second ischemic stroke hit me, vision in my right eye left me and it has not come back. I am told that it is highly unlikely to ever return and this event in my life at sixty-nine years old brought on a state of depression along with my PTSD and anger problem over what happened to us over there and what we have been put through after Vietnam.

No one knows how many people have died because of Agent Orange/Dioxin exposure in the Vietnam War. It is virtually impossible to find that answer. Yes indeed, many people have died from Agent Orange/Dioxin exposure, but when was the last time anyone read a death certificate that read "Death by Agent Orange/Dioxin"? Same with diabetes. Same with PTSD. They all cause death by causing heart attacks, kidney failure, and cancer. Many Vietnam veterans' deaths are from strokes, etc., associated with Agent Orange/Dioxin exposure—some directly, some indirectly. I believe that only those in the medical profession who know what to look for are able to detect a link between a specific chemical and a specific illness, but how many of these people are present at the funeral?

Pay attention to this: Eighty percent of cancers in the western hemisphere are caused by our own environment—pollutants, poisons and dioxins that enter our bodies along with those pollutants we choose to put into our body. Half of the cancers in the world during the twenty-first century occur among people living in the industrialized countries, but less than twenty percent of the world's population lives in the so-called developed world. The point here is that dioxins poison our everyday lives in our environment. Now, examine this scenario for a Vietnam War veteran:

> They are deployed to a war in a foreign country where the use of "chemical warfare" is killing most of the vegetation (including crops) thoroughly in the areas being sprayed. The level of Dioxin in the Agent Orange chemicals is several hundred times more toxic than the environment in the home they left behind. I said "several hundred" times. And then, IF they survive that full year, they are sent back to a toxic environment that will very likely escalate whatever internal problems are brewing inside their bodies from that place called...**VIET-NAM!**

If I have oversimplified this basic analysis, I'm sorry. It is my opinion so no one needs to take offense or chastise me. Form your own opinions and if you wish, please proceed in sending them to me at your convenience...please do.

If my Agent Orange/Dioxin chapter appears complex or confusing or both, that would be because it is. The Agent Orange/Dioxin story around the Vietnam War is still being road-blocked by those who do not want the story to continue to be told. The Agent Orange story and the Vietnam War have been called...**USA's Heart of Darkness**.

Well, my dear American patriots (if you are either or both), this is a reminder that the Vietnam War began as a war against communism, ended up being the American government's attempt to take the place of God. They experimented carelessly with our planet's environmental well-being. **Didn't our government tell us that Agent Orange would never hurt us...or our children? They lied.**

"What happened to those Vietnam War veterans who got screwed by the Department of Veterans Affairs?" This was a question asked of me recently by a reader of *Condemned Property?*, a non-veteran. My reply, after thinking about it for a minute, was simply this, "I'm afraid the only way you will be able to find those heroes is…buy a shovel and…dig them up."

Blunt response. Honest response. Sure, he was taken aback by my answer for a few seconds. After mulling it over, he understood the bluntness and anger in my words. I told him what a difficult and agonizing task it can be to address the result of the abused Vietnam veterans who have died so prematurely since coming home. I have found that when someone with the wrong attitude asks me Vietnam War-related questions, and they weren't there, that my response (or at least my thoughts of responding) can be borderline barbaric. To this day, I do not have very much patience or tolerance for the ignorant questions about Vietnam. At first, I attempt to ignore them and their question, and actually, I am overly anxious in providing an honest answer to them in quick and passionate fashion, not having the slightest concern how they will respond. But I am older now, not quite as quick (or as mean) as I once was, so I tend to be a little more diplomatic and civil with my answers. This can be difficult to do sometimes, but it is something I must attempt to do more often than not if I want to survive a few more years.

The Dying Will Go On

Many of the children and grandchildren of Vietnam War veterans will be cursed with the unlucky assignment of carrying on the legacy of their Vietnam War veteran parents and grandparents. For how long? Many Vietnam War veterans have abnormally high rates of lymphoma. It took the VA only a few decades to recognize the direct links between Agent Orange exposure to serious illnesses. Unfortunately, the effects of Agent Orange have been passed on to the children of Vietnam veterans into third generations. Sorry for being redundant here, but the facts cannot ever be told to Americans enough.

Children of Vietnam Veterans Health Alliance (COVVHA) was founded by Kelly Derricks and Heather Bowser. Both are daughters of Vietnam veterans, and both of them are disabled with illnesses or diseases related to their fathers' tours in Vietnam. Their problems can be classified as terminal, and the list continues to get longer, says the *VVA Veteran* Magazine.

Agent Orange, diabetes II, hypertension, heart attack, ischemic stroke, multiple cancers and suicide…connect the dots. It is very simple—watch:

> Agent Orange associated with diabetes II.
> Agent Orange associated with hypertension.
> Agent Orange associated with diabetes II, hypertension, heart attacks
> and ischemic strokes and…more hypertension.

Agent Orange and all of the above associated with Post-Traumatic Stress Syndrome.
Agent Orange associated with multiple cancers and increased hypertension.
All of the above...associated with SUICIDE!

My point? Any veteran who has experienced the torturous ordeal of being drilled by an ignorant VA Compensation and Pension examiner knows what my point is. They (the C&P examiners) cannot or will not see the forest through the trees on my simple connection of the dots scenario. Quite frankly, this narrow-minded procedure must come to a halt soon. And our modern thinking congressional representatives seem ready and willing to tackle this fight for us. We will see.

On paper, it would appear that the VA is devoting a lot of time focusing on the ongoing crisis around suicide veterans. Are their efforts sincere? Whichever the answer and whatever the VA goal to diminish the rate of veteran suicide is, it has not been working...or maybe, the VA plan is actually working perfectly? Nonsense. I know that.

Here is an average or typical day for most modern-day combat war troops and combat veterans as well:

Their day usually starts out with a headache for most combat troops and veterans. I mean a headache of earthquake proportions. The morning might even include a bloody nose. Some mornings will be far worse than others due to a poor night's sleep that was interrupted often for one reason or another. Some of those interruptions might include life-like visions of life-like images, which of course are not real; they are hallucinations. We tell our story to someone at VA. Most times, it never gets recorded or dealt with. This treatment or lack thereof drives the active troop of veterans closer to the dark side. Didn't the VA medical professionals know this would be the result? Maybe, they were perfectly aware...just maybe. So then, why don't these evil VA employees who resent us, even hate us... just step aside and let us do it...commit suicide?

Yeah, why not just let us do it since they don't seem to care about our fate anyway? In fact, why don't they "help us" do it? At one time, many veterans, specifically Vietnam veterans honestly believe or believed the following:

We were put on an overly generous dosage of medications to heal our illnesses or…to shut us up!

PTSD has become a label the VA puts on those with effects from a war that we were stupid enough to get sucked into.

We developed a low regard for life, even our own…over there and back here as well.

Few Americans today care to know the truth about the tragedies of the Vietnam War…even if they are the truth. How sad is that?

These are mostly my thoughts, just theory being put on paper. But it is extremely difficult to believe that all of the crimes uncovered and publicly broadcast in 2014 were just accidents from neglect. Could all of this have been part of a decade's long **ultimate conspiracy** by VA…to eliminate the generation of Vietnam veterans?

Don't answer that one to yourself too quickly. Here is an article that I uncovered awhile back — I have been hanging on to it for the right time, like right here:

(September 20, 1968) – U.S. Officials Defend Use of Defoliants - U.S. military spokesmen defended use of defoliants in Vietnam at a news conference in Saigon, claiming that the use of the agents in selected areas of South Vietnam had neither appreciably altered the country's ecology nor produced any harmful effects on human or animal life.

However, a paper released at the same time at the same news conference by Dr. Fred T. Shirley, also a U.S. Department of Agriculture expert, stated that the U.S. officials in Saigon were underestimating the extent of ecological damage caused in Vietnam by defoliating agents and that they had caused "undeniable ecological damage" and that "any recovery would take a long time." This happened forty-six years ago when Agent Orange spraying had peaked in the Vietnam War.

So what, some might say. Here is another article I dug up in my spare time:

April 10, 2010 Report: Agent Orange Risks Were Known by Maker - A *Chicago Tribune* investigation revealed that in 1965, Dow Chemical Company referred to dioxin, a contaminant in Agent Orange, as one of the most toxic materials known, causing not only skin lesions but also liver damage." The *Tribune* also reported that documents it reviewed noted techniques were available to drastically cut the amount of dioxin in the defoliant during manufacture. After examining court documents and government records in the National Archives, the newspaper concluded that soldiers were exposed to Agent Orange without being informed of the risks, making exposure more dangerous. Chemical companies that produced the defoliant have been sued by veterans and Vietnamese citizens who were exposed to dioxin.

The Agent Orange Wall?

You cannot see the Vietnam Monument (The Wall) from very far away. It does not have the attention-grabbing characteristics of the white stone pillars of the World War II Monument or the huge gray stone soldiers of the Korean War Memorial. It is just a long black wall, a long low slab of black granite with the names of the Vietnam War heroes who died in-country during the war. Visiting The Wall on Memorial Day or Veterans Day is a somber experience for all veterans of any war, especially for veterans of a war that was perceived to have been lost, thanks to our media. Today, those who came home from Vietnam and are still living never got to celebrate a mission that was accomplished over there. No one seems to know just how many "real" Vietnam War veterans are still alive. Shouldn't there be a source for this somewhere? If you look online, you will find a multitude of answers; all of them are general; none with specifics. These various sources will say that "approximately" 2.7 to 3.1 million troops served in the Vietnam War.

Today, the so-called sources cannot match their estimates of how many "real" Vietnam veterans are still living in society. The range of estimates goes from 850,000 to 1.5 million, leaving "about" 700,000 of us in the unaccountable category. Geez! The estimating process continues, and it is agonizing for surviving Vietnam veterans. So, if there are "approximately" one million to two million of our war buddies who are no longer with us, how did they die and how old or young were they and…how and why did they die? Was an Agent Orange cancer one of the causes? Very likely. Was PTSD one of the causes? Very likely. Was suicide one of the causes? Likely. How many more are fighting to hang on from the poisons and demons of their Vietnam War nightmare? How many more?

Today, many of us are wearing a hat or part of a uniform we wore over there. Some wear fraternal jackets; either way, whatever is being worn is now being worn by a Vietnam veteran (hopefully a real one) with utmost pride, almost in defiance of the disgraceful treatment many of us were handed for our "homecoming." And I hope, more of them begin to wear their hats, shirts or jackets adorned with patches and/or awards that were **earned.** Yes, wear your Vietnam War decor with pride. Wear it in defiance if you wish, defiance of who our longtime adversary has been since we came home. Of course, that adversary is not the Viet Cong or the North Vietnamese Army. The main roadblock that many

Vietnam War veterans have had to battle with is located at Vermont Avenue NW, Washington D.C....The Department of Veterans Affairs.

As mentioned elsewhere in this book, in the earliest days, the VA just denied everything and that usually discouraged even filing for a claim for service-connected disabilities. But of course, there was little evidence available in the 1970s that Agent Orange was the cause of or even associated with any health problems other than...a lot of strange deaths among Vietnam War's veterans!

What if there was a memorial for Vietnam War veterans, similar to the Vietnam Veterans Wall, built specifically for Agent Orange caused mortalities from that war?

Such a memorial could easily include 500,000 names rather than 58,000+.
Such a memorial could cover up to 17.24 acres.
Such a memorial could be up to 4,254.8 feet long.

The original, existing Vietnam Veterans Memorial has often been referred to as "The Vietnam Veterans Third Battle":

First being surviving in Vietnam.
Second being dealing with homecoming rejection.
Third being no one wanted to build this wall except Vietnam War veterans.

When the Vietnam Veterans Memorial Wall was dedicated, Cap Weinberger, Defense Secretary said this, "When your country called, you came. When your country refused you honor, you remained silent." My fellow Vietnam War buddies, I respectfully urge you to break out of that mode of silence and fight again for the benefits that you so bravely **earned**.

The Agent Orange Memorial Wall will most likely never happen and where would they put it? This was just a "what if" scenario. Besides, no one seems to know how many of us are still alive, let alone how many Vietnam veterans have died...prematurely.

Good news! We weren't the first ones to do it. Our buddies in Great Britain were the first to douse their foes with defoliants in the early 1950s in Malaya, then one of many British colonies around the world...before it became the independent country Malaysia. The Brits sprayed the Malayan tropical setting with chemicals to strip trees and large bushes to the ground. Unfortunately, the crops that the locals worked hard at cultivating for their survival just happened to be in the way, so they were destroyed as well. A decade later, we did the same thing in

South Vietnam on an enormously larger scale against the Viet Cong, NVAs and unfortunately, South Vietnamese peasants as well.

This plan seemed logical to the American government—simply starve everyone, even the friendlies and the enemy will surrender. How did that work out for us? Same way it did for the Brits. I suppose that one day our dedicated historians will get around to adding up the numbers. Should be double in this ridiculous high-tech age. I am referring to…just how many people did Agent Orange/ Dioxin spray kill in Vietnam's war and after? Millions? Possibly—probably. The trouble is, the meter is still running and running. No worries, the Vietnam War veterans will pass away quietly as they have been since they came home. They won't talk about it…even until the day they die and that will sadden me until the day they bury me.

Backing up a bit, according to the records of the American Air Force, Agent Orange was dumped on less than twenty percent of the forests and jungles in South Vietnam. Unfortunately, and as I have mentioned earlier, massive agricultural destruction resulted. It was so terrible that the soil in some parts of South Vietnam remain unproductive for farming crops. Another unfortunate result of Agent Orange's destruction of the countryside would result, forcing massive migrations of the civilian population from their rural homes to the urban areas. Sounds sad, doesn't it? Guess what, this was part of our fantastic leaders' plan in Washington, so I have heard.

Several species of plants and animals have reportedly vanished from the Agent Orange contaminated areas. Breathtakingly sad news.

Agent Orange Updates

VA has updated the list of ships that operated in Vietnam 12/2014

Ships or boats that were part of the Mobile Riverine Force, Inshore Fire Support (ISF) Division 93 or had one of the following designations operated on the inland waterways of Vietnam. Veterans whose military records confirm they were aboard these ships qualify for presumption of herbicide exposure. During your tour, did your ship or boat have one of the following designations?

- AGP (Assault Group Patrol/Patrol Craft Tender)
- LCM (Landing Craft, Mechanized)
- LCU (Landing Craft, Utility)
- LCVP (Landing Craft, Vehicle, Personnel)
- LST (Landing Ship, Tank)
- PBR (Patrol Boat, River)

- PCF (Patrol Craft, Fast or Swift Boat)
- PG (Patrol Gunboat)
- STABS (Strike Assault Boats)
- WAK (Cargo Vessel)
- WHEC (High Endurance Cutter)
- WLB (Buoy Tender)
- WPB (Patrol Boat)
- YFU (Harbor Utility Craft)

If your vessel is not included in the Mobile Riverine Force, ISF Division 93 or above designations, check VA's alphabetized ship list.

(Source: http://www.publichealth.va.gov/exposures/agentorange/shiplist)

VA Expands Dates of Agent Orange Exposure in Korea from 1968-1969 to 1968-1971

Veterans who served along the demilitarized zone (DMZ) in Korea during the Vietnam War now have an easier path to access health care and benefits. The Department of Veterans Affairs (VA) expanded the dates when illnesses associated with exposure to Agent Orange can be presumed related to their military service previously between April 1, 1968 and August 31, 1971, if a Veteran served in a unit determined by VA and Department of Defense to have operated in an area of the DMZ where Agent Orange or other herbicides were applied. The expanded dates took effect on February 24, 2011.

(See www.publichealth.va.gov/exposures/agentorange/korea.asp.) This presumption simplifies and speeds the application process for Veterans of the Korean DMZ. VA encourages Veterans who believe they have health problems related to Agent Orange to submit their applications for VA health care and disability compensation benefits. To apply for health-care benefits, apply online at www.1010ez.med.va.gov/sec/vha/1010ez or contact the nearest VA health-care facility at 1-877-222-VETS (8387). To file a claim for disability benefits, apply online at www.ebenefits.va.gov or contact the nearest VA regional office at 1-800-827-1000. Veterans who served along the Korean DMZ may also be eligible for a free Agent Orange Registry health evaluation. The regulation expanding the dates for eligible service in Korea is available on the Office of the Federal Register website or www.regulations.gov/#!documentDetail;D=VA-2009-VBA-0021-0007. (Source: www.va.gov)

I have provided substantial facts in this chapter, facts obtained from readily available sources today. However, when our Vietnam War buddies first started to file disability claims for alleged Agent Orange-associated illnesses, the VA compensation and pension examiners would have an easier time in denying them because the veterans were asked by the VA to produce information to substantiate that they were exposed to the Agent Orange spraying. And…that information **did not exist yet**. In 1980, the VA rescinded the requirement that veterans prove exposure when asking for information, assistance or treatment for what they believed to be Agent Orange-related illnesses.

I cannot imagine that the VA did not know there were no records available from the militaries or the Department of Defense that could verify a veteran's exposure potential to herbicides as no such records existed at that time.

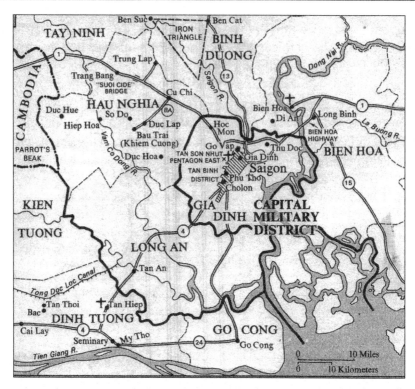

Charlie Daniels with Gainey (Deceased) and Ryan (Deceased)

One of the saddest things about the Vietnam War is…it continues to kill so many who have struggled to survive it after they came home!

- Author Unknown

CHAPTER 8

BETTER LATE THAN NEVER OR... TOO LITTLE TOO LATE?

My Vision for a Future VA...

I went to sleep one night recently, and I began with a dream, not a nightmare for a change. This dream was to be really dreamlike, almost like a far-away fantasy.

It was about ten years ago, and I was on my way to a new experience as I had recently entered into the VA system. I was excited but also apprehensive. Initially, I was told that because I was a Purple Heart recipient that my status would be upgraded somewhat. But I was also apprehensive because very few good stories had been told about the other veterans' experiences with VA. And this bad news had been coming back to us for decades.

My first physical went well. I was in pretty good shape at 190 pounds. Cholesterol was so-so, nothing to be alarmed about. My blood pressure was more than acceptable in the 130/80 range and there were no other problems, so I was told—except this news—I was found to be on the borderline of being a pre-diabetic and a full-blown Type II diabetic with an initial glucose reading of 151. (125 or under is a safe reading.) My medical professionals informed me that they could help me get this under control as I was in the very early stage of being a full-blown Type II diabetic. Sure enough, my VA medical professionals were true to their word. In quick fashion, I was set up on a diabetes management program, which included a mild but regular dosage of meds, consulting with diet experts and physical fitness advisors. I received my glucose meter and was scheduled for regular check-ups at VA to monitor my progress on getting and keeping my Type II Diabetes under control. I was determined to be one of VA's best patients with diabetes as I planned to adhere to all of their friendly and meaningful advice. I had also done my homework by reading everything I could about treating diabetes and keeping it under control. (This is still a dream.)

This was serious business now as it was the first health issue related to my heavy Agent Orange exposure in the Vietnam War. One exception—I had recurrent skin problems (jungle rot) from the Vietnam swamps and jungles, but that was external—so I thought. Anyway, the skin rashes did not hinder me from normal activities, but diabetes would become a life-threatening sickness if not taken care of as soon as having been diagnosed as having it. I kept my promise to myself. I remained a good patient with Type II Diabetes for all the years that followed. In fact, up until the age of sixty-nine, I was still engaged in:

- Bicycle rides of fifteen miles or so every other day.
- Two to three long walks daily, often with my big loveable dog in heavily wooded areas for several miles each time.
- Canoe trips on the Cuyahoga River as well as Florida's Everglades.
- Trips to baseball/softball batting cages with grandkids. I was still able to make good contact with 80-85 MPH fastballs (baseball) or 65 MPH softball pitches. This impressed the grandkids. Of course, my back was sore for a few days, and I had to lay off golfing for a while.
- Work-related travel. My sales job required me to be a "travel maniac", flying and driving to as many as twenty states or more each year—every year since 1980.
- Golf every week, sometimes twice a week, whenever possible.

I was still able to do all of the above at sixty-nine years old almost as if I was only thirty-nine years old—almost. Why was I able to engage in all of these activities at such a late age in my life? Because my medical professionals at VA diagnosed me with Type II Diabetes almost ten years earlier, and we kept it under control together. Then my dream ended, and I…WOKE UP!

Suddenly, I realized that everything I had just experienced in the dream-like fantasy was actually a nightmare. None of the activities, none of the events described in that dream actually happened as I described them—none except one. My glucose reading at my very first VA physical, which included a fasted blood work test, was…151. I was, in fact, suffering from Type II Diabetes at that time; however, no one at VA caught it back then, and I continued a somewhat reduced lifestyle of activity that most fifty-year-olds could not have maintained. Eventually, another VA doctor at a different location caught it after a lab test in 2010. I was diabetic, and I had been for at least the previous five years. My life would change dramatically from this point forward—changes that I have not adapted to as well as I should. It is psychological. It is like…now I have to start all over again as I have had to do many times before since the Vietnam War ended.

Within a matter of days or hours after *Condemned Property?* was launched and available for distribution to the world, I was stricken with consecutive ischemic strokes in December 2013, requiring immediate hospital care and critical surgery on December 13, 2013. Obviously, I have survived because here I am, just a year or so after surgery, doing exactly what probably caused the stroke, which is…writing a book about the Vietnam War and its ghastly horrors that followed.

Condemned Property? took me eight and a half years to plan for, organize, and write by longhand (thousands of pages, proofed, re-proofed and rewritten again and again). No complaints. I wrote that book with compelling passion, sometimes overwhelmingly so and sometimes with anger that had been stored inside me since the very evening I returned home from Vietnam in March 1969. That very unforgettable arrival back at Oakland, California still angers me. I offer **no apologies** for that anger and the things I wrote in that book. It was all the truth—hard hitting, controversial, sometimes meant to be offensive, but always truthful as I knew it or remembered the experiences around the Vietnam War for my war buddies, myself, our friends and families back in America.

Back to the ischemic strokes, which nearly killed me. Just a brief description of what happened with that and after that as there are too many other things I want and need to write about in this sequel to *Condemned Property?*

Here is a copy of the exact letter I sent to two congressmen and five senators pertaining to my ischemic strokes experience. I hope other veterans will take this example and use it if need be.

August 27, 2014

Subject: THANK YOU!

Dear Congressmen and Senators:

Thank you…THANK YOU and THANK YOU!!!

Each of you to whom this letter of gratitude is being sent has taken the time to communicate back to me in response to one or more of my letters on behalf of all veteran brothers and sisters, especially Vietnam War veterans. Thanks for taking the time away from your very busy days to address my grievances concerning the ghastly scandal at multiple VA hospitals and healthcare centers. Thanks for putting the extreme and very necessary pressure on VA that was <u>long past due</u>. In some cases, your actions are going to be timely and/or better late than never for many, mostly the younger veterans. As for my war buddies and me, the Vietnam veteran warriors, I am afraid that it is too little too late for tens of thousands (maybe hundreds of thousands) of us.

Anyway, without a doubt, because of this pressure put on the corrupt and in some ways, murderous VA bureaucracy, I will finally receive the badly needed healthcare that may be life saving for a proud old combat Vietnam War veteran…me. Here is a very abbreviated delineation of what should be considered an unsuitable series of events for me personally with the VA over just one of my health problems:

- On the week of 12/3/14, I was dealt what is called an Ischemic Transient Stroke as parts of the left side of my body went numb—almost paralyzed from my facial area to different parts of the left side of my body. When I informed a VA nurse, I was told that "it's probably just carpal tunnel" and nothing else was done. I went home, took aspirin and the events subsided. The next week, on 12/10/14 as I was driving to another VA facility to have tests done for something else (spinal problems), my vision was almost completely lost in my right eye as I was driving. Fortunately, I was already on my way to the main VA hospital facility in Cleveland, Ohio.

I explained my predicament immediately when I arrived at the VA. "Eventually" I was sent to the emergency room for further observations where I sat and waited far too long, in my opinion, given the nature of my problem, having suddenly **gone blind in one eye!**

Finally, after different tests and observations, it was determined that I had suffered from one or more ischemic strokes (brain attacks) and was admitted to the Cleveland Wade Park Hospital for further observation for the next several days and surgery was performed on my right carotid artery on 12/13/14 at VA Wade Park. I was released on 12/14/14 and sent home. There was no post-operation therapy or rehab suggested other than being told to take it easy over the next couple of months, which I did. However, it did not take me long to realize that I was not the same person anymore. Yes, the vision was apparently 70-80% permanently gone, but my problems went well beyond that as I still had one pretty sound eye. So, I expressed my concerns and frustrations a few times to the VA staff members I met with in each of the follow-up exams, regardless of who they were.

The problems I continued to experience from my ischemic strokes (brain attacks) continue to this day over a full year after the events described earlier took place. Just a few of the ongoing problems are (but not limited to) are as follows:

Trimmer (8116)
Ischemic Stroke After-Effects

Vision in Right Eye - About 80% vision loss remains in right eye since the initial loss of vision on 12/11/13. Seems swollen or drooping at times still.

Vision in Left Eye – Has been weakened since the stroke. Also blurred or double vision experiences on a daily basis.

Depth Perception – Walking can be challenging, and I will often stumble, so I wear a patch on right eye only when I am walking. I find myself bumping into people in public places of heavy traffic like Walmart or airports.

Memory Loss – Short term of thoughts within a 5 to 15 minute window have been escaping me since the stroke. I fear for vascular dementia.

Pain - Headaches have subsided in severity since first week after surgery, but they do occur from time to time. I never used to get headaches.

Balance - Still having problems going up and down stairs, constantly bumping into things, missing steps, etc., and tripping.

Speech – Was slurred at first but seems okay now, especially after speech therapy.

Muscle/Joint Pain - Was almost unbearable for the first few weeks after surgery on 12/12/13. Has improved as of this date one year later on December 28, 2014.

Numbness – Right side of face (jaw) and neck where surgery was performed, remained moderately numb for several months. Left hand continues with constant numbness and pain. Manual dexterity limits computer work time.

Sleeping – Sleep patterns greatly disturbed since surgery, having difficulty getting back to sleep after being awakened.

Depression – Has joined in with my moments of anger. VA medicates me for both and that can be awfully tricky.

Fear & Anxiety – I've noticed an elevated feeling of fear since the stroke with extreme fatigue during the day. My fear includes the fear of waking up with vision impaired in the left eye…leaving me with impaired vision in both eyes.

Hypertension Elevation – High blood pressure is often associated with PTSD, Agent Orange exposure and/or diabetes. I had all three before the stroke, and now, with an ischemic stroke behind me, my blood pressure readings are often 150/90 to 170/100 with medication.

PTSD - On top of my existing PTSD from combat in Vietnam, stroke after-effects have made me more hyper and extremely vigilant and even leery of going out in public places.

Incontinence – Has become an occasional problem.

Driving Problems – Long-distance driving of 100+ miles causes drowsiness and sometimes sleepiness, so I pull over to rest—or I just don't make the trip at all. Night driving is impossible. Driving for work purposes has stopped.

CONCLUSION: Overall strength, stamina and motivation to exercise are greatly diminished and has inhibited my personal rehab program. I have not been able to return to a regular work schedule, and doubt I ever will. I am a walking time bomb. However, here is a copy of a letter I sent to Congress and the Senate in July or August 2014:

Dear Congress members and Senators, just this week (yesterday) I was notified via a telephone call from a VA psychiatrist who I met with recently that I have been approved for a Post-Stroke Rehab Program outside of VA at a credible and convenient medical center…at VA's expense!

Gentlemen, regardless of whether this is too little and too late, which it may or may not be, I am accepting this happening as more of a "better late than not at all" mentality and I am embracing this as somewhat short of a miracle. And it was your pressure put on VA this year that made this happen.

I have no hard feelings for most of the VA medical staff members I have been associated with since entering the VA system almost 10 years ago in 2005. I have other issues with VA that I am embattled with and they could also affect my life's future, but I am not writing to you all about those pending issues…not yet!

Again, I thank you all for taking the VA to task. I have personally realized positive results already from the rehab program and this strengthens my faith that this is still the great country that my war buddies and I risked our lives for… and died for.

Very, VERY appreciatively yours,
Roland E. "Dusty" Trimmer
Combat Vietnam War Veteran
Author, *Condemned Property?*
Concerned Veterans for America-Strike Team

CC: Charles Moore, Veterans Affairs, 1240 E. 9th Street, Cleveland, OH 44199
     Joshua Rondini, DAV, 1240 E. 9th Street, Cleveland, OH 44199
     Robert Park, Veterans Service Office, 449 S. Meridian St., Ravenna, OH 44266

Make no mistake, my health issues caused by my Vietnam War experience and magnified by what I consider unconscientious misconduct and negligence by certain VA employees is not by any means as severe as many other veterans' issues. I consider my problems just an inconvenience compared to theirs. The fact that I am able to write and inform America about these unfortunate happenings is a blessing to me.

Rehabilitation After a Stroke. This is considered a vital part of stroke recovery, the sooner the better. In fact, the nationally recognized Cleveland Clinic's *Stroke Care Treatment Guide* offers the following information for its stroke patients entering rehab for memory loss at their Stroke Care Cerebrovascular Center:

Practical Tips for Memory Loss After a Stroke

Some memory loss after a stroke is common, but sometimes it's so subtle, you might not even notice the problem until the stroke survivor has to perform complicated

daily tasks. Memory problems can manifest either as trouble learning new infor-
mation and skills or trouble remembering and retrieving information.

- **Problems with verbal memory:** *trouble learning or remembering names,*
  stories or other information having to do with words.
- **Problem with visual memory:** *trouble learning or remembering faces*
  shapes, directions, or other things sensed by sight.
- **Vascular dementia:** *an overall decline in thinking abilities, with symp-*
  toms similar to Alzheimer's.

It's unlikely that a stroke survivor's memory will be completely restored. But for
many people, memory can improve over time, spontaneously or with rehabilita-
tion. Meanwhile, here are ways you can help:

- **If memory loss is dramatic, address the problem when the person is still in**
  the hospital. *If a stroke survivor can't remember his name or where he lives,*
  you'll need to arrange for more care than he had before the stroke.
- **Keep important items in designated places.** *For example, hang keys on a*
  hook by the door and keep wallets or purses on a hall table.
- **Set daily routines performed in the same sequence.** *For example, to get ready*
  for bed, he'll first put on pajamas, then brush teeth and use the toilet.
- **Repeat yourself often if a stroke survivor forgets what you've said.** *Though*
  it can be frustrating to say the same thing over and over, you're helping him
  by patiently repeating what you've already said.
- **Help him keep a notebook of important information.** *You might want to*
  divide it into separate sections with labels for doctor's appointments, medi-
  cation and personal information.
- **Create mnemonic devices to help remember simple tasks.** *For example, the*
  phrase "ALL OK" might help a stroke survivor remember what needs to be
  done before he leaves the house: appliances (off), lights (off), locked (door),
  oven (off), keys (in pocket).

Each year, more than half a million Americans suffer from strokes; stroke is one
of the leading causes of death in the United States and a leading cause of serious
long-term disability, according to the American Heart Association and American
Stroke Association.

A stroke or "brain attack" occurs when the blood supply is cut off from part of
the brain. When this happens, the blood-deprived brain loses its supply of oxygen

and nutrients. When the brain is deprived of blood for even a few minutes, it begins to die.

There are two types of strokes—ischemic and hemorrhagic. In ischemic strokes, brain arteries become blocked and prevent blood from nourishing the brain. In hemorrhagic strokes, brain arteries rupture from damage caused by high blood pressure and other risk factors or an aneurysm (an abnormal out-pouching of a blood vessel). This causes blood to flood the brain, creating pressure that leads to brain-cell death.

*Remember that for every minute brain cells are deprived of oxygen during a stroke, brain damage increases. The chances for survival and recovery improve when treatment begins within the first few hours of stroke warning signs. **Immediate treatment of a stroke may limit or prevent brain damage.***
(Source: *Cleveland Clinic Stroke Care Treatment Guide*)

The *Cleveland Clinic Stroke Treatment Guide* also notes these risk factors for a stroke:

- **High blood pressure:** strokes are four to six times more likely to occur in people with high blood pressure.
- **Diabetes:** diabetics are at a higher risk for a stroke.

There are many other risk factors, but for me and many Vietnam War veterans, these seem to be the two most important ones to get under control. So I have put a higher priority on trying to keep them both from getting out of hand with my post-stroke lifestyle.

The National Stroke Association offers these alarming facts about strokes:

1 in 4 Stroke Patients Suffer Post-PTSD Symptoms

One of four people who survive a stroke or transient ischemic attack (TIA) suffer from symptoms of post-traumatic stress disorder (PTSD) within the first year after the event, according to a new study. The study, led by researchers from Columbia University Medical Center also found that one in nine patients experience chronic PTSD more than a year later. The data suggest that each year nearly 300,000 stroke/TIA survivors will develop PTSD symptoms, the study noted. The new research builds on recent findings from the same team of researchers that PTSD is common among heart attack survivors, contributing "to a double risk of a future cardiac event or of dying within one to three years," according to first author Donald Edmondson, Ph.D., M.P.H., assistant professor of behavioral medicine.

- *PTSD in stroke and TIA survivors may increase their risk for recurrent stroke and other cardiovascular events, "given that each event is life-threatening and that strokes/TIAs add hundreds of millions of dollars to annual health expenditures.*
- *PTSD is not just a disorder of combat veterans and sexual assault survivors, but strongly affects survivors of stroke and other potentially traumatic acute cardiovascular events as well.*
- *"Surviving a life-threatening health scare can have a debilitating psychological impact, and health-care providers should make it a priority to screen for symptoms of depression, anxiety, and PTSD among these patient populations." According to data from the American Stroke Association, nearly 795,000 Americans suffer a new or recurrent stroke each year and up to an additional 500,000 suffer a TIA.*
- *PTSD is an anxiety disorder initiated by exposure to a traumatic event. Common symptoms include nightmares, avoidance of reminders of the event and elevated heart rate and blood pressure. Chronic PTSD is characterized by a duration of these symptoms for three months or longer.*
- *PTSD and other psychological disorders in stroke and TIA patients appear to be an under recognized and undertreated problem.*
- *Further research is needed to assess whether mental health treatment can reduce stroke induced PTSD symptoms. That treatment can "help patients regain a feeling of normalcy and calm as soon as possible after their health scare."*

(Source: http://psychcentral.com/news/2013/nearly-1-in-4-stroke-patients-suffer-ptsd-syptoms/56321.html)

In the words of one of America's politicians, he recently said:

Taking care of our veterans is a cost of war. If you can spend six trillion dollars sending people to war, you can spend a few billion dollars to take care of them when they are brought home.

Bernie Sanders, Senator – Vermont

Obama Begrudgingly (?) Signs VA Bill To Open Outside Care To Veterans…A Little Too Late For Some. Better Late Than Not At All For Others

IT happened in early August 2014 about forty-five years after my war buddies and I had finished our tours in the bloodiest two years of the Vietnam War, 1968 and 1969.

IT happened many years too late for the several hundred thousand Vietnam War warriors who lost their battles for survival after our war had ended and died prematurely after they came home.

IT happened for me eight and a half months after I had suffered two ischemic stokes in December 2013, but at least it happened. While some of the damages done by those ischemic strokes are permanent, some are not or don't have to be permanent. I will accept the fact that it happened with enough time to help me live longer.

H.R. 3230, the Veterans' Access Through Choice, Accountability and Transparency Act of 2014 is what I keep referring to as **IT**. Better late than never for today's veterans, and we Vietnam War veterans are extremely happy for all of them who will finally benefit this act, which we have been fighting for…forever.

Obama signed **IT** at Fort Belvoir's U.S. Army base in Virginia, a fitting and proper place. At that time, he had authorized sixteen billion dollars to begin funding and to begin "speeding up" appointments and seriously overdue health-care at VA health facilities across the United States of America. Love him or despise him; he signed into law a profound overhaul of America's veterans' health-care system. He deserves credit for that.

The battle to win the healthcare benefits was unbelievably long. No one can be sure how far back it goes when the first American veteran died because of the incompetence, negligence, apathy, arrogance and malpractice, to name a few, that has been all too common at VA facilities across our country. How amazing is this? Well, Americans have been calling their country the greatest country in the world, probably since the end of WWII. And yet, Americans left the warriors who defended them behind and unattended.

IT is just the beginning. It must not be the end. Our country's politicians finally came through for us. Now we must remain vigilant so as to never allow what has been going on to ever happen again…never.

I personally wrote and sent dozens of letters to every member of the House Committee on Veterans Affairs and many personalized acknowledgements came back to me. In fact, several letters included a personal invitation with open arms to my war buddies and I to visit with them personally. I may do that yet.

Many veterans are now free to seek and receive private care rather than wait for an appointment at VA, or if they live more than forty miles away from the nearest VA facility capability of attending to them.

IT also gives present Secretary McDonald more authority to terminate poorly performing VA personnel at all levels, including senior ranking executives. Why not? As Obama said at the signing of H.R. 3230…"our veterans don't have time for politics."

Commander in Chief Missing In Action?

In mid-October 2014, our country's decorated U.S. Marine Corps combat veteran Sgt. Andrew Tahmooressi celebrated his two hundredth day in Mexico… behind prison bars. My math shows that he had been held captive for more than six grueling months. In the same week, the President of the United States, also Commander in Chief of our Armed Forces played his two hundredth round of golf. Folks, I know many avid golfers. I used to be one until suffering an ischemic stroke. I don't know very many, if any who is able to play two hundred rounds of golf in…**fifteen years**.

If his majesty, Barack Hussein Obama has enough time on his hands to break away from his very stressful obligations to the American people to play on the golf course for five or six hours two hundred times, one should wonder…who else is in his golf group on those days? What was Joe Biden doing on those days? And by the way, two hundred rounds of golf could equate to three and a half to four months of time off from the most important job in the world.

Concerned Vets for America President Pete Hegseth stated this, "Six months into Tahmooressi's captivity, the president had yet to place a phone call to his counterpart in Mexico, President Enrique Peria Nieto, to discuss the matter and to urge the Marine's release. When asked, the president's spokesman puts the responsibility on the State Department."

As Hegseth also stated, "He had time to openly comment on the Trayvon Martin shooting and managed to carve time out from his busy schedule to film a pro-Obamacare video for a humor website called "Funny or Die" with comedian Zach Galifianakis."

Obama has boldly stated many times in public how strongly he supports our military motto of never leaving anyone behind. In fact, he has said it exactly like such, "The United States of America does not ever leave our men and women behind." Obama has also been quoted in stating, "We remain deeply committed to securing the release of American citizens who are unjustly detained abroad and deserve to be reunited with their families."

What was missing here? It appears that our President was missing. Someone please send out a search party to locate him, I thought to myself. But first, I prayed our Marine would have been brought home before this book publishes. That prayer was answered. Thanks, dear Lord.

CHAPTER 9

SHINSEKI URGED PATIENCE?

It is May 2014, and the scandal over the Phoenix VA has broadened to include several other VA facilities nationwide, so the suspense level was heightened. Federal prosecutors have joined the investigation as to whether criminal charges should be filed. There are calls for Shinseki to resign and Congress, senators and service organizations are furious with his lack of decisiveness to the accusations about long waiting lists and falsified records. Shinseki stated that the allegations made him "mad as hell", though his lack of emotion was not very convincing. Again, he asked for…"**patience**".

In Shinseki's Department of Veterans FY 2014-2020 Strategic Plan, he made promises to do some of the following, "We will achieve President Obama's vision for a 21st century VA. In doing so, we will strive to earn the trust and confidence of our veterans as their advocate."

- Empower veterans to improve their well-being.
- Enhance and develop trusted partnerships.
- Improve VA operations to deliver seamless and integrated support.
- Increase percentage of VA employees who are veterans.
- Improve high performance workplace score.
- **Keep the promises**.

Obviously, Shinseki's final five months on duty in 2014 revealed in an abrupt fashion that the promises were not being kept. While he was urging Congress and all veterans to use more "patience", the rains came down on his parade, and it will be a soggy world in VA land for a long, long time.

More "patience"? After his departure, the VA scandal was just warming up. Here is a short list of what was published in newspapers across the country:

"Scandal-plagued VA is overpaying its employees by millions, internal audits find."

"Officials review allegations of unsafe practices at VA Medical Center/Surgery Department."

"VA healthcare failed suicidal vets, families testify."

"Documents detail VA mistreatment of Vietnam vets."

"Veterans languished for years without proper treatment at VA psychiatric facility."

"VA misled public, vets on healthcare backlog."

"This VA scandal much worse than Watergate."

"Mental Health Services probed at VA in Maine."

"VA progress on claims backlog is a statistical illusion."

"Vietnam vet pleaded for help...has cancer."

"VA horror stories keep coming—VA downplays them."

"Tennessee veterans received inferior VA care for strokes."

"Patience," the former secretary of VA suggested just a few days before the pressure put on him forced his resignation.

With deserved respect to Shinseki, when he served as the U.S. Army's chief of staff, he "quietly" clashed with George W. Bush's administration as he warned that more troops would be needed in the Iraq War than the government had authorized. In most cases, when he was asked questions like "Were VA officials cooking the books?", Shinseki was very unemotional with his typical responses such as..."I'm not aware of any."

VA Secretary Shinseki Tells Second Biggest Lie of 2014!

Hello, it is still May 2014, and Secretary Shinseki came before the Senate Veterans Affairs Committee and smugly said—with a straight face—that the VA health-care system is..."a good system." Avid veterans advocate Pete Hegseth had these subtle words to offer about Shinseki's comment, "The totality of the

Secretary's remarks before the committee were not only deceptive, they were detached, defensive and unbefitting a leader who should be fighting mad about the scandals engulfing the VA."

Oh, I labeled this as the second biggest lie? Lie number one came from our country's chief of bureaucrats, none other than Mr. President Obama himself when he uttered these words, also in a smug manner, "If you like your health-care plan, you can keep it."

Two Top VA Executives Depart

Hello, it is still May 2014. What a strangely bizarre month to say the least, and it all happened abruptly one day after another. **VA's Under Secretary Petzel Resigns Amid Scandal.**

Hello again, it is still the month of May 2014 and…**VA Secretary Shinseki Resigned May 30, 2014.** This happened just a few days after he called the VA "a good system" and after he issued a plea for veterans to show more…"patience". Most veterans know that Shinseki is generally a good person, and he was a darned good soldier in the worst war in our history, the Vietnam War, of course.

Most of the pressure for the resignation came from Republicans in Congress, but that changed for the worse for Shinseki as an interim VA audit targeted over two hundred VA sites for misconduct. Shortly after that report was made public, more Democratic Senators broke ranks and called for the eventual departure of the Secretary and Sloan Gibson entered the scene as temporary Secretary of the VA. He was previously holding the office of Deputy Secretary of Veterans Affairs. Some VA officials and veterans alike defended Shinseki in that most problems were well in place long before he assumed the office. Some believe he was a scapegoat. Maybe so, but due to the severity of the VA problems, some heads had to roll. If you take the time to track his life, you will come away shaking your head in bewilderment, wondering what happened. Here is a very abbreviated bio of this fine American:

- Born of Japanese-American descent in 1942 in Hawaii.
- Active Boy Scout and president of high school class.
- Had three uncles who served in a Japanese-American U.S. Army Infantry Regiment.
- Attended the United States Military Academy, motivated by his uncles.
- Earned a master's degree at Duke University.
- Military career was too long to list here. He held a variety of command assignments in-country and overseas, including two combat tours in the

Vietnam War. (One of his tours was with the 25th Infantry Division—same that I served.)

- Awarded three Bronze Stars for Valor and two Purple Hearts in Vietnam. One of his wounds required hospitalization and rehab for nearly a year.
- Served as Chief of Staff of the United States Army in honorable fashion, but not without controversy.

I can devote a very long chapter to this true American patriot. Everyone should read his full biography. So what went wrong? Was he under qualified and overwhelmed? If so, the real culprit is Obama, who hired him.

Sacrificed and Abandoned? How Does it Feel, Erik?

How does it feel, Mr. former Secretary Shinseki—to be sacrificed and thrown under a tank when you know the VA scandal exposé in 2014 which cost your job was not all on you?

We know Shinseki was a good man, one of us—a real combat veteran and a victim of the Vietnam War. In the final phrase of his opening letter as part of his Department of Veterans Affairs FY 2014-2020 Strategic Plan, he said, "We will achieve President Obama's vision for a 21st century VA. In doing, we will strive to earn the trust and confidence of our veterans as their advocate."

Wow, did that public statement head south in a hurry in 2014. He did not stop there in this VA Strategic Report for 2014-2020. He posted a few more promises, such as:

- *We will keep the promises we have made to increase access, eliminate the claims backlog and end veteran homelessness. VA is committed to this promise.*
- *We trust our military service members to protect our freedoms every day. The men and women serving our nation can, in turn, trust VA to be an accessible advocate for service members, veterans, survivors and their beneficiaries.*
- *VA's five core values underscore the obligations inherent in VA's mission:*

  Integrity
  Commitment
  Advocacy
  Respect
  Excellence

- *These core values define who we are, our culture, and how we care for veterans and eligible beneficiaries. Our values are more than words.*
- *VA will provide timely, accurate decisions on veterans' disability claims and eliminate the claims backlog in FY 2015.*

Had enough? I could go on and on. Bottom line is, under Shinseki's reign, the VA lives up to its promises. Then again, the VA has been over-promising and under-performing since the first Vietnam War veterans started to return home to their unforgettable, inglorious welcome by Americans. Scapegoated at this level? On May 25, 2014, the following abbreviated article appeared on www.freebeacon.com:

House Passed a Dozen VA Reform Bills That are Dead on Arrival (DOA) in Senate

Harry Reid has not brought any of the House VA reform bills to the Senate floor for consideration while veterans are dying as they wait for care.

While the president pounds his fist and proclaims he's 'madder than hell' over the VA scandal and then just asks for more time to review and investigate, House Republicans are getting pretty tired of the do-nothing Senate and a president who claims to only learn about problems in his administration on cable news.

Rep. Jackie Walorski (R., Ind.) sits on the Veterans' Affairs Committee in the House and she told me Wednesday on WMAL radio in Washington D.C., that the House has passed a dozen bills for reform of the VA and they are collecting dust on Harry Reid's desk:

Larry O'Connor (Host): Are your colleagues in the house doing something about this decades-old problem so we can get something done for the vets?

Rep. Walorski: In the past 18 months, since I've been a member of Congress, we've passed, on the House floor, at least 12 reform VA bills. Mandating the VA to fix different things, mandating the VA to report different things, mandating them to fix their website, bipartisan bills that went to the Senate, and they are DOA on the Senate side.
(Source: www.freebeacon.com)

Shinseki never had a chance. I read a sad story in one of several news media sources that carried it. Not quoting it verbatim, I will paraphrase it for you here. "One of my Vietnam War buddies asked me this question," the writer said:

"If you were 18 again, with things the way they are now under President Obama, would you serve in the military?" I could tell that just asking such a question made this decorated combat veteran uncomfortable. After all, his career in the military spanned more than 30 years and included deployments to some of the world's hottest hot spots. More than once, this American patriot put his life on the line for our country, and more than once he came within a whisker of losing his life. For this good man, questioning military service must have felt like treason. The veteran answered his own question. "I would not serve in the military today—not with Barack Obama as Commander in Chief. Obama's treatment of the military and veterans is a disgrace. I am proud of my service in the United States Marine Corps and would not trade that service in the Corps because I joined at a time when my peers were burning their draft cards and slipping away to Canada to avoid military service. But I would not want to serve under the circumstances that now exist in the military. Those who wear the uniform have to know that their commander in chief has their back, will do nothing to undermine their effectiveness in combat, and will ensure that they are properly taken care of, even after leaving the military. For the first time in my lifetime, we have a president who not only fails to take care of our troops and veterans, but seems to disdain them. No president in my lifetime has shown less respect for active-duty personnel and veterans or done so much to undermine the effectiveness and morale of the military as Barack Obama.

(Source: Written by David Goetsch on June 16, 2014 for www.newsmax.com)

Hats off to The Military Order of the Purple Heart. Our fellow patriots in this organization (which I am proudly part of) stood by Shinseki during the turmoil leading up to his departure as well as after and not many others did. Bottom line—our former Secretary never had a chance to succeed.

The Department of Veterans Affairs (VA) has two large components, the Veterans Health Administration (VHA) and the Veterans Benefits Administration (VBA). Many say that both components are overflowing with incompetence and dishonesty. The VHA has been mentioned in the news for much of 2014 for falsification of records. There are hundreds of medical centers (VMACs) and clinics.

The large national veterans' service organizations make budget requests to Congress every year. Typically, Congress gives the VA a little less than everything the organizations ask for. The exception is facilities' construction. The budget for the construction of new buildings or wings at VAMCs is so small and inadequate that the VHA is often given an increase in doctors and other health professionals without corresponding space for them to work.

When doctors leave the VHA, it usually takes at least six months to replace them. The doctors are bureaucratically unable to step outside of their specialties, and veterans often are left without care until their specialists are replaced.

The money appropriated for the VHA is too often used for middle-level management, rather than for doctors and other health-care professionals. The number of injured veterans returning from our recent wars has grown substantially, in part because so many lives of severely injured soldiers and Marines can now be saved. Although the budget for veterans' health care keeps increasing, it is insufficient to meet the increasing demand.

Getting an initial appointment to see a specialist is a lengthy process. One reason for the delay is the requirement that veterans see general practitioners before they can see specialists for the first time. Another reason is the low skills and poor training of VA receptionists and telephone operators. The result is that VAMCs are unable to meet the national target of seeing every veteran within fourteen days of the date requested. Instead veterans often wait months for the first appointment.
(Source: http://www.veteranstoday.com/?=303209)

As for the VBA, their primary mission is to award (or in most cases, deny) compensation to veterans who suffer from service-connected injuries and illnesses. VBA is also in charge of administering GI Bill benefits for education and VA mortgages. Just like its sister component, the VBA runs way over quota for dishonesty and incompetence. VBA would be the target when a veteran throws out this old cliché… DENY, DELAY…TILL WE DIE! The long delays at the VBA are legendary for painfully long waiting periods of several years. In fact, I have heard a more profound version of this old cliché, such as DENY, DELAY, DECEIT and DUMB DISORDER. Most veterans I have known have a much higher respect for the VHA than they do the VBA. I am with them on this.

So, why has the VA been so bad for so long? Why hasn't there been one knight in shining armor to arrive on the scene and clean things up? I am dying to find out that answer as it seems as though "Bob" McDonald has made more changes, rocked more boats and actually fired people than his last several predecessors were able to do. But folks, "Bob" has only been in this position for a few measly months while others before him had several years to get things done, right? That is correct, right? Maybe not.

What I am simply implying in this chapter is that I am yearning so badly to know why and how the VA has been such a disaster when so many lives have been at stake. So I took a quick trip backward in time to look over the previous Secretaries of the

VA. I am not sure I found anything that will have quenched my thirst for an answer, but here is what I uncovered:

List of Secretaries of Veterans Affairs
2014 – 1989

Robert McDonald	7/30/14 – Present	Undetermined	Obama
Sloan Gibson	5/30/14 – 7/30/14	2 months	Obama
Erik Shinseki	1/20/09 – 5/30/14	5 years 4 months	Obama
James B. Peake	12/20/07 – 1/20/09	2 years 1 month	W. Bush
Gordon H. Mansfield	10/1/07 – 12/20/07	2 ½ months	W. Bush
Jim Nicholson	1/26/05 – 10/1/07	1 year 9 months	W. Bush
Anthony Principi (Acting)	1/23/01 – 1/26/05	4 years	W. Bush
Hershel W. Gober (Acting)	7/25/00 – 1/20/01	6 months	Clinton
Togo D. West Jr.	1/2/98 – 7/25/00	2 years 6 months	Clinton
Jesse Brown	1/23/93 – 7/1/97	4 years 6 months	Clinton
Anthony Principi (Acting)	9/26/92 – 1/20/93	3 ½ months	H. Bush
Ed Derwinski	3/15/89 – 9/26/92	3 years 6 months	H. Bush
12 Secretaries	**35 Years 5 Months**	**Avg. Term: 2.9 Years**	

I would love to spend more time on this as I am intrigued by it all. The U.S. Department of Veterans Affairs claims to have the most comprehensive system of assistance for veterans of any nation in the history of the world with its roots traced back to 1636. That means they have had 379 years to get this right. I think that shows an awful lot of…**patience**.

Hold on, glory be, could that be the underlying ongoing problem with the VA? Americans have been too patient for almost four centuries, so it is long overdue for the heads to roll at the top and anywhere on down where there is a rotten apple, or two or three, or three hundred.

By golly, I think I have accidentally stepped onto the VA problem. We have shown way too much patience towards VA and their arrogance has simply grown out of control. We pretty much had to shame them, whistle-blow on them and maintain our mission, which I liken to what Vietnam War veterans were trained to do in that war...**IN YOUR FACE, VA!**

VFW National Helpline: 1-800-VFW (839)-1899

CHAPTER 10

REAL VIETNAM VETS...HAVE STEPPED UP!

I t is October 2, 2014 when Terry Sharpe and Allen Brown are home again after a month on the road. They were angered by the Mexican government's treatment of Marine Sgt. Andrew Tahmooressi. The sixty-four-year-old Sharpe set out from North Carolina with a destination of Washington D.C., with hopes of voicing his displeasure to any government official he could get to listen to him. Brown joined Sharpe despite a major swelling of one of his legs that still contained pieces of shrapnel from a battle in the Vietnam War. Neither of the two knew each other, but they quickly realized they had fought in some of the same battles in Vietnam in 1969.

These two dedicated patriotic Vietnam veterans walked an average of fifteen miles a day on a three hundred mile trek to Washington. When they made it to Washington, they were not bashful in approaching people who would listen and had some clout to act on what the two were campaigning for...**to free an American warrior being held captive in Mexico.**

When Sharpe and Brown reached Washington, unfortunately, Congress had recessed, and the two men did not get to talk face-to-face with any legislator. But they managed to make contact with aides of Texas Senator Ted Cruz and Florida Senator Marco Rubio and were on hand for a Senate Foreign Affairs committee hearing where Talmooressi's situation was discussed.

They received a lot of media attention, received a boatload of promises to do something and they were flown back to Greensboro rather than having to do the three hundred mile trip on foot. After the plane brought the two back, they were asked if it was worth it. Sharpe said..."Yes." But Sharpe was not finished. He said that if the Mexican government did not release our Marine soon, he was willing to walk back to Washington.

NEVER question the heart of a "real" combat hardened Vietnam veteran.

There is no credible source that can factually confirm the number of Americans who served in the Vietnam War. One estimate from the DOD is that between 2,709,918 to 3,173,845 GIs served in country and in-waters Vietnam between 1954 and 1975. This excludes the few hundred Americans who served in Vietnam during WWII and the Korean War. Yet to this very day (2014), veteran groups have estimated that there are approximately 9-12 million Americans who "claim to be" Vietnam War veterans...SHUT THE FRONT DOOR!

Just how amazing is this? Various sources say there are approximately 800,000 – 1,000,000 "real" Vietnam veterans alive today. Yes, "real" Vietnam veterans have been dying at an alarming rate comparable to their WWII fathers and uncles...and few Americans realize this or they just don't care.

Let's investigate why America's agonizing perception of "Vietnam" has never been jarred. It's out of place in the American psyche, and it continues to fester in much the same way battle wounds fester when shrapnel or other foreign matter is left in the body. Americans do not idolize mass murdering communists or Islamic terrorists, champion the cause of human oppression, abandon friends and allies, or cut and run in the face of adversity. Why then, did so many Americans engage in or openly support these types of activities during the country's "Vietnam" experience?

That the American experience in Vietnam was painful and ended in long-lasting (albeit self-inflicted) grief and misery cannot be disputed. However, the reasons behind that grief and misery are not even remotely understood—by either the American people or the government. Contrary to popular belief, and a whole lot of wishful thinking by a crowd tens of millions strong that is made up of mostly draft dodgers and their antiwar cronies, along with their families/supporters, it was not a military defeat that brought misfortune to the American effort in Vietnam. The United States Military in Vietnam was the best educated, best trained, best disciplined and most successful force ever fielded in the history of American arms. Why then, did we get such bad press, and why is the public's opinion of us still so twisted? The answer is simple. But first, a few relevant comparisons.

During the Civil War, at the Battle of Bull Run, the Union Army panicked and fled the battlefield. Nothing even remotely resembling that debacle ever occurred in Vietnam.

In WWII at the Kasserine Pass in Tunisia, elements of the U.S. Army were overrun by the Germans. In the course of that battle, Hitler's General Rommel (The Desert Fox) inflicted 3,100 U.S. casualties, took 3,700 prisoners and captured or destroyed 198 American tanks. In Vietnam, neither were U.S. military units overrun, nor were any U.S. infantry or tank outfits ever captured.

WWII again. In the Philippines, U.S. Army Generals Jonathan Wainwright and Edward King surrendered themselves and their troops to the Japanese. In Vietnam, no U.S. general or any military unit ever surrendered.

Before the Normandy invasion ("D" Day 1944), the U.S. Army in England filled its own jails with American soldiers and airmen who refused to fight and then had to rent jail space from the British to handle the overflow. The U.S. Army in Vietnam never had to rent jail space from the Vietnamese to incarcerate American soldiers who refused to fight.

Desertion. Only about 5,000 men assigned to Vietnam deserted and just over 249 of those deserted while in Vietnam. During WWII, in the European theater alone, over 20,000 U.S. military men were convicted of desertion. On a comparable basis, the overall WWII desertion rate was 55 percent higher than in Vietnam.

During the WWII Battle of the Bulge in Europe, two regiments of the U.S. Army's 106th Division surrendered to the Germans. Again, in Vietnam, no U.S. Army unit of any size, much less a regiment, ever surrendered…not ever.

The highest ranking American soldier killed in WWII was Lt. (three star) General Leslie J. McNair. He died when American warplanes accidentally bombed his position during the invasion of Europe. In Vietnam, there were no American generals killed by American bombers.

As for brutality: During WWII, the U.S. Army executed nearly 300 of its own men. Again, in the European theater, the U.S. Army sentenced 443 American soldiers to death. Most of the sentences were for the rape and murder of civilians.

In the Korean War, Major General William F. Dean, commander of the 24th Infantry Division, was taken prisoner of war (POW). In Vietnam, there were never any U.S. generals, much less division commanders, ever taken prisoner.

During the Korean War, the U.S. Army was forced into the longest retreat in its history. A catastrophic 275 mile withdrawal from the Yalu River all the way to Pyontaek, 45 miles south of Seoul. In the process, they lost the capitol city of Seoul. The U.S. military in Vietnam was never compelled into a major retreat nor did it ever abandon Saigon to the enemy.

The 1st U.S. Marine Division was driven from the Chosin Reservoir and forced into an emergency evacuation from the Korean port of Hungnam. There they were joined by other U.S. Army and South Korean soldiers and the U.S. Navy eventually evacuated 105,000 allied troops from that port. In Vietnam, there were never any mass evacuations of U.S. Marine, South Vietnamese or allied troop units.

Other items: Only 25 percent of the U.S. military who served in Vietnam were draftees. During WWII, 66 percent of the troops were draftees. On a percentage basis, the Vietnam force contained three times as many college graduates as did the WWII force. The average education level of the enlisted man in Vietnam was thirteen years, equivalent to one year of college. Out of those who voluntarily enlisted, 79 percent had high school diplomas. This was a time when only 65 percent of the American military-age males in the general population were high school graduates.

The average age of the U.S. military men who died in Vietnam was 22.8 years old. Out of the one hundred one (101) 18-year-old draftees who died in Vietnam, seven were black. Blacks accounted for 11.2 percent of combat deaths in Vietnam. At that time, black males of military age constituted 13.5 percent of the U.S. population. It should also be distinctly noted that volunteers suffered 77 percent of the casualties and accounted for 73 percent of Vietnam deaths.

On the issue of psychological health: Mental problems attributed to service in Vietnam are referred to as PTSD (Post-Traumatic Stress Disorder). Civil War veterans suffered "soldier's heart." The WWI term was "shell shock." During WWII and Korea, it was "battle fatigue." U.S. military records reflect Civil War psychological casualties averaged twenty-six per thousand men. In WWII, some units experienced over 100 psychiatric casualties per 1,000 troops; in Korea nearly one quarter of all battlefield evacuations were due to mental stress. That works out to about 50 per 1,000 troops. In Vietnam, the comparable average was five per 1,000 troops.

To put Vietnam in its proper perspective it is essential to understand that the U.S. Military was not defeated in Vietnam and that the South Vietnamese government did not collapse due to mismanagement or corruption nor was it overthrown by revolutionary guerrillas running around in rubber tire sandals, wearing black pajamas and carrying homemade weapons. There was no "general uprising" or "revolt' by the southern population. South Vietnam was overrun by a conventional army made up of seventeen conventional divisions and supported by a host of regular army logistical support units. This totally conventional force (armed, equipped, trained and supplied by Red China and the Soviet Union), spearheaded by 700 Soviet tanks, launched a cross border, frontal attack on South Vietnam and conquered it in the same manner Hitler conquered most of Europe in WWII.

There you have it. No wonder that millions of "wannabes" have forged themselves into society as heroes of the Vietnam War. Can it be possible that many of the people who had been Vietnam War "protestors" have become Vietnam War "imitators"?

Whether you served in the "big one" during World War II or the "forgotten war" during the Korean War, the "living room war" in Vietnam or any of the more recent conflicts and wars, we all have many things in common, and we should all try to understand that and stand up for each other. Whether you were a mailroom clerk, motor pool mechanic, engineer, airplane pilot, Navy mate or a combat infantry grunt, we need to stand up for each other to…keep the pressure on Veterans Affairs. Our lives are at stake.

Every American veteran living today has experienced some devastation, some loneliness, and some super storm from weather or spirituality. When we look at another veteran—any veteran—we should think or say…I understand how you feel because I have been there myself. We must support each other because…each of us is more alike than we are different.

Each and every one of us should stand up and be heard when the opportunity presents itself. When would that opportunity be? When we read or hear news headlines or stories such as this, which is current enough to be concerned about:

Congressional Republicans are accusing the Department of Veterans Affairs of influencing an independent review of whether delays of healthcare resulted in the deaths of nearly three dozen patients.
(Source: politico.com/1BHAY, September 24, 2014)

When the VA inspector general released a report in August 2014 that said investigators could not "conclusively link the deaths of forty veterans to long wait times plaguing the agency", many Republican lawmakers were shocked. Many responded in saying there was no question that the two issues were connected.

Tired of fighting? I understand. Many, if not most, Vietnam War veterans who are still living today are exhausted from fighting their wars. I understand, but I still love them not only for what they did over there in the Nam, but also for their perseverance since coming home. They deserve to be admired, respected and… remembered.

When the Korean War veterans finished their service, most of them were tired, much older, and had little desire left to continue on as the Korean War was just warming up when it was thought to have ended. It just took a break and moved over to Southeastern Asia's Indo China region called South Vietnam.

The Vietnam War that was heating up in the late 1950s and early 1960s would require a new American warrior, a younger warrior, and a warrior who was just as loyal to and just as in love with their country as their fathers and uncles were who fought for their country and its people in WWII and Korea. This new warrior would be tested for courage, stamina and mental toughness as much, if not more than any American warrior in any previous war. These new warriors would be required (forced) to and called upon to defend themselves and what they did in the Vietnam War for the rest of their short lives. They are still defending their country…and themselves. No wonder most of them are weary.

When America's warriors began to return from the Gulf wars, America's Vietnam veterans welcomed them home first and with genuine sincerity. When President Obama closed down the Veterans Memorials (more than once) for ridiculous reasons not worth mentioning here, it was the Vietnam veterans who led the protests. Vietnam veterans who tossed the barriers aside and led other veterans past the police to pay homage to the various veterans' memorials. In fact, it was the Vietnam veterans who dragged one of the barriers down the street and tossed it over the fence and on to the lawn of the President's palace, the White House.

Today, America's often forgotten Vietnam War veterans have been leading the charge again to fight in another war. This time, the adversary is the United States Department of Veteran Affairs, the VA. But this is not a new war, not for Vietnam veterans. They have been waging this war since the day they came home from Vietnam. This war was similar to the war in Vietnam in this respect only… they were forced into it.

The war with the VA is America's longest war. Unlike the Vietnam War, its veteran warriors have lost more of their battles with VA than they have won, and it has cost too many of them their lives. The tide has turned for us, and we are now winning more battles with VA than we are losing. This war between America's veterans of previous wars versus Veterans Affairs is not likely to end soon. Hang in there my war buddies—hold the line because I do believe we can also win this one if we…stick together!

This Vietnam Vet…Gets It!

I found this story online somewhere; just cannot recall where I found it—sorry. Hey Nam vets, imagine this scenario:

- You are returning home from your very forgettable yearlong nightmare in Southeast Asia, along with a few hundred other Nam veterans. You are all arriving together at Fort Bragg. The anticipation is almost too exciting for you as there are a few thousand Americans, including family members, of course, assembled to greet their "heroes" with balloons, streamers, handwritten signs and the works. The hugs, the kisses, the tears, the ecstasy will remain as one of your greatest memories ever—this is what you have been looking forward to for what seemed like one hundred years. You are also greeted by one very thankful, patriotic combat veteran from the Korean War, or maybe a World

War II veteran, who none of you know. How special is that—such a day when you come home, my brothers.

I don't remember such a day in my life either. Here is what really happened not too long ago at Fort Bragg on December 22, 2014 just two days before Christmas Eve:

- More than three hundred U.S. Army infantry paratroopers from the 82nd Airborne Division have landed, returning from their year-long deployment to the war in Afghanistan, which the President has declared…"is over." There are several hundred people gathered, maybe a thousand or more with relatives and friends. The ritual for returning soldiers is dramatic. There is also one lone veteran in the crowd who is anxiously waiting to greet all three hundred-plus soldiers. He is a veteran from (you guessed it) the Vietnam War. His name is Roland Rochester, and this is not his first participation in a homecoming for Afghanistan and Iraq veterans. No sir, Roland Rochester has been doing this faithfully for the past decade. Can you believe it? Roland Rochester really exists. I hope to meet him someday and maybe join him on a homecoming greeting. Man, that is one GREAT AMERICAN!

Actually, Roland Rochester saw this particular group of 82nd Airborne soldiers a year ago. He was there to help send them off, and he just was not going to miss their return. Roland Rochester, a long-time Veteran of Foreign Wars (VFW), member and recruiter, has never missed a single deployment and homecoming since he started his ritual. It has meant so much to him, and believe this…it has cost him a few nights of good sleep.

I believe that one of the mediums that published the core of this story is the *Fayetteville Observer*. The staff writer's name is Roger Mullen. He can be reached at mullenr@fayobserver.com. By the way, Roland Rochester served in the U.S. Marine Corp in Vietnam in 1971-1972.

Nam Vets…STOP Being Ashamed For Serving

Make a choice. Which military ribbon are you going to pin on tomorrow, and the next day and every day thereafter? No, I am not kidding. I can almost remember (actually I can) when my Uncle Richard Jensen came home from the Korean War in his U.S. Air Force khaki-type uniform. Gosh, he looked good to me. Uncle Dick was never afraid to put on one of his medals after that, and I am glad.

I don't know how my Uncle Dick would have reacted to the non-welcome-home reception that Vietnam veterans received from America, but I am one who became sick and tired of hiding my ribbons and medals since coming home from Nam in 1969. Brothers and sisters, we Nam veterans are no longer youngsters, and those medals have been collecting too much dust, stuck in a closet or drawer. You earned them, so get it on. Start wearing one.

Nam brothers, if you don't think we have any clout on influencing our country's legislators, you would be dead wrong. You should take advantage of the power to influence and control America's future. We can do this by making sure "we" communicate our needs, concerns and opinions to our Nam brothers and sisters who still dominate the list of current Congress members that is made up of many veterans.

"More than ninety percent of America's troops do not support Obama" said former U.S. Navy SEAL, Carl Higbie in a statement to Greta Van Sustern, host of *On the Record* on Fox News in September 2014.

Former U.S. Marine, Thomas Sowell has warned us several times not to underestimate Barack Obama. He has mentioned that Obama's critics, referring to him as being incompetent with his foreign policies, are overlooking the possibility that Obama has "different priorities" than the protection of America's homeland. Sowell said, "This is a monstrous possibility" that should not be dismissed. Thomas Sowell was also a senior fellow with the Hoover Institute at Stanford University.

There are twenty-two million veterans in the United States as of November 2014. I think Obama's minions neglected or forgot to provide this information to him in the months leading up to the November 2014 elections. In fact, I am sure of it, and I am so happy for it. Veterans have been taken for granted at election time for many, many years—big mistake. Just ask John Kerry why he is not the President of the United States of America. Veterans prevented that disaster from happening…believe it.

Veterans Rally to Attend Vietnam Vet's Funeral

Winona, MN – Dozens of people who attended the burial service for a Vietnam veteran in Winona never had the chance to meet the man. Richard Rhodes died alone in his downtown Winona apartment about a week before Christmas. No family or friends could be found. The seventy-three-year old man left no will. A local funeral home took charge of Rhodes' body and learned that he had served in the Army during the 1960s. Hoff Funeral Home contacted area posts of Veterans of Foreign Wars hoping that other veterans would attend Monday's burial. KSTP-TV reports that more than one hundred people, mostly Vietnam veterans, attended the graveside service at St. Mary's Cemetery where Rhodes was given full military honors. Most had never met the man. The Vietnam War brotherhood lives on…

(Source: The Associated Press, January 20, 2015)

The 2016 Veteran's Vote Could Save America…or Not!

The results of several years of previous elections shows that approximately thirty-eight percent, maybe less, of Americans came out to vote. In case you are curious as to how many veterans came out to place their votes for America's future, I can proudly tell you that only fifty-seven percent of America's veterans voted on average. Only? Why do I say "only" when we exercised our loyalty and our right to vote by a 57% - 38% whopping margin over the average across America? Because **fifty-seven percent is not good enough**, not for those who did what we did for our country…not good enough. Of course, this is water over the dam now, but the 2016 election is hardly a long way off and many of you remain or "claim to" remain undecided up until the final moments. Why do you do that?

Right now, we live in an apathetic nation, one that is at war with itself. We are not the America left to us by that great generation that fought and won World War II. Our government is out of touch. Our society has degraded to a point where integrity is a thing of the past. Our education system has deteriorated. Our professional athletes are paid millions; they are idolized by an ignorant fan base. They couldn't pass a math course in college, but they are given a degree. Washington has gone way over the line to become utterly corrupt. My dear patriotic Americans, when the 2016 elections arrive…everything will be on the table.

All active military and all veterans must remember that your vote is the most important and most perfect weapon in our arsenal to get our needs and demands approved. USE YOUR VOTE THE RIGHT WAY IN 2016.

Over the past six-plus years and change, we veterans watched seemingly helplessly while the beloved country we and our war buddies risked our lives for, took a direction that had all of us worried. Some lost their faith. Some just gave up, thinking the end of America was just around the corner. It's time for veterans and our families to take back our country and it started at the polls in 2014. Oh, pardon me—I neglected to include this factual statistic in the earlier part of this section…along with those twenty-two million veterans in America today, guess what? They have families, and there are in-laws associated with them. My non-professional estimate is that sixty million family members can be at the polls at the direct influence of our veterans. United, we can be a profound influence on the outcome of any election as we were in 2014. Way to go, my war buddies. You did well. Remember this my war buddies…when the next election takes place…if not us, then who? If not now, then when? Let's take back "our" country and keep it.

Obama Warned…

He knew it was coming. They have been telling him it was coming and they kept their promise to him. I am referring to the veterans' vote that stormed Washington D.C. this past May 2014. The taking back of the Senate and keeping the majority in the House has for one thing, given our military a sense that once again, they will be appreciated and they feel safer. The deep fury of disgust was building up with America's active military, along with the veterans towards the indifference and incompetence of King Obama and his court jesters. They know that the so-called Commander in Chief has been AWOL for most of 2014 at least. The anger runs deep and their vote will only grow in power by the time November 2016 arrives. Warning served.

My dear war buddies, here is a book that we should all have on our bookshelves…*For Love of Country*. If that title is too mushy, forget it—go out and read Charles Manson's bio and then drown yourself in a heavily polluted river or pond. Anyway folks, this book is about a topic that should be dear to your hearts. It is to mine, but then it's just another average, everyday non-fiction story about the courage, dedication, loyalty and sacrifice of the present generation of American warriors on real battlefields. God bless them all! This book will teach the reader how our veterans can teach us about citizenship, heroism and sacrifice.

Illegals Before Aliens? Thanks, Barack!

Loyal soldiers and marines do not deserve this, and yet the current Commander in Chief, also our President, has made his choice public with utmost arrogance. Why is our present government helping illegal aliens before veterans who have fought to defend our country? Our veterans and our country's seniors are probably doing without because of the estimated twelve million illegal aliens who are mooching the generous and stupid American system for which Obama is responsible.

Democrats Kill Veterans' Pensions—Save Illegal Tax Credit (June 2014) —This headline ran in a few not-so-major news media venues. Mainstream pretty much ignored it, and now, look at what is going on regarding the Obama regime? It is true—when Democrats controlled the Senate, they killed an amendment from Senator Kelly Ayotte (R-NH) that has paid for unemployment benefits for many

Americans and replaced recent tax cuts to veterans' pensions by closing a tax code loophole that allows illegal aliens to access the Refundable Child Tax Credit. That vote failed by a 54-42 count with ALL Republicans except Senator Dean Heller (R-NV) voting for the amendment. Note — Senator Joe Manchin (D-WV) crossed the line, voting in favor of the amendment alongside the Republicans. Ayotte presented an argument that the amendment would pay for a fix to the military retirement cuts to the COLA (Cost of Living Adjustment) that also had negatively impacted Americans' wounded warriors. While Ayotte made the case for the amendment, lo and behold, Democrat Senator Barbara Boxer (D-CA), a Nancy Pelosi chum, argued against it.

My fellow patriots, let's keep the hope and prayers going that the resounding Republican victory in the mid-term election is in fact a victory for America. How can representatives of America's people vote down the pension of its military and then vote to subsidize illegal aliens via tax policy?

Are these so-called elite government asses aware that illegal aliens have been responsible for…countless deaths (60,000 plus) and…over one million sexual assaults on bona fide and legal American citizens? No wonder there is so much talk about taking back our country. But talking about it is old news. The mid-term election and…books like *Payback Time!* written by an everyday average American are the steps we need to take or support in a unified fashion. That is… if you are one who actually cares?

(Source: www.bookwormroom.com)

Here is another way to look at this. Okay, so Obama has blessed the existence of twelve to twenty-two million illegal aliens to suck the last few pennies out of our sick economy. How about this — we deport all of those who are arrested for breaking our laws after they have had their free pass to be here. Thousands of them are arrested every week if not every day, so I hear. That won't happen either, and neither the Democrats nor Republicans would go a long with this because of…cheap labor. The illegal aliens do not take jobs away from veterans or any other average American. Who do you know who works in the fields, on farms, picks crops or takes on employment as a pool boy or a maid?

On the other hand, there are approximately five hundred thousand veterans who need aid from the government—aid which they spilled their blood for in serving their government's commands. Don't forget that the stresses and injuries from war have made some veterans homeless or just unable to hold a job. VA hospitals cannot be expanded quickly enough and new facilities will take even longer to build. There are not enough beds for our tired and wounded veterans to lie down for a few days. Plain and simple, even for the most arrogant, complex mind—no illegal should be receiving any benefits from the USA's taxpayers, not as long as there is even one American veteran who is in trouble because of neglect by their own country. Take care of our own first…dispose of (deport) the illegal aliens.

If you are one of those who would disagree with the content of this chapter, that is the beauty of being an American. You have that right. You would not have that right if our veterans had not fought to preserve it for us. **Take care of our own first!**

One of the saddest things about the Vietnam War is…it continues to kill so many who have struggled to survive it after they came home!

- Author Unknown

Chapter 11

SECOND AMERICAN REVOLUTION?

Shhhhh…mention this term and the CIA locks on for sure. But unless you have been stranded on a remote island or have been lost in the Himalayan Mountains for the past year or two, you have heard it mentioned by someone you know or they know, that there have been rumblings about the need for a Second American Revolution. Duh, yeah that has been going around for at least one to two years, maybe five years. Even Christians have been mentioning this rumor. Really? Then again, the accusers would most likely be far, far left-wing liberals who view a Christian as a whacko terrorist.

Growing up as a Christian (Baptist), my experiences have been that real Christians are probably some of the most patriotic…brightest…most informed… most intuitive…and most prepared Americans. They also possess less positive traits, which I'll leave out for another discussion, and it's not the majority of Christians I refer to on the less flattering traits. I am not an expert on this subject by any means. I'm just an average everyday American with opinions that came to me from lessons learned in life the hard way, and I am a combat-tested Vietnam veteran, which says I am not an average schmuck.

I'm curious as to why they would refer to it as the Second American Revolution. What was the war between the North and South — the Civil War? The southerners revolted, did they not? They attempted to separate from the United States of America into a separate country, right? Jefferson was appointed as the President of the Confederacy, correct?

Oh well, makes no never mind. If they want to refer to it as the Second American Revolution, they have my ok, right! We have many battles to fight and hopefully win, before something as remotely possible as another American Revolution takes place. The next Presidential election would be one of those upcoming battles that *must* be won by the patriots, the "real" Americans. Party affiliation should not be the main priority for real patriotic Americans. The candidate's loyalty to our country should be most important. Come to think of it, our present administration just might be watching the wrong group of Americans regarding the eruption of the next revolt. How so?

Today's illegal aliens seem to be expressing little or no patriotic values toward America that the immigrants did after the World Wars, and even the Vietnam War. Think about it. Have the Vietnamese blended well into our society? Indeed, they came here legally, and they have been a positive contribution. The same is to be said for most Hispanics who did not arrive here illegally over our southern borders. Hispanics have always served bravely in our Armed Forces, even Vietnam or especially Vietnam and our wars since. Many immigrants have arrived in America legally from India, and they have also been a positive addition.

I don't see it happening unless, unless…our military is in on it. Remote as that sounds, I would not count anything out, not the way Obama and Clinton have treated America's military heroes.

Some say that the invasion of radical Muslims could stir up enough "I've had enough, and I can't take it anymore" type attitudes with patriotic Americans. If you are one who stays tuned to current news reports from mainstream or underground sources, you may recall the following event, which did not get much coverage from America's mainstream media outlets:

"Tens of Thousands of Germans Gather Together to Protest Against Islam—"
- Freedom Outpost, December 2014

Patriotic German citizens gathered together to sing. They sang Christmas carols, which were really traditional Christian songs. They gathered in non-violent fashion, but their mission was clear--to celebrate and promote Christianity over Islam. Their presence meant they are prepared to fight to prevent the "watering down" of their Christian-rooted culture. One German news correspondent reported this:

"The Anti-Islamization Movement in Dresden, Germany grew even bigger; the media is downplaying it. First, they said it was 10,000, then it was 17,500, but in reality, it was more than 25,000 people who sang Christian Christmas Carols. We also had a minute of silence for the 140 murdered children in Afghanistan just recently, as well as the victims of the latest terror attack in Dijon, France as well as any other victim of Islamic violence. All the Christmas songs we sang were Christian songs. Before each song, the words of the song were said loud and clear; therefore the Name of the Lord was said and sung from more than 25,000 tongues."

- Peter Schmidt

This group is one faction of a fast growing movement in Germany and it appears ready to continue growing. Amazingly, this group started out with a small rally of twenty to thirty people back in September 2014. They quickly became hundreds and just two months later, tens of thousands. They already had a name — Patriotic Europeans Against the Islamization of the Occident (PEGIDA). PEGIDA claims they strive and protest for the right to preserve and protect our Christian-Jewish dominated western culture and against the takeover of Christian culture by Islamic radicals in Germany. Even though some of the PEGIDA's critics, the liberal media, have tried to associate the group with Neo-Nazis, the group has made great efforts to distance themselves from the extreme far right where the neo-Nazis reside. Why would neo-Nazis be out in public, singing songs such as *Silent Night*? They seem to be genuine patriots, Christian patriots and their concerns are quite real.

That may come off as militant. But how would one confront radical Islam, which breeds the type of insane terrorists that attacked America on September 11, 2001? I see them more as crusaders if you will. As for me personally, and where I stand at the time of this writing, while I am not a "Bible verse toter," I am a Christian conservative and I am an extremist when it comes to being patriotic toward our great USA.

If this movement reaches America (maybe it already has), I am a likely recruit for them, and I am saying this publicly—obviously. If my endorsement of this group makes me a militant to some, then so be it. I am a Christian Crusading Militant who has vowed to remain a soldier for the rest of my life, which means I am prepared to put my life on the line for America…again.

My personal research comes up with an Islamic population in Germany of not quite five percent. That is not a significant number for now. I also saw a recent research study where the Islamic population in Germany and all of Western Europe could approach fifty percent by the year 2050. In case there are any readers who are not aware of the Islam threat in America, I have collected a mere handful of news clippings from American newspapers. Please read and heed…

Muslim Runs Down Dozens!

Just before Christmas 2014, several profound events took place in France.

- French police arrested a Muslim man after he deliberately mowed down a dozen innocent pedestrians in the city of Dijon. Two people were seriously injured and eleven others were also treated for injuries. During the thirty-minute demolition ride, the driver kept shouting "Allah hu Akbar." ("God is the greatest.")

France had already been on high alert for Islamic attacks on their country. Also at this time frame, as reported by the BBC, France had recently opened their borders to fleeing Christians who were being persecuted by Islamists. What does this subject matter have to do with *Payback Time!*, *Veterans Unite to Challenge VA for Overdue Benefits*? Think ahead, my dear patriots, think ahead to the November 2016 Presidential Election. What kind of person needs to be our military's Commander in Chief for the times that lie ahead for America?

Do you remember this?

The Muslim Brotherhood in American Schools

"I am waging a Bloodless Revolution in America's Public Schools..."
- Shabbir Mansuri
Founder and Director of the Council
on Islamic Education

Brigitte Gabriel spoke earlier this year at First Conservative Baptist Church and informed the people there that the Muslim Brotherhood is in the process of infiltrating American public schools, just as they have the United States federal government. Gabriel, author of two New York Times Best Sellers, Because They Hate *and* They Must Be Stopped *and founder of Act for America said that she is passionate about the subject because it has affected her life. Ms. Gabriel is an immigrant, who came to America after her home country of Lebanon (which was the only majority Christian country in the Middle East), was lost to fundamentalist Islam during the Lebanese Civil War. In the few minutes that she speaks in the video, Gabriel provides the evidence that the Muslim Brotherhood has infiltrated America's schools. She also warns that they will stop at nothing short of total domination of all non-Muslim countries.*

Gabriel went on to talk about the "behind the scenes" efforts by the Muslim Brotherhood to maintain an appearance of "moderation" with the goal of destroying Western society and establishing the Islamic State in America. This includes, but isn't limited to: Using our liberties against us, using "buzzwords," establishing non-profit and human rights organizations.

In referencing the Muslim Brotherhood's goals for America, Gabriel read the section of their goals regarding settlement, which came from the Holy Land Foundation trial. According to the document, Muslims must see their efforts in America as a 'grand jihad in eliminating the Western civilization from within and sabotaging its miserable house by their hands and the hands of the believers so that it is eliminated and Allah's religion is made victorious over all other religions."
(Source: *Freedom Outpost* / February 3, 2013)

The 1960s would have been an ideal time for a so-called Second Revolution in America. Everything was in place during a three- to five-year window for it to happen successfully. Think about the setting—the tragic events that took place in 1968 alone. Heck, just these few profound happenings alone in the 1960s sound like a Second Revolution already took place. We just did not recognize it then. Take a stroll back in time with me, please:

- The killing of President John F. Kennedy, one of America's most popular politicians ever, a conservative Democrat.
- The killing of Martin Luther King, also one of America's most beloved heroes for the average citizen of any race or nationality.
- The killing of Bobby Kennedy.
- Charles Manson was a child of the 1960s, and the drug culture rose to shocking popularity...in the 1960s, carrying over to the 1970s.
- Protests and riots in the streets, shootings at universities...the Beatles John Lennon pronounced that..."God is dead!"
- The Vietnam War...The Vietnam War...The Vietnam War.

Even Vietnam veterans became divided when it became obvious that the war had gotten way out of hand, that America's politicians were never going to allow a clear-cut victory. Actually, Vietnam veterans did earn a clear-cut victory, and then our country's politicians gave it away to North Vietnam. Vietnam vets would be betrayed and abandoned by those same politicians who sent their war buddies over there...to return home dismembered physically and psychologically...AND IN BODY BAGS!

Certainly, Vietnam Era veterans could have pulled it together near the end or at the end of the Vietnam War and united themselves enough to ignite a Second Revolution...back then. I am just speculating here. I am neither in favor of a so-called Second Revolution, nor is that one of the missions of *Payback Time!* In a sense, the present battle that veterans are waging against the Department of

Veterans Affairs has shown the makings of a so-called Revolution in itself, one that would be justified. But we are just fighting back to gain health care and benefits which we earned so that we can live a little while longer. Is that asking too much of our country?

When my war buddies and I served in the military, we were taught or "brainwashed" into the mindset of...never ever surrendering. And for the most part, Vietnam's warriors lived up to what they were taught in that respect. Yes. He really did say this:

We the people...are the rightful masters of both Congress and the Courts, not to overthrow the Constitution but to overthrow those men who would pervert the Constitution.

- Abraham Lincoln

There has been a lot of rhetorical garbage thrown out by left-wingers toward patriotic conservatives that they are the lunatics, anti-American, even terrorists. What total bunk that is. The real lunatics and terrorists within our country are those who came here (mainly illegally) and think they are going to change us. Many of them do not subscribe any patriotic loyalty to our country, especially during a time of war. Those are the lunatics and terrorists or...the enemy within!

Ask yourself this question: When was the last time the United States had a sizeable population of immigrants who have warned us they would not be loyal to America in a foreign war? All you have to do is read up on the dangerous problems our friends in the land down under have been experiencing. Don't stop there. Take a hard look at similar threats facing Europe, Canada, even Russia, China and...the USA.

Millions of Muslims are invading our countries and bringing with them a culture and society, which they are loyal to and they believe their way of living is superior to ours. They have no intention of adopting our ways or embracing our country as we do.

Is there any other immigrant group that has warned their new western homelands that their loyalty may be elsewhere during a global conflict? Those hordes of illegals invading our southern borders are not all from Mexico. Read up my dear patriots. It will shock you. It will sicken you. And under which of our presidents has this invasion been at its worst? If you said "Bush", you would be dead wrong. Try again—like someone named Barack Hussein Obama.

Of course, many of the comments in this book are just my opinions and a consensus of other conservatives I know. Most are veterans. However, make no mistake on this opinion...**Muslim culture has never blended into the culture**

of whatever country they have immigrated to. Here is a suggested reading— The *Post American Presidency: The Obama Administration's War on America* by Pamela Geller.

In most wars, America was confident that immigrants from lands we were fighting in or against would be loyal to their new country, America. Those days may be over, and if that doesn't spell D-A-N-G-E-R for our country, then you should not even be reading this book because you may be one of them. Hold your horses. Don't get bent out of shape. I am aware that there are not enough admitted Muslims residing in our country to threaten us the way they seem to in other parts of the world. Not yet. There are nearly five million professing Muslims in the U.S. It just seems like there are more. And why is that?

> "The U.S is one of the biggest Muslim nations."
> - Barack Hussein Obama
> French television interview, October 2014

Absurd statement, yes. But since he is the president, one can only imagine how many uninformed Americans took Obama's statement seriously. Remember this old saying…"Perception is reality."

If there is ever a Second American Revolution, the immigrant Muslims will not be a factor of concern. The sides would be more than likely be patriotic Americans—Republicans and possibly Democrats of all nationalities and races versus those who are responsible for attempting to give our country away. Who would that be?

Currently, the Muslim population in the U.S. is about three percent of the world's Muslim population of 1.5 billion. Heck, there are six to seven million Jews in the U.S. and have you heard anyone saying that the U.S. is one of the biggest Jewish nations?

India, a very America-friendly country, has one hundred fifty million Muslims making it the world's third largest Muslim population after Indonesia and Pakistan. I don't think there are very many of the one billion non-Muslim Indian civilians who think their country is a Muslim country. America is centuries away from becoming a Muslim country, but Obama's comment could be a damaging example of "false teachings." Think about it.

While we need to keep an eye on the Muslim immigrants because of their potential for terrorists entering the country, please know that America has been a Christian nation for over two hundred thirty-five years. When our constitution was signed, our first enemy was the Muslim pirates from the Barbary Coast. It was then that we built a Navy and created the first Marines to fight them. They were a Satanic-like cult back then and today, they are still beheading completely innocent and defenseless people…for fun!

Ruling by Michigan Judge Lets Muslims Silence Christians with Violence

(May 15, 2013) - *Federal judge Patrick J. Duggan dismissed a civil rights lawsuit brought by Christian evangelists who were violently assaulted by a hostile Muslim mob while preaching at an Arab festival last year in Dearborn, Mich., the American Freedom Law Center said. The AFLC filed the lawsuit against Wayne County, the Wayne County Sheriff, and two Wayne County Deputy Chiefs alleging authorities refused to protect the Christians while threatening to arrest them. A 22-minute video showing the Christians being attacked and stoned as police watched went viral last year. Instead of controlling the crowd, authorities threatened to arrest the Christians under attack for disorderly conduct. Despite the video evidence, Judge Duggan, sitting in the U.S. District Court for the Eastern District of Michigan, granted Wayne County's motion for summary judgment, dismissing the lawsuit.*
(Source: Examiner.com)

Muslims Stone Christians in U.S.!

The full U.S. Court of Appeals for the 6th Circuit has decided to review a First Amendment complaint brought by Christians who were assaulted by a rock-throwing Muslim mob at an Arab festival in Dearborn, Michigan. The case arose from the annual Arab International Festival in June 2012 when Wayne County sheriff's deputies stood by while a Muslim mob threw rocks at Christians, bloodying them. The officers then threatened the Christians with arrest if they didn't leave the event. The Christians brought a lawsuit against Wayne County over its officers' actions, and a three-judge panel dismissed it. But a majority of 6th Circuit judges has agreed to re-hear the case. The case, shepherded by the American Freedom Law Center, isn't the first time that Muslim mob violence has erupted at the Arab festival. Earlier, a group of Christians was awarded more than $100,000 in damages because of attacks there. In the latest case, Robert J. Muise, senior counsel for the AFLC, called the decision to re-hear "great news for religious freedom and the freedom of speech."
(Source: www.wnd.com/10/27/14)

Yesterday it was just stones. What will it be tomorrow and who will rise up to confront it or…end it?

Obama Never Saw This Coming?

The "red tide" rolled in and rolled over the opposition on November 4, 2014 as red states once again prevailed in what was supposed to be a tight battle between Democrats and Republicans for control of the Senate and for control of the direction of America the Beautiful's future. It was a massacre. Obama seemed somewhat unimpressed at the massive defeat his party suffered. In fact, he made statements like this just a couple days after the Dem's Waterloo—that he is still preparing to use his executive authority to rewrite the nation's immigration policies because…Congress has been unable to pass legislation to do so. "Before the end of the year, we're going to take whatever lawful actions that I can take," said Obama. Unfortunately, Obama successfully came through with his brash promise on November 20, 2014.

On the other side, members of the "red tide" seem unimpressed with the President's bold comments after his "blue tide" forces were overrun, stampeded, trounced, overpowered, out-foxed and subdued. Yep, he said these things and a lot more, and the smoke from the battlefields was still hovering in many states. Well, some of his rejuvenated opponents retorted back in a fashion that clearly showed that they were more than up to the task. Senator Mitch McConnell even warned Obama that his statement of his intent was "not a good idea." McConnell also indicated that some of Obama's statements came off like "waving a red flag in front of a bull."

Well, I could get all wrapped up on the tit-for-tat verbal sword rattling exercises between both sides, but I have to stop and back up to the reason I wrote this section. As a former U.S. Army combat infantry pointman in one of the worst wars of all wars, to even be a point man in the jungles of the Vietnam War, I have a pretty keen sense of what is going on around me as far as my neighbors, customers, prospects, friends, family business associates, etc. are concerned. I don't have a wave of minions all around me on every street corner and on top of every tall building who are pulling watch for me. Obama sure does or did. And yet, he got the taste of a good old-fashioned AMBUSH by the Republicans in 2014!

Fellow patriots, there can be little doubt that active military and veteran warriors rose up and cast their votes in proud fashion. And our President created this uprising towards his own political party and the military he claims to command and lead.

The Christian stoning disgrace in Michigan happened on October 27, 2014 and I would bet most sleepy Americans never heard of the details, possibly because they don't want to be aware of such a violent problem. Do they think that they can hide on their farms in the country and those situations will evaporate? America needs the "silent majority" to wake up. Speak up ASAP.

Damn. They were…*stoned* in their own country by immigrants who have made it profoundly clear that they have little or no allegiance to this country. We are undoubtedly in unsettling times. Our country seems to be trembling as though a coast-to-coast earthquake was saying, "hey, I'm coming." Our Secretary of State's Iran nuclear negotiations revealed that.

Today, we are faced with dealing with Sharia Law, Islamic Caliphates, border invasions—south and north and unparalleled lying at every level of our government, including the highest levels. Ignore the news headlines—good luck. That is for those who have their heads buried in the sand for too long and their brains have been fried into burnt sausages. Good luck with that.

If I threw stones on someone and hit him or her—causing bodily injury, I would be arrested, charged and punished. And I should be, so I won't throw stones at others…unless they throw stones at me first. As one of Hollywood's more patriotic stars once said:

"They drew first blood."
- Sylvester Stallone, *First Blood*

Muslim converts all over the world are frantically looking for safe communities to live in and the good old USA is one of their best bets. Trouble is, the Muslim converts also bring Muslim thugs into our country who are on a mission to kill Christians converted from Islam. An example of this happened in England on December 19, 2014 when a Pakistani man who had converted, fled to England in hopes of living out his life in peace. No such luck as a group of chosen Muslim assassins found him, beat and stabbed him repeatedly and left him in a street, taking it for granted he was dead or would soon bleed to death. Fortunately, the would-be murderers were wrong as the Muslim convert survived, was taken in and cared for by an Anglican priest. Unfortunately, he has to live the rest of his life in hiding simply because he chose to change his religious faith.

There are tens of thousands of people who would convert from Islam if it were safe. How should the American government address this growing problem? After all, our President has helped millions of "illegal aliens" seek and find safe refuge in our country. Maybe one of our other enemies has an answer that American should follow.

America's good buddy, Vladimir Putin, Russian President, has delivered numerous speeches about the tensions that unwanted minorities are causing in Russia. In one of Putin's speeches, he basically said this:

In Russia, live like the Russians; learn to speak Russian, respect Russian laws. If they prefer Sharia Law, and live the Muslims' way of life, then I strongly advise them to leave Russia to go to those places where Sharia Law is. Russia does not need Muslim minorities—minorities need Russia, and we will not grant them special privileges or change our laws to fit their beliefs. We will not tolerate disrespect from the Muslims. They will not take over Russia's culture as they have been succeeding to do in other countries such as England, Holland, France, Canada, Australia and America. When a legislative body creates laws, it will have in mind the Russian national interest first, keeping in mind that the Muslim minorities are Muslims first; they are not Russians.

Putin received a loud and long-standing ovation from the Russian Parliament (the Duma).

The United States of America has been trying to befriend the entire planet Earth along with the multitude of America haters, even welcomed them into our homes. Yeah, we have—we even elected one of "them" as the president of the greatest and most powerful countries in the history of the world. Simple solution to the above might be…welcome into our homes again, offer them permanent residence, bring their families and their families' families, and I am sure everyone will be living in ecstasy—right?

Try Stoning This Marine

Remember this…Corporal Nathan Cirillo was murdered by Islamic fanatics on an attack on the Canadian Parliament in early November 2014. It was another example of despicable, ruthless, and savage rancorous, cowardice by a group of people living in the fifteenth century but who are unaware it is the twenty-first century.

Corporal Cirillo is gone—lifeless in an instant, ambushed as he was performing his duty to his country, which offended no one. I am so frustrated by the fact that I have "suddenly" become seventy years old. Frustrated because I cannot once again embark on a mission alongside our war buddies of today's wars. So frustrated. Have no fear because Sinke is here (not sink).

The following event took place on November 8, 2014 with very little fanfare. Unannounced and in full-dress uniform, a Marine showed up at the Canadian War Memorial where Corporal Cirillo was ambushed in the most shameful manner by the Islamic terrorists. As the story went…Major R.E.G. "Fox" Sinke Jr. (retired) made his unexpected heroic appearance and beforehand had issued a challenge to any Islamic would-be attacks to "take your best shot." Sinke is an established author, including *When None of Their Dreams Were Dead*. He did receive several cowardly death threats and oh yeah, those really scared him. He was quoted by one news source in responding to a jihadist threat to kill him, "Hey, you looking for another target, try me—give it your best shot. We'll see how it works out for you."

What a spirited guy, and guess what, my readers—he is one of those "losers" from…the Vietnam War! These are the kind of men I served with in the Vietnam

War, the kind of men who continue to make me proud as hell that I served my country over there…when most were not willing to serve. Here is another spirited American story relating with a Muslim encounter.

Could Have Used "Her" in Vietnam

Indeed, I am talking about Ann Barnhardt of Lone Tree, Colorado. This is one bad dude. Here is her abbreviated story that I amended from an underground patriotic media. Please enjoy—I did.

A Muslim man issued a death threat to an American woman and her family this past November 2014. His exact words to her follow:

"I am going to kill you when I find you. Don't think I won't. I know where you live and I know where your mother and father live. All I need to do is make one phone call and you will all be killed."

Mufcadnanu123!

Patriots, this is going on in America more than most of you know, and you could be next. Can you deal with it if this trouble comes your way? Well, here is how our American girl, Ann Barnhardt, took to her Islamic radical's threat—a typically cowardly type from these sorts…

"I'll be waiting for ya', but please do me a favor so we can even this thing out a bit for your benefit. If you would kindly wear body armor when you arrive, I would have an opportunity to test my new body armor piercing ammo and quite frankly, close quarter body shots (if you even get close) without body armor would be almost unsporting from my perspective. That and the fact I'm probably carrying a good fifty IQ points on you makes this confrontation you are threatening, morally incumbent upon me to spot you a tactical advantage. You see, I like a fair fight."

Then Ann proceeded in providing our Muslim coward perfect directions to her residence from multiple directions to make sure he did not get lost. As the story goes, Ann issued some very unsavory digs to her Muslim would-be killer, about his religion, his manhood and his almighty God…Mohammed. Ms. Barnhardt added a closing comment to the email conversation they were engaging in to keep him motivated for the possible confrontation. She told him how disappointed she was that not a single "musloid" here in the USA has made any attempt to rape or behead her. "Regardless, you miserable coward, I am prepared to fight you and your satanic evil Islam with every fiber of my being for as long as I live. You are going to have to kill me if you have the guts to come after me. Watch your own back."

Don't ya' just love the American spirit? I do.

194

Please keep in mind that I have written this book after being diagnosed with PTSD from the Vietnam War, and dealing with another PTSD enhancement, so to speak, after suffering from an ischemic stroke, presumably caused by my Vietnam War vacation. Therefore, I must be one of those troubled Vietnam War veterans to whom Nancy Pelosi has referred.

PTSD or not—the beauty of our great country is that I have the right to continue and finish this book…God willing. So the Republicans kicked the Dem's butts at the mid-term elections. Bravo. What followed was something like this:

> Democrats' favorable rating fell to an all-time low of 36%. Special attention should be made that their favorable rating in 2012 was 51%.

> Many of their losses came from their 'used-to-be-loyal' independents.

> Following the mid-terms, the majority of Americans made it clear that they were counting on the Republicans in Congress—and not President Obama— to have the major influence on the direction our country takes over the next couple of years. It was 2012 when Americans indicated that they were trusting Obama's leadership to take them to a better life.

Following this, Obama took the offensive and counterattacked the Republicans' position on the illegal alien situation by granting amnesty to how many million illegal immigrants? Some critics referred to this move as a "Legacy of Lawlessness." Many referred to Obama as a self-proclaimed Emperor who ignored the American people when he announced an amnesty plan that even he has said many times that he really has little or no constitutional authority to enact. Lawlessness by our own President? How about something far more criminal? How about…**God lessness!**

Obama finally announced his executive action on amnesty, defying all those who opposed him and all hell broke loose in our country on November 21, 2014. The after-effects sent shock waves across America. Plain and simple…illegal aliens are unauthorized visitors who have entered or "invaded" a country without legal authorization and overstay during this unauthorized visit. It is quite likely that many of these people turn out to be good people who are just trying to better the living conditions and opportunities for their families. Everyone has that God-given right. But not if those unauthorized visits infringe on the rights of those Americans who arrived or were born here legally. However, Obama has stated that "U.S. taxpayers must pay for children of illegal aliens."

Hey patriots, do you think that the Republicans know they were elected not to work with Obama, but to *stop* him? Obama is going to be obnoxiously defiant at every step as long as his term lasts. He will not let up until America can be pushed over the cliff to destruction. Those who have not come to realize this or refuse to will remain dumb and blind lemmings. In the meantime, my dear Republicans, the independents, the "real" conservatives in the middle, on the right and even somewhat on the left, did not elect you guys and gals to sit down and "work with" Obama's regime. You were elected to *stop* the speed with which our great country is getting closer to the edge of that cliff. You were not elected to slow it down.

Republicans, you were elected by Americans who really care about reversing the direction our country has taken toward destruction. The winners need not work with the losers this time. Republicans, we put you there to stop the people who have been ruthlessly and carelessly breaking America. You were not elected to just "fix" things. STOP THEM!

On that note, I can only pray that God gives wisdom to the Republicans that *we* voted into office to understand *why* we put them there and kicked out so many Democrats. Not all Republicans are conservatives as not all Democrats are far left liberals. But Americans in general spoke loud and clear that they want Obama stopped, that liberalism is not the path desired by the majority of Americans. The true patriots in this country banded together at the mid-term elections and now, we have a badly wounded tiger as our President, and he wants to strike back and inflict pain on his attackers. We who voted all those Republicans back into office need to know that the fight to take back our country won a major battle in November 2014, but the adversaries are licking their painful wounds and regrouping for a long, grueling war that will linger on up to the BIG BATTLE, which will take place in November 2016.

How does this subject help veterans pull themselves out of a hole? How does this jargon help educate or inspire a veteran to continue their battle with another faction of our country's government, that "nine-hundred-pound gorilla"—the VA? It doesn't--then again yes, it does.

[Washington] November 4, 2014 – Veteran Democratic Sen. Mark Pryor of Arkansas lost his seat Tuesday to a freshman House Republican, putting the GOP a step closer to its goal of controlling the Senate for the first time in eight years. Rep. Tom Cotton's win brightened an already happy night for Sen. Mitch McConnell of Kentucky, who won a sixth term of his own and was poised to become the Senate majority leader if his party could gain six new seats overall. Cotton, an Iraq combat veteran and Harvard Law School graduate, joined virtually every other Republican nationwide in relentlessly linking his opponent to President Obama, whose popularity has sagged.
(Source: The Associated Press/Charles Babington)

The new Senator Tom Cotton is part of a recent trend as more veterans seem to be entering the political scene in hopes of changing things and in hopes of stopping our current President. Stay tuned, folks. I like Cotton, and I don't care if he is a Democrat or Republican.

On October 23, 2014, I found this alarming headline—I believe it was from the *Military Times* or *Army Times* media: ***USA Military Elite Dismissed or Fired Under President in Overwhelming Numbers.*** Most of us have been aware of the drastic and dangerous military cuts under Emperor Obama's reign. I was not aware that he had inflicted so much damage to our country's defenses by discarding an alarming number of our military's most seasoned, most capable leaders, which included at least five dozen generals and admirals from the Army, Marines and Navy.

Since Barack Obama has entered the White House, high-ranking military officers have been removed from their positions at a rate that is absolutely unprecedented. Things have gotten so bad that a number of retired generals are publicly speaking out about the 'purge' of the U.S. military that they believe is taking place. Dozens of highly decorated military leaders have been dismissed from their positions over the past few years. So why is this happening? What is going on right now is absolutely crazy especially during a time of peace. Is there a deliberate attempt to reshape the military and remove those who do adhere to the proper 'viewpoints'? Does someone out there feel a need to get officers that won't cooperate out of the way?

Throughout world history, whatever comes next after a military purge is never good. If this continues, what is the U.S. military going to look like in a few years? Perhaps you are reading this and you think that 'purge' is too strong a word for what is taking place. Well, just consider the following quote from a very highly decorated retired officer:

-Retired Army Major General Paul Vallely: "The White House protects their own. That is why they stalled on the investigation of Fast and Furious, Benghazi and Obamacare. He's intentionally weakening and gutting our military and Pentagon and reducing us as a superpower and anyone in the ranks who disagrees or speaks out is being purged.
(Source: *Freedom Press*)

President Obama, Please…WAKE UP!

Wake up, Mr. President or…just get out of there and take Joe Biden and John Kerry with you, please. American's priorities have changed. Anyone who cannot see that is never going to because they refuse to. In a 2015 poll taken by The Pew Research Center's annual policy priorities survey among a sample of 1,504 adult American citizens, it was found that the strengthening of the military has increased to become a top priority. Here is a brief recap of those results:

Pew Research 2015
Center for the People & the Press
Fifteen Top Priorities

Priority		January 2013 (%)	January 2015 (%)
1.	Defending country from terrorism	71	76
2.	Strengthening the nation's economy	86	75
3.	Improving the job situation	79	67
4.	Improving the educational system	70	67
5.	Making Social Security system sound	70	66
6.	Reducing the budget deficit	72	64
7.	Reducing health-care costs	63	64
8.	Making Medicare system sound	65	61
9.	Reducing crime	55	57
10.	Dealing with problems of poor & needy	57	55
11.	Strengthening the U.S. military	41	52
12.	Dealing with issue of immigration	-	52
13.	Protecting the environment	52	51
14.	Addressing race relations	-	49
15.	Dealing with moral breakdowns	40	48
16.	Reforming the nation's tax system	52	48

Survey conducted Jan. 7-11, 2015

While there have been increases since 2013 in the percentages of both Republicans (from 58% to 71%) and Democrats (from 31% to 41%) rating a stronger military as a top priority, this is now a leading goal for Republicans. It now ranks above the economy, jobs and the budget deficit among Republicans' top priorities. Terrorism by a wide margin ranks first among Republicans (76%). The survey finds little change over time in many of the public's other priorities: 67% rate improving education as a top priority, 66% cite securing Social Security, 64% reducing health care costs and 61% securing Medicare. However, the budget deficit—which surged in importance between 2009 and 2013 has lost ground since then. Currently, 64% say reducing the budget deficit is a top priority. (Source: Pew Research Center)

The message here is a clear one. Americans are more worried about the defense of the country against terrorism than anything else, and this should be a greater focus for the government than the economy, jobs, education, social security, etc. This means a stronger system for protecting our borders from... illegal aliens.

Patriots, if you want to see a safer, stronger America for your family and friends, do plan to get out and vote for the "right" person as the next President of the USA. You have that right, and you have that power to get our great country back on track. This is apparently what most of us want, so please show you mean it when November 2016 arrives.

Stars & Stripes ran an article about the following a few weeks after the Paris shootings, **"European law enforcement agencies are rethinking how many police should re-arm."** Even Scotland Yard openly stated that it was increasing the deployment of police officers allowed to carry firearms in Britain. I wonder if they remember how to "lock and load." Therefore, the unarmed "bobby" will soon be no more, thank goodness. Belgium has made a similar declaration... bravo for them too. And guess what, fellow patriots? In light of all of this and what might have happened while this book was in the proofing stages at the publisher, our President still has no idea what American citizens want!

Obama wakes up? Well, sort of. On January 29, 2015, it was quietly reported in several low-key media resources that "The Obama administration is now seeking an increase of $20.4 billion or thirteen percent for weapons and research in an apparent attempt to offset some of the massive defense budget cuts that have reduced America's military strength to pre-World War II levels. Nice try, but isn't this similar to the premature exit from Iraq, then we are forced to go back? I remain confused with this President's actions. How about you, my dear patriots?

King Obama giveth...and he taketh. Elsewhere in this book, I attempted to bestow credit to our much-maligned president for something he had at least a part in doing. Six months after Obama signed off on a bill granting veterans permission to use medical care outside of the VA, our king had called for "cutting the program" in his 2016 budget. This is and was the choice card program that our Congress came up with and pushed for to try to ease the long, long waiting list of veterans who were not getting timely or quality health care. It was this program that I had been taking advantage of for badly needed and long overdue stroke rehab at outside facilities. I had already gone through fourteen weeks of extensive therapy at two different clinics outside of the VA and I began another post-stroke rehab program with a retina specialist at an ophthalmologist's office in February 2015. I will keep my fingers crossed that it will not be cut by Obama. It wasn't much to begin with, a mere ten to fifteen billion dollars that was set aside for us, and he had threatened to deplete it anyway. Heck, the program had barely gotten started. Many vets were still learning about it, and he wanted to make cuts in it already.

Representative and veterans' champion Jeff Miller, a Florida Republican was leading the charge to stop Obama from reneging on yet another promise. When this book comes out, this should have been settled one way or another. STOP IT, OBAMA!

Our vote has never been more important in our great country's history as it was at the November 2014 mid-terms and as it will be in November 2016. Our active duty troops are fed up with the Obama politics, and he has made them feel that way. The young veterans feel the same way. Most older veterans from WWII to Iraq feel the same way. Several studies—one from the VA itself, have projected that eighty to ninety percent of the military is not in favor of Obama's ways. They don't necessarily favor one party over another by a landslide, although Republicans do have an edge. In fact, a poll taken by the *Military Times* of more than two thousand active duty troops showed that forty-four percent believed that both major political parties have become less supportive of military issues in recent years. I do not believe a Democrat in Congress would be much less supportive than a Republican would; however, I do believe very strongly that our current Democratic President may be the least supportive President that the USA has had in my lifetime.

In November 2014, a U.S. Marine called out Obama at the White House on election night. When the Republican victory became certain at the mid-term election, Sgt. Manny Vega, a former Marine who is now reported to be a Patriot Militia member, left the celebration party in Virginia to personally deliver a message to Barack Hussein Obama, while standing right outside the White House. Vega was 'armed' with a megaphone and a copy of his First Amendment Right to free speech. Vega said that he did not vote Republican. He voted "American". Manny Vega is Hispanic, by the way. Vega exercised his First Amendment Right and let Obama have it in no uncertain terms. Can any of us imagine the dedication and intestinal fortitude that Manny possessed that night? Oh—Manny did respect-fully ask Obama for his resignation and to vacate the White House.

A great American veteran strikes back. I hope there will be more of us doing that, many more. I wish—oh, how I wish—that I was thirty five years old now rather than seventy years old. Regardless, as I have said often…**I am still a soldier, and it is still my duty to fight for my country when it needs me.**

Great news! In 2015, Congress unleashed the largest class of veterans ever, even as Obama decreases the numbers of our active military. Already mentioned earlier was Senator Tom Cotton's election. He was joined by another twenty-one veterans who won their respective elections. The new class will include six Democrats and sixteen Republicans. Why is this great news to my ears? Because our country needs more young "bravehearts" to bring justice on the Obama administration and this appears to be happening and not in slow motion either. God bless our veterans.

Bravehearts, step up! Remember the true story of William Wallace. Most of you know him as "Braveheart." William was told by the "Nobles" of Scotland that it was impossible to defeat the tyrannical King of England and his minions (which held Scotland in captivity to their tyrannical ways). There were too many, too strong in every way for Scotland…or so they thought.

This one man, William Wallace, knew more than the "Nobles" of Scotland. He knew that freedom was not a gift granted to them by mere men or a tyrant king, but freedom was a right guaranteed to every man by God, which has been summed up in our Declaration of Independence. Freedom was not a thing to be stripped away from the common people by a tyrant because Wallace knew that rights were granted by God. The people of Scotland, outnumbered, outmatched, starving and without even the proper weapons to fight with, followed William Wallace, and eventually Robert the Bruce, into victorious battle. Although it was a high cost to pay (namely the life of William Wallace himself), they won their freedom and were delivered from the tyrannical King of England.

How could this be? How could the starving commoners defeat a skilled, pro-fessionally trained and heavily armored army? It was because their freedom was more precious to them than anything in the world, and they would rather die than have it taken away. They were resolved and were willing to follow one man who believed they could secure it.

Now take that to America. The "Nobles" which are most of our Congressmen and women, will not stand up against the crimes that have befallen "we the people" from this administration. They have titles and positions, which they don't want to lose much like the "Nobles" of Scotland in the day. But the tyrannical King of England was not defeated by the "Nobles." **He was defeated by the people.**

America, it can be the reality that we leave our children, the way that our forefathers left it unto us. America, God is willing to give to His people what His people are willing to fight for.

Looking back, sometimes I almost wish we Vietnam War era veterans had teamed up with all of those hippy protestors and gone after the politicians who sent us over there to die. But we were a tired lot when we came home, much older, as our Korean War brothers were, and burned out from the worst and longest nightmare of our lives. It's like we are just now waking up and all of a sudden, we are almost half a century older. How did that happen?

Some of today's politicians are wimpy enough to suggest we change for the benefit of the incoming aliens, but "real" Americans are not wimpy, and we are not going to lie down and give up our country to those who never risked their lives for our country and probably never will.

American history worth repeating again. It took approximately three percent of the population to take the fight to England's King George III and his horde of minions and defeat them soundly, securing America's independence from the mighty England. Never underestimate the power of the true God and the people who will stand in his name.

Sometime in November 2014, a smaller fight for freedom took place, and the victors were also Christians fighting in the name of their God. This small force of just seventy or so fighters was Iraqi Christians, and they drove out a much larger force of Islamic state militants. The town was called Bakufa. The Iraqi Christians were not experienced soldiers by any means, although some of them had received some training from Americans. The article went on to say that these brave warriors could very easily triple their numbers or more, *if* they were armed properly.

U.S. Army Veteran Attempts Overthrow…of a country. The details of this veteran "fighting back" can be found in *The Daily Beast*. Although too long to reprint here, the gist of this story recounts a true combat-trained Gambian-American, Papa Faal, along with other American veterans who plotted to overthrow the government of the African country, Gambia. Faal served seven years in the U.S. Air Force when he became a U.S. citizen. Later, he spent another three years in the U.S. Army. He also served in Afghanistan for nearly a year.

His goal for the overthrow? "To restore democracy to the Gambian people." He is not just an ordinary revolutionary. He is a published author of political history, working on his doctorate, and of course, a U.S. Army and Air Force veteran, of which he is extremely proud. Investigators found a handwritten note that appeared to have described Faal's vision for Gambia, which read as follows: "Gambia Reborn: A Charter for Transition from Dictatorship and Development." Unfortunately for Faal, the attempt did not succeed and as of this writing (1/10/15) he was in custody and was being tried—along with others—for the crime of **plotting to overthrow the West African government of Gambia.** One has to admire the heart here, if nothing else. I would have liked meeting up with him when I was a few years out of Vietnam.

A Conservative (Patriot) American Revolution

Few may be aware of the 2002 book release, *The Conservative Revolution: The Movement That Remade America*, authored by Lee Edwards. Untold by the mainstream media (no surprise), Edwards told the story well about the post-WWII conservative movement that reshaped our country's political structure. Don't be hard on yourself if you are one who is not familiar with this book's existence. I just became aware of it as I was researching for information to support my book. The reviews are not plentiful; however, they are intriguing enough to have the book added to my shopping list. The well-known *Kirkus Reviews* gave the book one of their hard to come by positive reviews and credited Edwards for his knowledge, his writing ability and especially his even-handedness in showing the errors made by his conservative pals as they took control of the branches of government, a process that has not seen its final chapter.

Senators Taft and Goldwater, President Reagan and former House Speaker are the foundation of *The Conservative Revolution*. From what I can take away from all of the reviews, this book will engage you; it will peak your interest with every page. It will surprise most as Edwards shows how so much of what happened forty years ago when the modern conservative movement was born, is re-occurring in the rebirth of the conservative movement today. I dropped my pen long enough to order this book, and I will probably add it to my agenda along with finishing *Payback Time!*

WARNING: While the conservative movement of today seems to have received an impressive vote of confidence with the Republican takeover of the Senate, I hope we are all watching the White House just as closely in the days ahead as we should have been doing over the past six years. If we do not maintain vigil, do not let your silver out of close sight or it may disappear. I say this because of what seemed like—no, actually was…an anemic response by the Republicans to Obama's executive amnesty. It was like they went on an early vacation to celebrate their resounding mid-term romp.

Keep your faith, my patriotic buddies. I liken the Republicans' victories across America in the mid-terms as the new beginning of real changes to come. I like to think of the 2014 mid-terms as the…**Second Patriots American Revolution.**

Patriotism means to stand by the country. It does not mean to stand by the president or any other public official, save exactly to the degree in which he himself stands by the country. It is patriotic to support him insofar as he efficiently serves the country. It is unpatriotic not to oppose him to the exact extent that by inefficiency or otherwise he fails in his duty to stand by the country. In either event, it is unpatriotic not to tell the truth, whether about the president or anyone else...

- President Theodore Roosevelt

American braveheart saves grandmother. It happened in Charlotte, North Carolina in December 2014 when two would-be burglars were spotted by one of the home's occupants. Immediately, the two criminals were confronted and warned with these words, "Stop, I have a gun." The intruders ignored the warning and broke through the glass, but they were greeted by three shots fired by the owner's fourteen-year-old grandson. It turns out that this brave young American was defending the home's other inhabitant, an ill grandmother, so he was pretty motivated. The young hero, grandson to the Wyants had been properly trained and taken to shooting ranges by his grandpa, so he knew how to use a gun properly. One of the intruders was killed by the fourteen-year-old. The other one fled but was captured and booked by the police. There were no charges against the fourteen-year-old who had been living with his grandparents since 2008 when his father was murdered. What would have happened had the young man not stepped up to meet the challenge?

Call to arms? Please don't fret and think that I am promoting an actual revolution like the War for Independence or the War Between the States, and if I were, what would one little book like this accomplish? No, my freedom of expression does have limits, and I love America way too much to ever want to see anarchy in the streets. My call to arms in this chapter is directed more at using our God-given rights to speak up for ourselves. We, the People...have so much more power than the average American could ever imagine because they have never tested that power by doing anything with it.

My fellow patriotic Americans, I invite you; I appeal to you to become more proactive in letting your feelings be known to our politicians in Washington, D.C. We put them there. They did not inherit their powerful position from their bloodline. We can put them out of there, too...use your power or lose it.

Almost every day, it seems like our freedoms are being challenged and devoured from within by those who believe that socialism would be better for all of us rather than a culture of dependency. I, for one, refuse to accept these unbelievable assaults on our country's traditions, our economy, and our government.

I have hope that more Americans will continue to wake up and rise up. Without hope…we are hopelessly lost. Do you have hope? I hope so. If you do, then we must pray to God together to save our great country. But God helps those who help themselves.

"Ben Carson Scares GOP and the Left with His Unfiltered Truth."

You will read more about this man in this book because *Payback Time!* is about telling the truth, and Dr. Ben Carson speaks the truth as fluently as anyone I have ever heard. But with truth comes controversy, hurt feelings, resentment and untruthful retaliation. In case you might have missed these controversial truisms from Dr. Carson, they are worth mentioning again. Please read and please keep an open mind…it is imperative that you come away with an accurate understanding of what this fine American is telling us.

Once, Dr. Carson made a comparison between the current U.S. government (Obama Administration?) and the Nazi government. Of course, this infuriated the left-wingers as well as some of those in the middle. Dr. Carson's intent was simply to say…both governments attempted to silence their critics.

On a separate occasion, Dr. Carson made another famously controversial comparison when he spoke of the similarity of ISIS fighters and America's patriots. At first, this fired up those on the right until they understood exactly what he meant, which was—American patriots should be praised for their willingness to die for what they believe, similar to the ISIS fighters. Although they have the wrong philosophy, they are also willing to die for what they believe. Oh, by the way, one of the left's favorite media sources, CNN (Communist News Network?) spun this story about one hundred eighty degrees from what Dr. Carson had intended.

One more—this Dr. Carson comparison really set off the left. He said that Obamacare was the worst thing to happen to America since slavery because it is trying to make all of us submissive or subservient to the government. Wow! Dr. Ben terrifies the left because he will have a decent shot at winning a presidential election, and he has shown interest in tossing his hat into the ring. Dr. Ben is your and my kind of American, harvested from the old days when real Americans walked more commonly than they seem to today. Dr. Ben Carson has one glaring fault in that he is not afraid to call a terrorist a terrorist or a communist a communist. These days, that is politically incorrect.

IF Dr. Ben has decided to enter the brutal presidential election, may God be with this fine gentleman. Too bad he wasn't our first black President instead of Barack Hussein Obama who is not a great American. Actually, if Dr. Ben runs and wins…he would officially be our first black President. Isn't Obama of black and white mix? What I like best about Dr. Ben is this…IF YOU TELL THE TRUTH, THEY DON'T WANT YOU IN THEIR CLUB, and he doesn't care!

Here is a ticket I would support in a heartbeat or less—Dr. Ben Carson and Trey Gowdy, Marco Rubio and Rand Paul and any combination of them if they can stand each other. I am certain that any of these men would step up and bring to a screeching halt what Obama is ignoring.

America doesn't only seem to be traveling down the same path as France or Germany and other European countries regarding Muslim immigration, America is well on the way and dark days are ahead if we do not change our path…abruptly.

Here is a recap of what has been happening to our country as noted by Ian Tuttle, a William F. Buckley fellow of political journalism at the National Review Institute:

> In 1992, forty-one percent of new permanent residents in the United States came from the Middle East, North Africa, Asia-Pacific or sub-Saharan Africa. Ten years later in 2002, the percentage had grown to fifty-three percent. Over that period, the number of Muslim immigrants coming to America each year had doubled from fifty thousand to one hundred thousand (each year).

> The present total of Muslims in the United States is not factually documented because religious affiliation is not tracked by the Census Bureau, but the Council on American Islamic Relations estimates that there are approximately seven million Muslims in our country, as mentioned elsewhere in this book.

Guess what else has grown? The incidence of Islamic radicalism. To get a good idea of what could happen in your community, take a trip to Detroit, Michigan. Drive over to Dearborn, spend a couple days there—even visit a Mosque exercising your American freedom of worship. If you do, feel free to communicate your experience back to me if you wish.

Each of these "peace loving" Muslims has something in common: Dzhokhar Tsarnaev, Tamerlan Tsarnaev, Abdul Rahman al-Anoudi, Mohammad Hassan Hamdan, Mohammed Hamzah Khan and Aafia Siddiqui have been involved with radical Islamic practices in the 2000s, arrested, convicted and/or imprisoned for their activities. Their crimes will undoubtedly be carried out again and again by more like them, whether it happens in Boston, Chicago or Dearborn. And do we presently have a President who recognizes this problem? Does he have a plan to stop it? Do you…Mr. Barack Hussein Obama?

At the end of the day, could there be a second American revolution and what could cause such a disaster? My basic answer is…only if our government is no longer capable or willing to protect legal, patriotic Americans.

January 2015 ended as it began, as radical Islamists were in the news from all parts of the world. As I was attempting to close this chapter on January 30, this report came in from *Freedom Outpost* by way of the *Philippine Star*—"**Forty-nine police officers were killed in a no-go Islamic zone.**" The mainstream media pretty much ignored this news. The forty-nine member police unit's mission was to arrest suspected terrorists; however, the feeling of the Moro Liberation Front guerrillas involved in the slaughter was that this area was clearly under Islamic law (Sharia) and not under the jurisdiction or national or local police. Listen up, patriots—if this can happen in the Philippines, it can happen anywhere, including America. Even in America, radical Muslims seem to believe that they are above the law of our country…on guard, patriots!

Have you seen *American Sniper*? Judging from the response that this excellent movie generated from some American Muslims…every legal, patriotic American citizen should have seen it. Here is a news release I caught on January 27, 2015:

"American Muslims Attack American Sniper—Demand Eastwood and Cooper denounce fictional Islamophobia."
(Source: *Freedom Outpost*, January 27, 2015)

Muslim groups alleged that Muslims have become targets of "violent threats" because of the movie, *American Sniper*. Few of us believed it—I still don't. Gotta remember, free speech is unknown in the Muslim world. *American Sniper* is about a true American patriot. Nuff said…see it.

CHAPTER 12

VETERANS STRIKE BACK ONE BY ONE IN MASSES!

NEWSFLASH: VA negligence and misconduct is not a new thing. It just seems new to most Americans, mostly because the media, Congress and veterans themselves have never made themselves noticed in the way they have in 2014. I am proud of our veteran brothers and sisters, and I pray that we can remain a strong and unified voice for as long as it takes to force the VA into doing what they are supposed to do in taking care of ill and deserving war veterans.

L ong before 2014, Vietnam War and other Vietnam era veterans were taking issue with the overall care they were seeking or attempting to receive from their main health-care providers, the Department of Veterans Affairs. Here is an abbreviated recap of a war buddy of mine who served with me in Vietnam during the Tet Offensives of 1968:

"Never Giving Up" From 1979 – 2004

In 1979, I found myself on the tenth floor of the VA in Durham, North Carolina. All the doors were locked so that the mental patients could not escape. I had a nervous condition, is what I told them and I couldn't understand why things weren't working for me. I just had this strong feeling that I needed to blow something up. Well, they put me through these tests where they'd ask questions like: Do you ever hear voices? Yes, I do. How often? Every time someone speaks to me, I said. You got out of the army in 1970. What have you been doing? I went to a community college for a couple of years. There were a lot of draft dodgers so I didn't do too well. They talked me into joining the National Guard and <u>all</u> of them were draft dodgers. How's your love life? Well, I got problems there, too. My girlfriend is nice enough, but she's got three kids. I get along with the kids o.k. But her husband *doesn't care for me a whole lot. You see, they were separated when I met her, but then he found out how much the divorce was going to cost him, so he just moved back home. His kids told me not to worry, that he would be gone pretty soon, but he didn't.*

After two weeks, they gave me a personality disorder and sent me home.

May of 1981 found me right back at VA in Durham, N.C. again. I can't remember his name, but my doctor was pretty good. I was obsessed with the loss of the war. Back in April of 1975, I watched as President Ford went before Congress and asked them to help the South Vietnamese. Every Democrat voted no. The Senate was the same. The Democrats controlled both. All I could see with the fall of Saigon was the loss of 58,000 men for nothing. To this day, I have never voted for a Democrat for President, for Congress or the Senate.

I had some problems with the law too. I got extremely drunk the night Saigon fell. Got to where I couldn't even to go sleep without a few drinks. Bourbon and coke was my main drink. If I was sick with a cold or something, the doctor always said to drink plenty of orange juice. So I would switch over to screw drivers. Bottom line, I ended up with a driving record about seven pages long. It used to be eight computer printout pages long, but they condensed it down to seven.

This time they sent me home with a general anxiety disorder. I applied for disability. Before I left, the doctor had asked me to stay on and do a 12-week program. I said I would, but that I needed a few days to take care of some things. He said no, you need to do it now. I said look, I've got an appointment tomorrow and I promised I would make it. He said that I needed to make some sacrifices. I told him that I had two Purple Hearts and that was enough of a sacrifice. Then I left.

The next day I went to Little Washington, North Carolina. It was May 20, 1981. I kept my appointment with Kay Currie and filmed about fifteen minutes on her program. One of the questions she asked me was, what did I think about Israel's ultimatum to Syria. I said that Israel had given them thirty days to remove the missiles they had set up, so within the next thirty days those missiles will be gone. You can take that to the bank. Then she asked me if any other country was going to have any problems. I said that I believed that Bolivia was due to have another coup attempt. The reason she was asking me these questions is because the year before I had told her that El Salvador would be next since the Sandinistas had taken over Nicaragua and that the attack would come after the first of the year, which happened.

Anyway, the show aired on May 24, 1981. Two days later, some Colonel in Bolivia took over a whole city. The next day, Israel bombed the missile sites and that was that. Next thing I knew, I was in Washington D.C. at the Salvadorian Embassy. Eventually, I went on vacation to El Salvador. I'd have to check my passport for the dates, but I did visit during the 1980s – 1992.

After my visit to D.C., I went back home and back to the VA. I told them that I was willing to go through their 12-week program. They told me that they didn't have a bed for me and that it would be quite a while before they did. I refused to leave. They called security on me and I was escorted off the property. Thank God they wrote it down in files. This was at the end of May 1981.

In the meantime, my lawyer called me on a traffic ticket and told me that he thought that the judge was going to give jail time this time. I said, don't worry about it, I'll take care of it. Then I packed my bags and left N.C.

*I went to Virginia Beach, got a job at a hotel. Then I got a job pouring cement. I slept on the beach using a black garbage bag to cover me, to keep sand off of me. Then I spent the winter at a homeless center. The summer of 1982, I was back at the beach working as a bus boy at Sambos. Then I got a job that took me to Houston, Texas. I traveled all over until 1985. I ended up in Lawton, Oklahoma selling life insurance. Occasionally, I took a vacation to El Salvador. Then in 1989, around January, I got sick with bronchitis. The motor in my car blew up. I lost my business. I was homeless once again. One day at the hospital, this guy asked if I would come into his office. He said he had gotten my records in from the VA in Durham, North Carolina. He asked me if I was getting any disability. I said no. He asked, didn't you ever apply? I said yes, but they turned me down. So I just forgot about it. They didn't want to help me anyway. Then he asked if I had ever heard of PTSD. I said no. He says, well, here is a list of symptoms. I said, which ones do you think I got? Sitting at his desk, he looked up at me and said, **I think you have got them all.***

He sent me to the VA in Oklahoma City. I was in the hospital for eight days. Then they recommended that I go to a special hospital in Topeka, Kansas. However, I had to wait until July 16, 1989 to go. That was four months I had to wait. In the meantime, Disabled American Veterans took my case and filed for disability for me. About two months later, I went before a psychologist to determine how much disability I should get. Then I got a letter telling me they had turned me down again. So I went to the Oklahoma City VA and signed a release form to get a copy of all of my records. When they came in the mail, I started reading everything. While in the hospital, my psychologist (who was also a lawyer) had asked me to write three pages on any combat I had seen in Vietnam. I started writing and before I knew it, I had written six pages. She wrote that I had written this as if it were yesterday and recommended that I receive compensation. The doctor that decided that I should not receive any compensation wrote that he admitted that I had stressors (as he put it) if I was telling him the truth. This guy was calling me a liar! It was ninety miles to Oklahoma City, VA from Lawton, Oklahoma. I got there about 3:00 in the afternoon and I was as mad as I have ever been. When I hit those doors to the Mental Ward and walked in, nobody even said a word to me. I went from office to office looking for Dr. Baker. I wanted to pound him into the floor! Naturally, security was called again and the DAV guy came down and assured me that he'd take care of everything. Bottom line, I was never allowed in there again.

In July, I went to the PTSD ward in Topeka, Kansas. It was supposed to be a 90-day program. They kicked me out after sixty days. But while I was there, I learned a lot. I had a really good doctor by the name of Dr. Horne. He had been in artillery in World War II. Then he became a psychologist. After I had been there thirty days, my DAV guy called me to let me know that I had been awarded 30% disability and I would be back-paid to February. After I got out, I received 50%. Also, they agreed to allow me to come back and try again in July of 1990.

I got kicked out again after thirty days. They said that I needed to do this on an outpatient schedule because I could not conform to their structure. However, I ended up with 100% disability.

In 1991, I applied for back pay. The struggle lasted for thirteen years. Finally, in April of 2004 I received my back pay all the way back to 1979.

-Robert (Bob) Best
Sergeant, 11 Bravo, 1st & 2nd Platoon Bravo Company
3rd 22nd 25th Infantry Division
U.S. Army, Vietnam 1968 – 1969
U.S. National Guard 1972 – 1975
2 Purple Hearts
Army Commendation – Valor

For twenty-five years, this Vietnam War hero took on the United States Government's Veterans Administration. You veterans of the Gulf Wars think that your waits of one hundred days or one to two years is unthinkable and terribly wrong, it is, so hang in there because times have changed. Resilient veterans like my pal, Bobby Best are the heroes of today's victories in our ongoing war with VA. Hats off to all of the Bobby Bests of the military.

During my pre-planning and during the actual writing of this book, I had a difficult time not dedicating an entire chapter to sharing the "horror stories" from other war veteran buddies, and I could have because the truthful episodes are plentiful, unfortunately. Trouble is, I would have had to dedicate an entire series of books to those horrible and unforgiveable acts over the last four or five decades of which the VA has been unquestionably guilty.. But I thought *Payback Time!* would provide a better service and be more helpful to all veterans from all wars by talking about the fight that is still very alive in so many of us. Therefore, building this chapter on war buddy Bob Best's story has been one of the most gratifying experiences for me since coming home from a war most Americans were selfishly too eager to block out of their minds for the rest of their lives... and they mistakenly believed we who fought in Vietnam should forget it too. WE WILL NEVER FORGET VIETNAM... WE WILL NEVER FORGET OUR WAR BUDDIES, AND WE WILL NEVER ABANDON ANY VETERAN FROM ANY WAR... NEVER!

Since 2009, the Department of Veterans Affairs has come under withering public criticism for their growing backlogs in handling the rightful claims for healthcare and compensation from disabled veterans. The pressure being put on VA officials has been so great, so vicious and so fact-based, that the Secretary of Veterans Affairs was forced to resign in 2014. The accusations of VA medical centers across the country fraudulently doctoring records and patient appointment information to conceal the massive lists of backlogs, causing hundreds of veterans to "die while waiting" was enormous. It was about time.

Payback Time! will more than likely reach just a few thousand people, lucky for the criminals who committed the inexcusable and unforgiveable acts of murder at the VA. The book should be read by millions, but this old Vietnam veteran "grunt" just does not have the contacts with the media giants or the resources of people like Bill O'Reilly or Oprah Winfrey. Just the same, I know this book will impact enough people at all levels to raise some eyebrows, just as *Condemned Property?* did.

On the next several pages are some blurbs about veterans fighting back. These stories rarely made the powerful mainstream media outlets, but to me, they are worth mentioning to my veteran buddies. Maybe they will provide some inspiration for some of them to…**never give up.**

I love hearing and reading about how my veteran brothers and sisters are no longer just sitting around and taking whatever the VA has been begrudgingly willing to let them have. I love hearing and reading stories such as those to follow:

Veterans sound off at VA medical center in town hall meeting

More than 100 veterans and their supporters were ready to be heard Wednesday at a town-hall style meeting hosted by the Canandaigua VA Medical Center. The event, prompted by an order from new Veterans Affairs Secretary Bob McDonald to all VA health and benefits facilities, gave citizens a chance to ask questions and comment about issues of importance involving the local VA.

This won't be the last meeting of its kind in Canandaigua, according to VA Medical Center President Craig Howard, who took questions and comments for two hours Wednesday night, along with VA department heads. "I think the timing is right for this," said Howard. "I think folks were ready to engage in discussion. I think it was very positive and balanced. And I thought everyone respected everyone else."

Among the issues brought up by attendees were lengthy wait times for services, lack of transportation funding for veterans in need of services, colder pool temperatures that serve some but hurt others, the new aquatic therapy program, the upgraded canteen, the golf course closure, the absence of a Catholic priest at the VA, frequent truck traffic on Fort Hill Avenue, and the lack of visibility of veterans driving motorized scooters on roadways.

"I appreciate the veterans focusing on specific issues and even having some solutions," said Howard. "Even the most passionate comments included a solution too—something we can work with."

On the issue of lengthy wait times for services, Laura Stradlay said her husband has been waiting nine months to be assigned a primary physician. In the meantime, he has been given doctor appointments, which the VA has then canceled and rescheduled and canceled again. "Anyone who's waiting too long for care or knows of someone who's waiting too long, bring them right up to my office in building 1 and we'll fix that," said Howard. "If you're not getting service, come to me."

Rose Rossi Williams, a volunteer at the VA's outpatient clinic, asked for an update on a new outpatient clinic. Howard said the project was targeted to break ground in summer of 2015, with completion in 2016.

Veterans Affairs Secretary McDonald promised lawmakers in early August he would move quickly to help restore public trust in VA operations following months of scandals about lengthy wait times, questionable record keeping and management practices designed to protect employee bonuses. The meetings in Canandaigua and at other VAs nationwide were designed to gather feedback from veterans and their families, but were also open to lawmakers, veterans groups and other local individuals who work with the facilities.
(Source: *Daily Messenger*, Canandaigua, NY, September 14, 2014)

Minneapolis town hall meeting gets attention

Over one hundred very fed up veterans went to the microphone in Minneapolis, Minnesota to call for a change in culture of the massive Veterans Affairs bureaucracy and demanded more accountability from top local VA leaders who recently were accused of seeking retribution against employees who complained of secret scheduling lists and canceled appointments.

This week, the VA's inspector general was in town to investigate claims by two former workers that the Minneapolis VA ordered them to falsify records in the hospital's gastroenterology department. The former workers also claim they were fired in retribution.

The Minneapolis VA system also has been flagged in a national audit for potential problems with how wait times were calculated, both at the Minneapolis hospital and at an outpatient clinic in Rochester.

"I fully commit for us to investigate those allegations, to call on the appropriate oversight bodies to help us understand where we may have made mistakes if that's the case, and to correct those mistakes," said Janet Murphy, network director for the VA's Midwest Health Care Network, which includes the Minneapolis hospital. "We probably have some work to do to regain the trust and confidence of veterans and our stakeholders."

Several vets focused on the recent allegations. Jason Quick, Minnesota State Director for Concerned Veterans for America, asked why the local whistleblowers were fired while higher-level VA officials are permitted to take administrative leave when accused of wrongdoing.

Minneapolis VA Health Care system director Patrick Kelly said a process is in place to determine whether whistleblowers suffered reprisals because of their actions. Both the VA's inspector general and its Office of Special Counsel have been asked to investigate the recent local claims. "When they do, there will be actions to hold people accountable if they took the wrong actions in those cases," Kelly said.

Vets had to brave a long wait to even get into the parking lot for the meeting at the Bishop Henry Whipple Federal Building at Fort Snelling. They were then required to go through a security screening to get through the door.

Veterans detail VA hospital problems

One angry veteran tells of his bout with cancer that was diagnosed too late at VA hospital as vets voiced their concerns at a Tennessee VA Medical Center. There were plenty of harsh words directed at the Memphis VA to local and regional directors. Veteran Luther King, a Vietnam veteran, was not going to be unheard as he told his horrible stories of one misdiagnosis after another, which included two heart attacks and a moving blood clot. King also launched these comments at the VA directors present, "I was given outdated insulin that had expired over three years ago. When I confronted my provider, I was told to be grateful my situation was not worse." King also said, "I think they would rather just get rid of us than help us. It's a form of genocide to eliminate all of the Vietnam era veterans to have enough money and funding to take care of the veterans coming home now. (Source: WREG News Channel 3, Memphis TN, September 14, 2014)

Does Vietnam veteran Luther King's comments hold water? Is it true that the VA has been committing an unthinkable form of genocide against its own kind, against brave American warriors who risked their lives and lost their lives…on behalf of those same VA employees? That's a question, not an accusation on my part. A question that needs to be asked again and again.

Well, in support of King's bold statement, here are some factual statistics that were current as of September 29, 2014, available to anyone who cares enough to search for them:

Clearing the Veterans Benefits Backlog

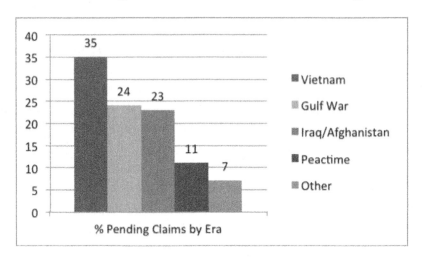

Total Pending Claims by Era
(Source: www.va.gov, September 22, 2014)

Anyone see anything wrong with this picture? If not, I will spell it out for them...**TOTAL PENDING CLAIMS BY ERA REMAIN TO BE...VIETNAM WAR ERA VETERANS!**

Veterans air out concerns to Cincinnati VA officials

Tri-State veterans sharing passionate pleas for reform to care from the veteran's health-care system aired their concerns at the first of several expected town hall meetings. The town hall meetings come by the direction of new Secretary of Veterans Affairs Bob McDonald. He has directed all VA healthcare and benefits facilities to have these types of meetings by the end of this month to improve communication with veterans nationwide.

The whole idea is to give veterans an open forum, and to give VA officials the chance to hear straight from veterans on how to improve services and maintain trust with the system. This comes on the heels of a scandal plaguing the system related to chronic delays for patients at VA facilities and the ousting of former secretary Eric Shinseki.

"We want veterans to feel comfortable bringing their concerns forward to us. It's clear that mostly what we attracted tonight were veterans who had issues and

wanted to be heard," said Linda Smith, medical center director of the Cincinnati Veterans Affairs Medical Center.

Scheduling and efficiency of care dominated the crowd's concerns. There was even a call for the resignation of Linda Smith, the head of the hospital. "I had a gallbladder problem and from the time I started yelling 'ouch' until I got the gall-bladder out was 13 months. My son had a gallbladder problem out in the world. From the time he started yelling 'ouch' until he had the gallbladder removed was a day," said one man at the meeting.

"There's no accountability in this system, and Bob McDonald, right now, is doing a bang-up terrible job," said Tony Kohl, who attended the meeting.

"The thing that drives me the most crazy is that I've seen a lot of HIPA (Health Insurance Privacy Act) violations. Patient information laying out in the open," said Jacob Redmond, a veteran.

As hands shot up in the air from those ready to air out concerns, for two hours Monday night, praise of the system merely peppered the sometimes-heated con-versation. "Things are getting better. They've got to start somewhere," said vet-eran Rick Olson.

Hospital leadership says the Tri-State's VA system sees almost 1,700 people a day. They're using $4 million in federal funds to help veterans be referred to other places who see scheduling delays more than 30 days for certain procedures. But, they realize there's still a long way to go. At the meeting, many veterans were able to immediately have their concerns addressed by members of the hospital staff. "We're not perfect in providing care. We work as hard as we can to provide the best care possible, but the more we can communicate directly with the veterans, the better that healthcare will be," Smith told FOX19 NOW.
(Source: FOX News 19, Cincinnati, Ohio; September 14, 2014)

U.S. House Veterans Affairs Committee Criticizes VA

The Associated Press
Published September 13, 2014

Two members of the U.S. House Veterans' Affairs Committee have expressed concern over the ability of the Department of Veterans Affairs to handle a costly brain research program in Waco. *U.S. Rep. Jeff Miller, R-Florida and U.S. Rep. Bill Flores, R-Texas, said in a statement Thursday that the VA is mismanaged and cannot successfully handle the project at the Waco Center of Excellence for Research on Returning War Veterans.*

"With Traumatic Brain Injury being the signature wound of our recent conflicts, every research resource must be shared to its fullest potential," Miller said. "VA must hold employees accountable if that potential is squandered. So far, VA has failed to do that."

Flores agreed, adding that the program should be handled by a different agency, such as the National Institutes of Health. "I just don't trust the VA on something like this," said Flores, whose district includes Waco. "They have proven themselves not to be worthy of taxpayer funds."
(Source: Associated Press, *Stars & Stripes*; Waco, TX)

Medical Board Sues VA for Records

Mississippi's State Board of Medical Licensure has sued the U.S. Department of Veterans Affairs over its refusal to release the names of patients who may have suffered because of the misconduct of a former radiologist at the G.V. (Sonny) Montgomery Medical Center.

The VA is apparently still fighting state efforts to get records, despite a pledge by acting Secretary of Veterans Affairs, Sloan Gibson that he would look into the matter when he spoke in July at the hospital. The licensure board says it needs the names to obtain patient records and complete its investigation into Dr. Majid A. Khan. The board could restrict, suspend or revoke his medical license.

A spokeswoman for the Jackson VA hospital declined to comment, citing the litigation.

Another radiologist who won a discrimination suit against the VA claims Khan didn't properly read images and that some patients may have died as a result. Multiple VA reviews have absolved Khan of wrongdoing, noting that all radiologists sometimes miss abnormalities. That didn't satisfy Dr. Charles Sherwood, former chief of ophthalmology at the hospital, who complained to medical licensure board and the VA's Office of Special Counsel. The suit was filed July 29 in Hinds County Chancery Court. The Department of Veterans Affairs filed to move it into U.S. District Court in Jackson on August 29, saying it's a federal matter because it seeks to force action by a federal officer.

Khan worked at the hospital from 2003 to 2008. Today, he is the chief of the division of neuroradiology at the University of Mississippi Medical Center. UMMC spokeswoman, Ruth Cummins wrote in an email that Khan "was subject to the same recruiting procedures as other faculty hired at that time, including reference checks."

(Source: *Clarion Ledger*; Clarion Mississippi, September 13, 2014)

My Heartbroken Letter to Congress

July 4, 2014
Subject: Heartbroken Loyal American
Dear Fellow Patriots:

I am Roland Earl "Dusty" Trimmer, a combat-wounded, partially disabled veteran of the Vietnam War, arguably America's most tragic and unpopular war. In fact, I wrote a recent book about what Nam vets encountered when we entered the war and when we returned from the war. This book is full of pure emotion. It fights for Vietnam veterans' rights to get well deserved and earned benefits. But why should we have to fight back here when we already fought for our country's freedom and safety?

Condemned Property? is not likely to make any of the so-called Best Sellers lists. Its subject matter is too painful for most Americans, including Vietnam veterans themselves. However, *Condemned Property?* is about healing, about bringing Vietnam veterans home…finally! We "walked the walk", we can "talk the talk", and yet we still get put at the back of the line at the Department of Veterans Affairs.

I am presently on a 362 day waiting list for an appeal—actually **Notice of Disagreement** for claims that were DENIED over one full year ago. Before that, I was kept on hold for 2+ years for service connected medical claims. In *Condemned Property?* I refer to brothers of mine from the Vietnam War who have been delayed and denied for 20 to 30 years. My opening statement in my book is a dedication to one Nam vet brother who died waiting for VA help that never came. These are atrocities against our own, and they are common.

Congressmen and Senators, it is documented that well over 35% of all backlogged claims from veterans are for Vietnam War veterans. It is awfully depressing and insulting when we go into a Compensation & Pension Evaluation with an "alleged" concerned professional and it becomes obvious to us that they NEVER opened our file…then they take the easy road to eliminate the claim with a simple, cold, heartless…**DENIED!** Then the painful DELAY process starts all over again.

It may take an Act of Congress to stop the damage STILL being dealt to my brothers and sisters who fought and are still suffering from the Vietnam War.

Most sincerely,
Roland Earl "Dusty" Trimmer
Author/Vietnam Veteran

P.S. Please note that *Condemned Property?* has received hundreds of endorsements and/or very favorable reviews from my peers as well as from non-veterans. I have enclosed a couple. You can find my book on Amazon.com, BarnesandNoble.com or on www.condemnedpropertybook.com.

Dorn VA Hit with Class Action Lawsuit

Two days after Dorn VA Hospital notified more than 2,100 patients that their personal information may have been compromised, a class action lawsuit has been filed.

In July, four boxes of pathology records had been reported missing. The documents contained veterans' names, social security numbers and pathology reports from 1999, 2000, and 2002. The Mike Kelly Law Group filed the suit on Wednesday, citing that the hospital is in breach of the U.S. Privacy Act. Attorney Brad Hewitt said that they're seeking at least $1,000 per claimant. Hewitt also said that some veterans that were affected by this incident were also involved in a privacy concern when a laptop went missing from the hospital containing more than 7,000 veterans' personal data. The firm also filed a lawsuit for that incident.

The hospital notified affected patients and are offering one year of free credit monitoring through Equifax.
(Source: WLTX, Columbia South Carolina)

'Inexcusable' changes in Veterans Affairs IG report slammed by veterans' groups

AMVETS and Concerned Veterans for America issued a joint statement calling changes made to the IG's final report "inexcusable."

[The] IG (Inspector General) investigation was initiated to get to the truth of these allegations and to hear that VA administrators may have manipulated its findings is outrageous," the joint statement said.

"The tainted report sought to absolve the agency of responsibility for veterans who died waiting on secret wait lists at the hospital by setting an impossible causation standard for patient deaths. If this is due to deliberate tampering by VA officials, Congress must find out who ordered the changes and bring those people to justice."

The joint statement was issued by Stewart Hickey, executive director of AMVETS and Pete Hegseth, chief executive officer of CVA.
(Source: *Washington Examiner*)

Syracuse VA Medical Center officials get an earful from veterans at town hall meeting

Syracuse, N.Y. -- Brad Edwards, 66, a military veteran from Rome, N.Y., said he got the run-around when he tried to make an appointment to see a neurosurgeon at the Syracuse VA Medical Center three years ago.

"We will get back to you," Edwards said he was told by a staff person at the VA's Rome outpatient clinic. Edwards said he called the clinic every month, but no one returned his calls. So last year he found a neurosurgeon on his own outside the VA system and got the operation he needed. "I felt like one of those veterans they forgot about," Edwards told VA officials today at a public town hall meeting at the Syracuse VA Medical Center. He was one of more than a dozen veterans who spoke, offering a mixture of criticism and praise of the Syracuse VA. About 70 people attended the event. All VA health care facilities nationwide are holding town hall meetings in an effort to improve communications with veterans. Secretary of Veterans Affairs Robert A. McDonald ordered facilities to hold the meetings in the wake of the recent controversy surrounding long waits for appointments at some VA facilities nationwide.

James Cody, director of the Syracuse VA, opened the session by telling veterans the Syracuse VA consistently ranks among the best in the nation in terms of quality, patient satisfaction and access to care. But after hearing complaints from several veterans, Cody said, "Statistics show we are doing pretty well, but obviously we have a lot of room for improvement."
(Source: Syracuse.com, September 18, 2014)

Vets share VA troubles at Hampton town hall meeting

By Dianna Cahn
The Virginian-Pilot
© September 25, 2014

Hampton – *One veteran said he waited a year and a half after biopsies of his lung and his lymph nodes to finally find out he has cancer.*

Another said she can't get her pain medication because her doctor no longer works at the Hampton VA Medical Center, and staff physicians can't see her for weeks. In the meantime, hospital staff told her to go to the ER if she experiences narcotic withdrawal symptoms.

Still another was assaulted years ago when she was a young recruit in boot camp. When she finally went to the VA for help, a counselor listened to her painful story, but after baring her soul, she was left to her own devices for months, waiting for a follow-up appointment.

"The VA is supposed to be there to help us," the woman told U.S. Rep. Bobby Scott during a town hall meeting in Hampton. "You open up these wounds and then you have no provisions to deal with it."

"We can talk all day," she added. "But the bottom line is, we need some action fast. The Virginian-Pilot does not identify victims of alleged sexual assault.

Close to 200 veterans turned out for Tuesday evening's meeting with the Democratic lawmaker, many complaining that VA waits were so long, their health has suffered.

They're not alone. Since 2009, the Department of Veterans Affairs has come under withering criticism for backlogs in handling disability claims and long waits for medical care. The Secretary of Veterans Affairs resigned this year following rev-elations that some medical centers had doctored their books and tampered with patient appointments in order to camouflage the enormous backlogs.

At the core of the issue: a severe shortage of doctors and other primary med-ical staff while the system is experiencing an influx of new veterans from the Afghanistan and Iraq wars.

Scott said solutions have been put in place and some efforts are working, albeit slowly. The backlog has been cut in half since early last year, when more than 600,000 veterans were waiting more than 125 days for a claim to be processed. The goal is to bring that number to zero by the end of the next fiscal year.
(Source: *The Virginian-Pilot*,© September 25, 2014)

Regional VA director gets an earful at town hall

PENSACOLA – About 100 veterans and family members came out for a face-to-face meeting with the leader of the Veterans Affairs Gulf Coast Health Care system on Monday night.

The meeting was one of the first steps taken by the new director of the Veterans Affairs department, Bob McDonald, who ordered all VA healthcare systems to hold town hall meetings to hear veterans' concerns. The VA has been scandalized in recent months by reports of exceptionally long delays in care and some cases where veterans died while waiting for appointments.

"It is my honor to be here and listen to you to hear how we can do things better," said Mark Morgan, acting director of the Gulf Coast system, which serves about 66,000 veterans and their families from Panama City Beach to Biloxi, Miss.

A long line of veterans spoke during the meeting, detailing various concerns including delays in accessing mental healthcare, difficulty obtaining prescriptions and neglectful care. The most common issues raised were with disability claims, which fall outside the healthcare system's oversight.

Gary Cooper, a 62-year old Vietnam veteran from Mobile, asked whether a new Mobile facility was in the works to replace the current one, which is about 50 years old. Morgan said there was but acknowledged that with a patient population growing by 1 to 3 percent a year, often by the time clinics are built they have already been outgrown.

Cooper who has advocated for better medical care for veterans for years, was thankful for the opportunity to address the system's leadership. "I was never told in my military career –and I was in Vietnam – that the hardest fight was going to be getting veterans benefits," he said.
(Source: *Daily News*, September 8, 2014)

Angry Utah vets get VA's attention. If you have never heard of a town called Ivins City, Utah, you might want to look it up sometime. A large group of very angry veterans, mostly Vietnam-era veterans took the southern Utah VA to task in impressive fashion. Unfortunately, the level of anger got a little out of control, forcing many onlookers to leave the scene in a hasty fashion. It is hard to blame these vets. They have been lied to and mistreated for so long; it can be difficult for some of them to keep waiting while nothing happens, which is what we usually get by going through what VA officials refer to as "proper channels." Way to go, "Utes." This was reported on January 22, 2015:

Vets in Toledo Sound Off to VA

The Veterans Affairs Department held a town hall meeting on November 12, 2014 to give veterans a chance to voice their opinions on how the VA is run. Dozens of veterans from Northwest Ohio talked healthcare. VA leaders raked in complaints about backlogged medical claims and compliments about Toledo's doctors. The director of the VA Ann Arbor Healthcare System which oversees the Toledo outpatient clinic on South Detroit Avenue says it's all about listening and building trust. Last May the Secretary of Veterans Affairs resigned after allegations of a systemic cover-up of long delays in care for veterans.

The new VA Secretary said his agency had taken disciplinary actions against more than 5,000 employees and is also instituting major reforms to customer service. "If there are broader issues, things that we need to work on as a system, we're here to listen," says Robert McDivitt, the Director of the VA Ann Arbor Healthcare System. "A new veteran coming to Toledo today looking for a primary care appointment would likely to able to get that in about two and a half weeks."

"We're still dealing with the fact that there are too many bureaucrats that are just there to collect their paycheck, are just there to collect their retirement," says

one anonymous veteran who says he receives therapy for PTSD and has anxiety simply going to a store. "They don't care about us."

"Things are much better now, but I'm only hoping no other spouse, no other wife has to go through what I went through," says Mae Randall of Sylvania. Randall says her husband Charlie served in World War II, the Korean War and Vietnam. She says the VA largely ignored his medical issues and the family's struggles until he died in 1998.
(Source: 13abc.com/ChristineLong/November 12, 2014)

Irish-American Still Fighting...

When this book launches, the content of this piece will have become about one and a half years old. No matter, I value its message, and I am sure most readers will not have known about it.

Did you know that more than 2,500 Irish (from Republic of Ireland) volunteered to fight side by side with Americans and Australians in the Vietnam War? And that there is a memorial in County Clare of Ireland called the Irish Vietnam Veterans Memorial? There are twenty-two names on this memorial, written in Gaelic and English. Just like The Wall in Washington, visitors have the opportunity to make rubbings to bring home and treasure for the rest of their lives. There is also an inscription at the bottom of the Memorial. It reads:

The people of the allied nations express their heartfelt gratitude for the service and the sacrifice of those above and to the families, loved ones and the Irish nation.

The Irish-American who started this project back in 2012, I believe, and saw it through is Matthew Carroll from Tidewater, Virginia. Carroll made it known throughout the project that he identified with and honored the names on the memorial for their Vietnam veteran status first and second, because they were Irish. "They are my brothers and sisters, and for them to be remembered is the proper thing," Carroll said.

Vietnam Veterans of America (VVA) President John Rowan has honored and endorsed the project in 2013 and encouraged VVA members to contribute or volunteer for the project. To me, this is another example of why all Vietnam veterans can be and should be proud of the war buddies they served with in that war. By the way, Matthew Carroll served with the First Infantry Division (Big Red One).

Anyone interested in contributing to the project or learning more about it, please visit www.theirishvietnamveteransmemorialproject.org.

THIS is what you could do. Broken Gear is the name of a company formed by wounded veteran, retired Sgt. Steve D'Amico. He founded his company on the principle of disabled veteran athletes, empowering themselves to get back into athletic condition to actually compete in their daily lives. D'Amico reaches out to disabled civilians as well as disabled veterans.

D'Amico attended a series of classes offered at the University of Connecticut Entrepreneurship Boot Camp for veterans with disabilities. It was then that he came up with the concept for Broken Gear after he suffered from an on-duty accident that severely injured his leg and ankle, forcing him to retire from the military. D'Amico thought to himself, "Now what do I do. I am broken just like so many other disabled veterans. What can I do?" Once, a local businessman donated a Dodge Durango to a charitable organization called Work Vessels for Veterans and D'Amico was selected to receive the vehicle. The article I read from a New London, Connecticut newspaper told how honored D'Amico was to have received this donation. To him, the Dodge Durango was what a Broken Gear vehicle would be—rugged, tough, kind of beat up—just what he was looking for. It looked like it had been through the ringer and that was okay, he said. I guess that was because that is what a disabled veteran often looks like, and that is okay.

D'Amico started a clothing line. You can find it at www.brokengearwear.com. I looked it up, and I am getting some gear—also telling others about it as I am doing in this book. Here is one small example of what Broken Gear does:

- A veteran wants to start riding a bike again and cannot afford to buy one. Broken Gear would sponsor the veteran, get the bike for the veteran, get him a Broken Gear jersey and free admission into the company, which is like a club. (I hope I explained that one correctly.)

D'Amico plans to hire other veterans and views his business as a way to "build up a fraternity." This concept is precisely what I am working towards with my introduction of the following products or services for veterans' benefits:

1) Condemned Property?, my first book (December 2013)
2) Veterans Strike Back LLC, my new company (November 2014)
3) Payback Time!, my second book (May/June 2015)

More about Veterans Strike Back LLC another time. Back to Steve D'Amico and his company, Broken Gear. Before D'Amico's service-connected injury, he was actively studying Muay Thai Kick Boxing and Brazilian Jiu Jitsu for nearly five years. He is making an attempt to get back into that game and we all wish you the best, Steve. Huuuah!

As the VA scandal continued to make national headlines in all media venues, more individual heroics by lone veterans became more popular to the media, although they rarely merited front page or featured headline material. Some of the stories were old, but worthy of being brought up again.

There was a medal presentation in Portland to present U.S. Navy veteran, Dario Raschio with a neatly prepared case of medals he had earned for his heroic participation in World War II. While attempting to accept the medals on behalf of all who had died in World War II, the proceeding was interrupted by more than one hundred protesters who pushed on doors and banged on windows, shouting and hoisting signs with messages against the present wars and the unfortunate shooting of Michael Brown by a white police officer in Ferguson, Missouri. While the presentation was being given by U.S. Senator Ron Wyden, the protests erupted. Order was achieved when Navy veteran Raschio got up, took the microphone in hand, and spoke to the protesters, and the story goes that his words to the crowd were, "Give me a chance." He chastised the invading protesters and said, "Let's show a little respect for this occasion." The crowd applauded and cheered, and the protests subsided. Folks, this feisty, brave veteran was no spring chicken... he was one hundred years old.

Marine Corporal Michael Jernigan suffered from devastating injuries from a bomb blast during the Iraq War in 2004 and has shared his story often and by unique means to help motivate others, veterans or not. He was blinded in both eyes by the IED. His wounds from that attack went beyond losing his eyesight. He has put his motivational story into a video, which was released by Honor Courage Commitment Inc., a nonprofit organization focused on helping veterans with their transition back into civilian life, something that every Vietnam War veteran can appreciate as they had no such benefit available to them after their war. Jernigan's story is inspiring to put it mildly. You should look it up online, and tell others to check it out.

Army veteran fought cancer...till his end. U.S. Army Captain Justin Fitch had a dream while he was dying from cancer at the age of thirty-two. The Iraq combat veteran wanted to see a heroes' retreat project completed before he died. The retreat is called...The Action Heroes' Veteran and Family Retreat. Therefore, he pushed and motivated himself to tell his story to various news media, including Fox, CBS and MSNBC. Fitch's story can also be found online, and it would be well worth your time to look it up. He had spent nearly ten years in the U.S. Army as an infantry officer in Iraq, and later as a personnel officer, supporting

227

Special Forces in Iraq. His main goal during his last days was to take on the terrible problem of veterans' suicides. He did that by creating extra awareness to the problem, doing this with little energy left in his failing body. Fitch was a candidate for ending his own life by his own hands. He felt there was no way out for him, and he came within split seconds of pulling the trigger on a gun he was holding to his head. He put the gun down when the voice of one of his fallen war buddies came to him, and he sought help from there. The result of that close call was that he made the decision to devote the rest of his life to saving others. And folks, he has done just that—saving others—while he was dying.

Vets March on the White House

These vets had guts. Just a few dozen of them and yet they boldly marched, each with an American flag in hand on a very cold, windy day last December, protesting the fact that they do not believe the VA or Congress are doing enough to prevent the masses of veterans' suicides going on in our country. Specifically, the vets had Senate Majority Leader Harry Reid on their radar. What did they accomplish? They made a statement, the kind of statement that more veterans should be making. Come on guys and gals...**do it.**

Don't mess with a combat-trained vet. This altercation took place in early 2015 in the Seattle, Washington area. A former U.S. Army Airborne Infantry veteran was confronted in his own home one evening by a would-be robber. The full details of this incident can be found online. Mr. Andrew Myers jumped on the opportunity to utilize his army infantry training to lay down a pretty thorough ass-kicking on the intruder of his dwelling. After subduing the intruder and pinning him down, a friend called 911, and the local police arrived shortly after to apprehend the villain, who became the victim in this case. Way to go, grunt! Airborne – Airborne, All the Way...Huahh! By the way, fellow grunts, brother Myers suffers from PTSD, as most real combat troops do, but he also spends some of his time raising money to help his fellow veterans by assisting them in adopting service dogs.

Don't mess with Cincinnati, OH-IO! Listen to this (I mean read it, of course.). Even VA employees are stepping up to the plate for veterans because of our rotten treatment by the rulers of the system. In Cincinnati, scores of employees at the VA medical center have issued their protests of the bad conditions at the facility. The protesting workers also cited problems of understaffing and mismanagement at the top and demonstrated that this situation is unfair and harmful to veterans.

The Town Hall Meetings Continue...But?

From Virginia to Ohio to Arizona to Oregon, veterans shared their stories openly at town hall meetings that became most popular after Secretary Bob took over. VA officials who were surprised with all the dissatisfaction of the veterans had to have been on a long siesta for the last few years or decades, or they were fresh recruits from college.

Some of the VA directors have really reached out to the vets by meeting with them on a one-by-one basis after some of the meetings. After all, that is what the town hall sessions were held for, to improve communications with the veterans, the patients, or the victims, in some cases. As one veteran told director, Thomas Smith at an Alabama town hall meeting, "I'm fed up with coming to VA with my pains, and then leaving there with the same pains. Enough already," he said.

My brothers and sisters, I am proud of those who attended so many of these town hall meetings as you are standing up for the American rights you already fought for and risked your life for...Freedom of Speech! I have attended two town hall meetings in northeast Ohio in 2014, and I am extremely pleased that I did. I will participate again, but plan to pick and choose, depending on who the mediators will be.

Our American right to freedom of expression is officially recognized as a human right under Article Nineteen of the Universal Declaration of Human Rights and recognized in international human rights law in the International Covenant on Civil and Political Rights (ICCPR)—whatever that is. Seriously, Article Nineteen states that "everyone shall have the right to hold opinions without interference" and "everyone shall have the right of freedom of expression; this right shall include freedom to seek, receive and impart information and ideas of all kinds, regardless of frontiers, either orally, in writing or in print, in the form of art, or through any other media of his choice." **Shall include the right to seek and receive.** In a nutshell, this is the goal of my first two books... to help veterans seek out what they earned and deserve.

Freedom of speech has always been a sensitive subject, especially when that act of speech infringes on the respect, or rights or reputations of others or the protection of national security, public moral, public health or public order. Therefore, every government has to put some restrictions to free speech. Some limitations could relate to the following:

- Classified information
- Copyright violations
- Ethical or racial hate

- Public nuisance
- Public order and security
- Right to privacy
- Trade secrets
- Threatening words
- Religious offenses

The cornerstone of America's freedom is freedom to express. Heck, there have been many revolutions fought around the world to maintain or to restore freedom of speech. The right to freedom of speech and expression has a long history. It is believed that the ancient Greeks' democratic ideology of free speech may have emerged in the fifth or sixth century B.C. Even the Roman Empire included freedom of speech and allegedly, freedom of religion. It was officially made part of England's Bill of Rights in 1689—Freedom of Speech in Parliament, and it remains in effect to this day. One hundred years later, in 1789 during the French Revolution, the Declaration of the Rights of Man and of the Citizen was adopted, specifically for freedom of speech as an inalienable right. Article Thirteen of the American Convention on Human Rights enshrines this right in our country.

Vietnam Veterans...Power of the Pen!

Private First Class David Rice was nineteen years old, serving in Vietnam. He was drafted and he went. He remembers, as you and I do, just how important "mail call" was to us. It actually helped get some of us through the day. Unfortunately, those who were cursed to be grunt-like troops out in the boonies rarely enjoyed mail call on a daily basis. Then on some days, you would receive a couple of weeks of backed up mail, and that was okay. You read them all eventually.

Rice remembers that some of his buddies rarely received letters, and they stopped showing up for mail call. He received an occasional letter from home and treasured it as though it was written in gold ink. He also remembers that some guys never received mail because—get this—they never told anyone they were in Nam because of the war's unpopularity back home. One day, Rice saw one of those "Dear Abby" columns in which GIs were asked what they wanted for Christmas that year in 1967—not knowing that the enemy would greet them with a post-holiday present of their own...the Tet offensive. Rice wrote a letter to "Dear Abby." It read, "Please ask your readers to write to 'Any Lonely Soldier'" in care of him, and he would distribute them. Well, "Dear Abby" published Rice's letter in hundreds of newspapers across America with his mailing address.

Get ready for this…on November 12, 1967, Rice received four large packages, which contained twenty thousand letters. How large were the packages? It took two trucks to deliver them. The next day on November 13, another ten thousand arrived.

This barrage of letters raised the eyebrows of the FBI and the DOD as they had suspicions that Rice might be orchestrating a money-making scam, so they had seventy thousand letters sent back to the senders (I wonder how much that cost taxpayers). The mail also caused bottlenecks at the San Francisco post office, prompting Congressman Bob Wilson to intervene. Naturally, Rice was cleared of any wrongdoing, and the mail delivery resumed. More soldiers started lining up for mail call because they would be given a package and a couple of letters from some anonymous but very patriotic American from home. You can read all about this uplifting outpouring of support in the Delaware Public Archives, as Rice put together a scrapbook recalling everything that happened during his vacation in the land over there between 1967 and 1968. Rice donated the scrapbook to them.

So troops, if you don't think one little old letter can make a difference, change your thinking on that and get to it. Write to you know who (Congress or VA or both) and then write again. I do, and I know for certain they are making a difference. Just another…veteran fighting back.

Plain and simple, freedom of speech or expression is understood to be fundamental in America. So, my dear war buddies and all other patriots loyal to our great country…exercise your fundamental right to Congress and to senior VA officials. Here is a short list of responses, which I mentioned in an earlier chapter.

Congress Replies to Dusty

March 24, 2014

Dear Mr. Trimmer,

Thank you very much for your very insightful letter. I am truly sympathetic toward your concerns and the concerns of your fellow veterans and my office has been working closely with others to see that all veterans within our district and throughout the state of Ohio are properly taken care of.

Also, I am intrigued by your description of your recent book, as I feel compelled to acquire it. It is always great to hear of those Americans that are making a difference and spreading awareness of today's issues.

If there is any way I can ever be of any assistance to you with regards to our state matters, please do not ever hesitate to call my office. Additionally, I would like to congratulate you on the completion of your book, *Condemned Property?*

Sincerely,

Troy Balderson
State Senator, Ohio
April 10, 2014

Dear Mr. Trimmer,

Thank you for contacting my office with your passionately written letter. My staff and I firmly believe that our veterans, be they from the Vietnam War or any other time in our history, deserve our complete respect. It is our goal to ensure that all of you have a chance to pursue the American dream, as you pointed out in your letter. We take note of every piece of mail that comes into our office, and yours received a personal response from me. Thank you for your service to our country.

Richard Burr
Ranking Member
United States Senate

Dear Mr. Trimmer:

Thank you for expressing your experiences and thoughts regarding health care for veterans exposed to Agent Orange during the Vietnam War. Senator Gillibrand's office forwarded your book *Condemned Property?* to my office and my staff who work on veterans issues have taken a look at it.

Our service members exposed to Agent Orange during the Vietnam War deserve VA benefits for exposure to the agent and must receive the health care our nation has promised them.

Currently the Department of Veterans Affairs (VA) requires veterans who served in the waters off Vietnam during the Vietnam War to prove exposure to Agent Orange before receiving service-connected benefits based on such exposure. Veterans who served on the ground in Vietnam or in a craft on Vietnamese rivers are entitled to the presumption of exposure to Agent Orange if they make a claim for service-connected benefits.

I will continue to support veterans who served in the airspace above, inland waterways, and offshore waters of the Republic of Vietnam for VA benefits from Agent Orange exposure. As a member of the Senate Committee on Veterans' Affairs, I will certainly keep your views in mind as the Senate considers related legislation. Thank you for contacting me.

Sincerely,

Sherrod Brown
United States Senator

May 8, 2014

Dear Dusty,

Thank you for your letters sharing your concerns for the bureaucratic disaster at the VA and just as importantly, I greatly appreciate and admire your service in the Vietnam War. (My Uncle Jim also served over there from 1968-1970.) I serve as a Senator in Columbus. Please continue to email, mail and call your Washington D.C. Senators and Representatives as…this is a federal issue now.

May God Bless You,

Bob Peterson
Ohio State Senate

May 19, 2014

Dear Mr. Trimmer,

Thank you for your March 13, 2014 correspondence and referring me to your book. I appreciate your observations and your profound passion for supporting our Veterans. I will always, without apology, argue the business case for potential employers to hire from our states' 877,000 Veterans and their families.

All veterans, regardless of the era they served, deserve acknowledgement and our gratitude for their service. I am especially mindful of our Vietnam Veterans, their health challenges, of their reluctance to overcome their concerns regarding the Veterans Administration and shortfalls in the public valuing their service. I assure you that the Governor, the Ohio Department of Veterans Services, and I personally are committed to facilitating change and perpetuating the much deserved and earned benefits for our Vietnam Veterans and their families.

I have purchased *Condemned Property?* and I look forward to reading it. Thanks for your service and for writing to me.

Sincerely,

Timothy C. Gorell
Director – Ohio
Department of Veterans Services

Dear Dusty,

We received your letter today and on behalf of the Congressman, I want to first of all, thank you for your service. As you know, this is the Congressman's first term in office and I can assure you that he knows the plight of Vietnam Veterans and is appalled at how you all have been treated. The Congressman's first choice for committee assignments was on the Veterans Affairs Committee. He is 100% committed to reducing the backlog at the VA, determining how we increase healthcare services to our veterans, and most importantly, showing you the respect you deserve.

Our number one caseload in our office is veterans' cases and we have been able to secure over a million dollars in benefits. We actually have a Wounded Warrior on staff to assist our veterans. I encourage you to please contact me if we can be of any assistance in your personal case.

Please don't hesitate to contact me again. We are listening to you and doing everything we can to make up for the wrongs that our Vietnam Veterans experienced when they returned home and still continue to experience today.

Once again, thank you for your service.

Greg Rodriguez
District Director
Office of Representative Raul Ruiz, M.D. (CA-36ᵗʰ)

June 13, 2014

Dear Dusty,

Thank you for contacting me to share your thoughts about supporting our nation's veterans of all wars. I appreciate hearing from the veterans themselves and thank you for your honorable service in the Vietnam War. As Vice-Chairman of the House Veterans Affairs committee, I am dedicated to ensuring that veterans receive the support they need, especially in these critical economic times. One of my top priorities while serving in Congress is working to honor our nation's veterans. During my time in Congress, I have introduced and co-sponsored many pieces of legislation intended to ensure that our veterans receive the compensation and benefits that they earned by serving our country.

I support increasing veterans' benefits and I believe these benefits represent just a small token of the nation's tremendous appreciation for those who have defended our country.

Your comments and opinions came from your heart for comrades from the Vietnam War. Congratulations on your book in their behalf. Your comments and opinions are an important source of information to help me carry out my duties as your federal representative.

Again, thanks for sharing your thoughts with me.

Gus M. Bilirakis
Member of Congress
Vice-Chairman, House Veterans Affair Committee

July 29, 2014

Dear Mr. Trimmer:

Thank you for contacting me regarding H.R. 3230, the Pay our Guard and Reserve Act. As a new Member of Congress, I am excited to have the opportunity to represent you and the 14th Congressional District.

As you may be aware, H.R. 3230, Pay our Guard and Reserve Act was passed through the House on October 3, 2014, with my support. This bill seeks to improve the access of veterans to medical services from the Department of Veterans Affairs. The Senate passed their own version of this bill and currently the two chambers are resolving the differences in the bills. I have a special admiration for former and current service men and women, being the son of a World War II veteran. Should any more legislation be presented dealing with the VA, I will make sure to keep your opinion in mind.

Sincerely,

David P. Joyce
Member of Congress

December 19, 2014

Dear Mr. Trimmer:

Thank you for your honorable military service and for contacting me with your concerns about the Department of Veterans Affairs (VA) claims process. It is unacceptable for those who have served their country to wait months, or even years, to have their claims accurately processed. This delay puts a tremendous financial strain on veterans and their families, many of whom need—and deserve—help immediately.

VA has been making progress. For each of the last four years, it has successfully processed over one million disability claims. Despite this achievement, incoming claims have greatly increased in recent years. The increase is due in part to the number of veterans returning from the conflicts in Iraq and Afghanistan with complex injuries, but it also the result of Secretary Eric K. Shinseki's decision to grant benefits to veterans who experienced certain exposures during military service. Unfortunately, the VA's ability to process the larger workload has not kept pace. To address this problem, VA is working aggressively towards creating a more efficient paperless system in support of its goal to process all disability claims within 125 days, at a 98 percent accuracy level, by 2015.

Recently, the House and Senate voted in an overwhelming and bi-partisan manner to pass Public Law 113-146, the Veterans' Access, Choice and Accountability Act of 2014, which President Obama then signed into law. This law provides the Secretary with authority to immediately remove incompetent senior executives based on poor job performance or misconduct while guarding against the politicization of VA or other inappropriate uses, such as whistle blower retaliation, of such authority by providing an expedited appeal.

I will keep your concerns in mind as I continue aggressive oversight in order to hold VA accountable, measure progress towards eliminating the claims backlog in 2015 and work to find solutions to the challenges of the claims system.

Sincerely,

Bernard Sanders
Chairman, Committee on Veterans Affairs
United States Senate

On January 25, 2015, I read an article in an off-the-track newspaper that the Senate Affairs Committee, now under Republican dominance of course, has declared that they will make it a top priority mission to keep a closer eye on the troubled VA, including holding hearings at Secretary Bob's headquarters. Bravo. While the firings have taken place of deserved VA officials, it was also announced on January 27, 2015 that the House Veterans Affairs Committee has considered new legislation that would allow Secretary Bob to take back bonuses paid to VA workers if evidence shows there was mismanagement or criminal activity. Committee chairman, Jeff Miller (Republican – Florida) is the main sponsor of this move. Bravo.

The Best for Last…Allen West Quotes!

Since this chapter features veterans fighting back, I could not leave out one of our scrappiest veterans. I thought it would be interesting for readers and inspirational for troubled veterans who may think they are all alone and no one else of political stature is fighting for them. Allen West is well known for telling it like it is, as he sees it and more often than not, I agree with his outspoken statements. Here are a few of my favorite quotes from Allen West. Enjoy!

"I think we have to understand that when tolerance becomes a one-way street, it will lead to cultural suicide. We should not allow the Muslim Brotherhood or associated groups to be influencing our national security strategy."

"We must never forget why we have and why we need our military. Our armed forces exist solely to ensure our nation is safe so that each and every one of us can sleep soundly at night, knowing we have guardians at the gate."

"I believe the election and reelection of Obama were among the most conspicuous acts of denial in recent years. Voters just stopped paying attention. They accepted consistently bad behavior and rewarded it. Then they wonder why they get more bad behavior."

"Leadership is about being a servant first."

"The only plausible explanation for many actions taken by President Obama and his administration is that they are working counter to the security of the United States of America."

"The republic I fell in love with, the republic I risked my life to defend, the value I hold dear, the integrity that we all share—these do not know prejudice and they do not accept partiality."

"Conservatives understand that the power that binds our republic together is fierce independence held high on the shoulders of compassion."

CHAPTER 13

SECRETARY MCDONALD'S SCORECARD?

In my opinion, this VA scandal, which went public in 2014, is worse than Watergate. No one (that we know of) died over Watergate. But we don't even have a handle yet on how many veterans were killed by the VA's system. Big problem when you have a clear case of wrongdoing by government officials. It will inevitably become a conflict of interest for the government to investigate and prosecute. The only solution is…to bring in someone from outside the system.

That outside person must have an unquestionable track record of integrity. He or she must have total independence from the government to exercise his full authority and power to turn things around that have been so bad for so long. Lives are at stake here. Lives have already been lost. How would you like to take on the responsibility to deal with that? This person has to have real "juice" to make things happen. This person needs proven military or executive experience.

Robert McDonald was chosen to be the new Secretary of the VA. Unfortunately, he was hired by Barack Obama, and McDonald needs to separate himself from the President as much as possible. And then Obama has to get out of his way. We will see how that has worked by the time this book releases.

It was sometime in October when I heard that our new Secretary of Veterans Affairs had attempted to do something that should have been done a long time ago and that was—recruit medical and nursing students in college to consider careers in the VA.

Was this for real or just another VA-type smoke screen to cover up something? I looked into it and found it to be true. In fact, Secretary McDonald has made numerous recruiting trips of this nature with a mission of course, to remedy the long-waiting backups that he inherited with his position. Kudos to our VA secretary for this effort, which could offer short-term but also long-term ways to improve the VA problems. He has made stops from Vermont to California and states in between. For this, I personally give him an **A**.

Also sometime in early October, the Veterans Affairs Department announced that it was firing four senior executives as part of their crackdown on the VA internal problems with long waiting lines and record of falsification reports. These would have been the first actual firings at VA at the senior level since Congress passed a law in the summer of 2014, making it easier for veterans on holding delays to seek medical treatment outside of VA. This law also eased the firing process of senior officials suspected of wrongdoing. The VA hospitals affected by these firings were located in Pittsburgh, PA, Dublin, GA and Alabama. This was a short step forward for the journey that lies ahead for McDonald and his staff, but it's a start. More terminations must come…people lied, veterans died and more may die prematurely before they receive long overdue proper care while I am writing and publishing this book. I would like to give Secretary McDonald a rating of **B+**.

Robert Morgan, 2nd Battalion, 7th Cavalry, U.S. Army, Vietnam, served with a recon unit in the Vietnam War. Those survival instincts that kept him living over there motivated him to stand up and challenge the VA for quicker medical care. He told them he would die if he did not receive timely care soon. Morgan was right. It was later confirmed that he had pancreatic cancer that had already spread to his liver. As of this writing on October 20, 2014, Morgan was still battling VA for his service-connected claims due to his Agent Orange exposure, diabetes, PTSD and cancer. What does VA need to make the right decision and why the wait time? **Deny, Delay… Until Forced to Approve?**

Many VA officials are getting the hell out of Dodge in quick fashion since VA came under the microscope, meaning they have been taking early retirements before they would most likely be fired. This means that criminal acts will probably remain unpunished unless some Congress members are game enough and care enough to dig deeper into the history of these VA cowards.

While the VA bureaucrats will tell you that forced retirements are just as good as firing them, and if my war brothers and sisters swallow that as a fair and just ending for some of these scumbags, then we should all choke on our stupidity! So far (as of this writing), none of these early out retirees have been held accountable for their unethical acts. Even House Representative Jeff Miller has been quoted as follows, "Quite simply, any VA administrator who purposely manipulated appointment dates, covered up problems, retaliated against whistle-blowers or was involved in malfeasance that harmed veterans must be fired rather than allowed to skip out the back door with a pension."

Secretary McDonald does not seem to be looking the other way on this issue. However, he has said that the VA had no legal authority to stop employees from retiring early or to take away their pensions. He has also noted that many of these retiring in lieu of being fired will have it reflected in their records that they were targeted for termination. They will have great difficulty in getting employment elsewhere.

Okay fine, this scenario needs work. But McDonald seems genuinely concerned. Then again, those chicken shit weasels who ran would have been entitled to hearings and appeals that lasted for many years because the judicial system is so terribly backed up itself. But under the new law, which passed after many VA scumbags slithered out of harm's way, firing a VA official takes less than thirty days and this eliminates the appeal option...that is a good move and McDonald seems to agree. My grade for our secretary in dealing with this scenario is a **B-**.

Some of you out there may be wondering who the heck do I think I am putting out a book, which includes my own personal ratings of the VA Secretary's job performance so far? *Come on, give us a break,* some of you may be thinking or saying out loud. Come on yourselves. Who is better qualified to evaluate Secretary McDonald than a maligned, bruised and battered combat infantry grunt who survived the...twilight zone of all wars? NO ONE is more qualified. Most "real" Vietnam War veterans are more than qualified to send their grade in to Secretary McDonald on his job performance or to Congress...please get off your couch and DO IT!

During an interview just a few weeks after assuming his new position, Secretary Robert McDonald was quoted: "Many people want to call me Secretary or Mr. Secretary. I'm asking that they call me Bob because we've got to flatten the hierarchy. We've got to get rid of the hierarchy because it may get in the way of people communicating what's really going on." On this move, I would like to give "Bob" a grade of...**A+**.

$270 Million Towards Homeless Veterans

One day after our new VA Secretary "Bob" McDonald announced a lump sum of $207 million in new funding for rapid assistance grants to help up to seventy thousand veterans and their families keep their homes or return to some other permanent housing, the VA said they would dedicate another $63 million toward a rental assistance program that could rescue close to ten thousand chronically homeless veterans from their street lives.

More than $1 billion has been committed by the VA in 2014 to strengthen programs that attempt to end homelessness among veterans. Of course, much of this was already in progress when "Bob" McDonald stepped in, but his quick adoption and support of trying to prevent and end veteran homelessness deserves more credit. I give "Bob" **B+** for his quick action here.

This scorecard will not affect "Bob's" pay grade at the VA, nor is it likely to get noticed—but you never know. One thing about this little fantasy exercise of mine, which I chose to do is…If "Bob" cares what the real veterans are thinking about him, the grunts who fought in the trenches and dug their own foxholes, he can take this commentary on him with a little more credibility than the reports he may be getting from the minions who cater to him every day.

Fighting in the trenches is known as ground warfare, and it was most prominent on the Western Front in World War I. Trench warfare battles usually sustained severe casualties. Actually, one of the first known trench-style battles took place on or about March 31, 627 at the siege of Medina (Yathrib then). An estimated combined force of ten thousand Arabs and Jewish tribes attacked some three thousand Medina defenders, which were mostly Muslims, led by Islamic prophet, Muhammad who fought from trenches they dug. The well-organized defenders prevailed despite being badly outnumbered.

Anyway, the term *grunt* is used in the Marine Corps and the U.S. Army's Infantry. The opposite of grunt in Marine slang is *pogue*, which is an uncomplimentary reference to virtually everyone who is not a grunt.

It is understood that a pogue does not resent being called a grunt. Many relish it. But if you call a grunt a pogue, an unpleasant discussion will follow. Grunts are a proud lot. In fact, they have an old saying that goes like this, "**If you ain't a grunt, you ain't SHIT!** Hey, that's the Marines talking. Take it up with them.

It's the fourth week of November 2014 and VA morale still seems low at each of the four facilities where I spend my time. I am not just speaking for VA patients and their attitudes—who are the victims, I mean the VA employees' attitudes are pretty much at rock bottom at this point. What a quagmire our new leader, Secretary Bob walked into in July.

One good thing came from Secretary Bob's mouth in late October, which was "I am going to try to improve VA by creating a non-hierarchal organization for the VA employees who work directly with veterans to get all the support they need." Of course, that would be a good thing, Secretary Bob, but I hope you put your watchdogs on duty to keep track of your VA employees that reside on the top floor of most VA facilities. Your predecessors were complete failures in doing this.

Credit Secretary Bob with a couple of gold stars with his trust building moves for launching a national recruitment drive shortly after he was barely unpacked in his new office. He has made a good start on his promise to fire VA executives. Both of these moves should be great morale builders--it is for this Vietnam veteran. I will watch and listen closely to the situation, as all veterans should…those who really care.

Finally! Sharon Helman, Phoenix VA Healthcare Director became the "former" director as was announced in the *Arizona Republic* on November 24, 2014. FINALLY…after allowing her the undeserved luxury of being put on leave of absence—with pay and benefits—she was canned. Helman faced a barrage of withering criticism from veterans' advocates and lawmakers but little came of it for seven months. She was accused and eventually found guilty of…mismanagement, dishonesty and delayed care for veterans. Sharon Helman…Good riddance. Secretary Bob gets an **A+**.

500 VA Criminals Fired…1,000,000 Vietnam Vets Died!

In early December 2014, various media sources reported that under Secretary Bob more than five hundred employees had been relieved of their services…fired actually. From me, Secretary gets a rating for this of B. This is not enough. The crimes committed far outweigh this punishment. Then again, many of those VA schmucks that were guilty of negligence, incompetence to the level of causing deaths that could have been prevented are no longer living themselves. Here is a thought for someone to pursue—dig into past records of veterans' deaths from five or ten years ago or more. If VA still has useable and findable records on veterans who were under their care in the 1990s and 2000s. Then again, I don't think America wants to know what happened with these premature deaths, nor do I think America could deal with the findings. It would be painful and shocking.

The fact remains that well over one million Vietnam War veterans are no longer with us and it just seems like someone should be held accountable. One place to begin would be to investigate those who preceded Secretary Bob, including the recently terminated former Secretary Shinseki. I'll leave that one out there. Maybe someone who reads this will get mad enough to open "Pandora's box" on this horror show…maybe.

Is a mere firing enough? After all, some of these people have received bonuses—bonuses while at the same time, they may have denied proper medical treatment for our veterans. As of December 2014, Secretary Bob had been on the throne at VA for less than six months. And yet, he has acted swiftly and decisively. Overall, I would like of grade him with an A- for a job very well done under extremely challenging circumstances.

NEWSFLASH: Just in as I was writing this chapter—Secretary Bob's office announced considering disciplinary action against more than one thousand employees as it struggles to correct systemic problems that led to long wait times for veterans seeking health care and falsification of records to cover up delays. My fingers are crossed.

Secretary Bob has stated that there could be up to one thousand staff members terminated because of their improper job performance in taking care of our country's veterans. He said this in mid-November 2014, just months after becoming the troubled VA's latest Secretary. I believed him at the time of his vows to fire VA employees like they have never been fired before. I believe Secretary Bob to be a man of action, and I believe the President of the United States has bequeathed him the almighty power to exercise the mass axing of jobs that was needed inside the VA. Thanks, Obama for giving us Secretary Bob.

The trouble is, I don't know if replacing only one thousand or thereabouts of the tens of thousands who could be targeted will be enough to make much of a difference. It might satisfy some of the Congress members who have finally stepped forward to put intense and continuous pressure on the top-level bureaucrats who have been sitting safely and smugly in their guaranteed employment positions for too long. Will this gesture really help those Secretary Bob means to help—the veterans? When this book launches, the answer may be known by all.

Here is my personal example of what might need to be addressed and rectified immediately:

> I returned home from the Vietnam War in March 1969. (It might have been February.) It is old news now about how we were unwelcomed home. What is not common knowledge today is how we were not at all prepared by our government when they turned us loose into a world that had changed as though several decades had vanished rather than the one to two years we were held captive in the jungles of South Vietnam...ten thousand miles away from home sweet home.

Turned Loose is a subtle but very accurate way to describe our release from the twilight zone called the Vietnam War. How about—we were more like dumped back into society like raw garbage to face our fate...extermination! I am not even sure if these words were even uttered by any of the officials who out processed us... Veterans Affairs or VA Health Care or VA Benefits? While I was wrecking automobiles at lightning speed during the 1970s and even the 1980s, definitely on a suicide mission—an unsuccessful one—I could have used some helpful counseling. I could have benefited from a *lot* of it. Hey, no one ever told me that there was a VA that offered free psychological therapy. Actually, VA did not really have it then because we were just beginning our decades-to-be battles with VA and Congress, to get them to acknowledge a couple of terms most of America was not familiar with. Those two would eventually become household words to just about anyone who was breathing—Agent Orange and PTSD.

I took my first official Agent Orange physical at the Cleveland Department of Veterans Affairs in October 2005. I opted for this because I saw it being promoted in the *Vietnam Veterans of America* magazine, which was the first time I became aware that there was such a physical...thirty-plus years after my full obligation or commitment to Uncle Sam's United States Army had been fulfilled to the U.S. Army Reserves in 1973. Keep in mind that some of the survivors of our platoon kept in touch after we were all dumped back into the real world as we used to refer to it during our pleasure stay in steamy South Vietnam. Most Nam vets just wanted to try to bury the memories of the most dreadful year or two of our entire lives. Tried to bury them. None of us knew back in the 1970s or 1980s what was in store for us in our future years—those of us who would actually live into our fifties, sixties and seventies. Of the estimated 2.8 million who served in the Vietnam War, about one million of us have not made it that far. You are reading this part correctly—one million Vietnam veterans have died very prematurely and never had the opportunity to live out to their so-called "Golden Years."

Backing up to my VA Agent Orange physical of 2005. Everything seemingly went well. Yeah, my head was badly screwed up from Nam and from the scores of car wrecks I had been in. My estimate is that I may have suffered nine or ten concussions from those car accidents. But...never was anyone else hurt or involved. All of the objects I crashed into were done "solo"—Evil Knievel style. The list of targets I drove my cars into inadvertently or "unintentionally" at speeds of one hundred miles per hour ranged from the following in no particular or favorite sequence:

- At least four telephone poles.
- Several full gainers or rolls while heading for the bottom of a ninety-foot deep ravine at a high rate of speed, of course.
- One very stationery mailbox located just a couple blocks away from my parents' house in lovely Twinsburg, Ohio.
- One very, *very* stationery pine tree with a four-foot wide trunk. One of its branches drove through my front windshield, missing me by inches.
- I count three steel guardrails that I managed to put dents into at a high rate of speed, of course. The guardrails remained in place, so I did not have to pay for them.
- Two concrete dividers. I remember my Hyundai Sonata sliding, spinning, twirling in circles during a tornado-like rainstorm, driving home from Michigan on the Ohio Turnpike and this happened only a few years ago in 2008.

Back to the Agent Orange physical of 2005. Here I go again, jumping around. Can't help it. I mentioned that the results seemed fairly positive, and I was in pretty good shape as I've always prided myself for that. But…and this was a big BUT, I just didn't know it at the time. One of the readings from the lab tests of the Agent Orange physical was noted with a small and barely legible "H" next to it. The "H" next to the reading was to suggest that this particular reading might be high. That lab test, which I fasted for as I was instructed to do, was my reading for…glucose at 151. Okay, so I had a little sugar problem. And it wasn't even mentioned to me by the VA doctor who reviewed the lab tests with me. Hey, I wasn't a doctor and I thought I felt pretty good, except for my banged up head (inside and outside), so I moved on with my life, living as I always lived and constantly taking risks, never dwelling on a high glucose reading of 151—especially since "they", the VA doctors did not consider it an issue. Today I welcome readings in the 150s.

This personal example of the educational process I received from the VA is factual. In fact, most of my readings for glucose thereafter were at least that high, which was well over the 60-120 level recommended on the VA lab test reports. I believe that today, a glucose reading at 125 or 126 is considered to be pre-diabetic, but my readings were well past that and the VA's record stayed unblemished with me as no one—no doctor, no nurse ever alerted me that…I WAS A DIABETIC.

One day I heard from another Nam veteran who said that he had received really good care at a small regional VA in Ravenna, Ohio. Heck, with that location being half the driving distance for me that the Cleveland Wake Park VA was, I requested to "take my services to South Beach." (Just kidding you, LeBron James fans from Cleveland.)

Ravenna VA was going to be where my next physical would take place. This was October 2010 I believe, and my new health-care provider was and still is Dr. Paul Fantauzzo. It was nice to know that I would be taken care of by the same health-care professional every time I went to Ravenna VA. At Cleveland's Wade Park VA, I was being seen by a different "intern" almost every time I went in, which was terribly frustrating and not much of a confidence builder that I was in good hands, but hey, it was on Uncle Sam's dime, and beggars cannot be choosy.

It was a couple days after my initial visit to Ravenna VA that I received a personal phone call from Dr. Fantauzzo. Can you believe it? An actual personal call from a VA doctor. I was impressed. He asked to see me again at my earliest convenience. He said it wasn't urgent, but he wanted to discuss my lab tests in person, not over the telephone. Myhealthvet.com was not in place at that time. I made it into see him ASAP, anxiously wondering what the news was. Usually, the VA doctors who reviewed lab test reports with me were always impressed at how great my "good" cholesterol was, especially for someone my age. As I mentioned earlier, I have always tried to keep myself in pretty good physical shape…on the outside.

When I came in for the meeting with Dr. Fantauzzo, he asked me to please sit down, that he had bad news for me. I knew that my blood pressure usually ran high, and VA was giving me medication to treat that. I could never really understand why my blood pressure read on the high side as I thought I was in pretty good shape.

"Mr. Trimmer, you are diabetic." Those were the first words out of his mouth. I did not hear a lot of what he said immediately after that as I went into a temporary daze, sitting there, wondering if this was true. Maybe there was a mistake with the recent lab test at Ravenna VA. After all, it was my first lab test at their facility. Then Dr. Fantauzzo uttered this shocker in a very sheepish, almost apologetic way…**"Mr. Trimmer, your health records show that you have had Diabetes Mellitus Type II from the very first lab test you had at VA. Hasn't anyone ever brought this to your attention?"** Wow! I was stunned into disbelief.

When I told him that there was absolutely no family history of diabetes on either side going back to my great grandparents, he said "but you were exposed to Agent Orange, weren't you, so you can and should file for service-connected disability with VA and it should be a given." Okay, so I decided to do that. So now I found out one of the reasons for my high blood pressure as diabetes does have an effect on that, as well as several other 'life threatening' illnesses.

Okay, so it is not the end of the world for me. Lots of people are diabetic, and they live normal lives if and when they get it under control and keep it under control. I still had two legs, two arms, two eyes and ears, about half a brain, a terrific wife, a loyal band of friends, wonderful family, a devoted dog, a great job with great customers, so hey…on with it!

I can only imagine how my health would be today IF the VA medical staff I counted on from 2005 to 2010 had been more alert, more caring and informed me that I was in fact a diabetic. I would most certainly have altered my lifestyle back then as I have since the official diagnosis was shared with me by the very caring Dr. Fantauzzo. What we have here is a serious case of…**communication failure** from VA to the veteran, only this time I was the victim, like so many others before me. A communication failure process that has been in place for more years than anyone can document or wants to document. This failure to communicate critically important medical information, let alone, receive actual health care itself has cost an untold number of premature deaths of veterans of every war since the Vietnam War.

Secretary Bob can fire ten thousand or one hundred thousand VA employees and that won't be the ultimate answer or remedy that will save scores of veterans who are in the dark about where to turn and who to seek help from next. Secretary Bob will not be able to help the veterans who have already been victimized by VA's inability or total disdain for communicating valuable and life-saving information and healthcare to veterans in need and their families. Okay, not his fault. He is trying very passionately to move forward. At least Secretary Bob offers something for the veteran that has been missing all these years. It is called…H-O-P-E.

I think Secretary Bob took the position of Secretary of VA because he wanted the job. He didn't need it, not like the rest of us need our jobs. He appears to have a soft spot in his heart, a genuine affection for veterans. He really truly wants to help us and we need to ease the difficulty of the seemingly impossible task he faces… by *supporting him.*

Bad news will almost always be more newsworthy to the American public, so we are the victims of our own ignorance. We dictate what the media feeds to us. We do it by our response. Heck, I can remember when Secretary Bob had been in his new position or predicament for barely two months and nearly everyone from Congress, the media and then, of course, the people in the streets were already giving up on him because he did not come in and provide them with instant action and instant terminations. Did everyone suddenly forget that the VA is part (a very large part) of the U.S. government? Bureaucracy, red tape and road blocks one after another, but everyone expects it now…instantly. Here are a few more noteworthy events that occurred under Secretary Bob's watch, but of course you would not have seen it in a mainstream media outlet:

(August 11, 2014) – Program for Homeless Vets gets $300 Million Infusion. This is a program that helps to keep tens of thousands of veterans off the streets. Is this not interesting news? Well, in a very short time, this program has grown from $100 million in 2013 to $300 million in 2014. This program is known as *Supportive Services for Veterans Families*, launched in 2012 with just $60 million in available funds.

(December 8, 2014) – Former VA Official Gets Prison for Agent Orange Benefits Scheme. David Clark was former Deputy Chief for VA at a Maryland facility. He actually retired in 2011, but has since been sentenced for fraudulently obtaining VA compensation for himself and as many as seventeen others and in some cases the claimants had served in Vietnam when they had not. Previously in May 2014, six others pleaded guilty to receiving over $500,000 in compensation as part of this scheme.

(December 17, 2014) – Ex-Palo Veterans Affairs Official Indicted in Bribery Case. Conrad Lopez Alfaro was charged for receiving illegal gratuity by a public official in an indictment handed down by a grand jury in San Jose, California. Two other VA employees have also pleaded guilty in this case as reported by Hearst newspapers.

Is there any wonder that real Vietnam veterans continue to get screwed with delays and even unfair denials in some cases with such corruption going on within the VA? We can use more watchdogs out there…lots more. Just saying. This corrupt system was solidly entrenched before Secretary Bob joined the VA. Give him a chance.

(January 26, 2015) – Secretary Bob will investigate Tomah Medical Center. He made this impressive statement to the media, "While important changes are being made to improve services to Wisconsin veterans immediately, we must ensure that we fully investigate the issues surrounding the alleged wrongdoing of possible overuse of powerful medicines and to share these lessons learned throughout our health care system." For the prompt response, I will rate him an **A-**.

(January 28, 2015) – Secretary Bob was caught red-handed at a Washington D.C. VA Medical Center…handing out coats to homeless veterans as part of a nationwide point-in-time homeless count of January and February of 2015. On a given night in the month of January 2014, it was estimated that 50,000 veterans were without safe, stable shelter in the United States. Secretary Bob is passionately involved with volunteers across the country to measure the scope of homelessness of veterans in America. Secretary Bob gets another **A**.

(April 13, 2015) – I took a small break from my watchdog activities on the VA. While I was working on other sections of this book, a few events whizzed by me regarding our Secretary Bob. One year after Phoenix, the VA is under more scrutiny than ever. They have made little headway in their fight to shorten waits for care. In many Ohio VA clinics, the percentage of veterans with long waits for treatment has stayed the same. As one can imagine, the Secretary Bob rating during the month of March-April 2015 took a hit, and I would grade his VA staff for that period, no better than a **C-**.

The news got worse as President Obama himself appointed Rob Nabors as new Chief of Staff under Secretary Bob. This undercutting move by Obama could set the progress of fixing the VA back several notches. Nabors has no experience with veterans' affairs, nor is he a veteran himself. He is just one of Obama's lemmings at the White House. Here is what one of our more outspoken veterans' advocates thinks about Nabor's appointment:

"We at Concerned Veterans for America truly sympathize with VA Secretary McDonald for being forced to accept a complete undercutting of his authority, which we highly doubt he had any say in. And we'd like to thank the White House for finally bringing Rob Nabors out from the shadows and admitting who's really running the show at the VA."
- (Source: Concerned Veterans for America, April 10, 2015)

On that unfortunate but necessary statement, I will just say that you let us down here, Secretary Bob, and your past few weeks have earned you a very average rating.

Just like Secretary Bob, I also have a burning passionate desire to help our veteran brothers and sisters from any war to take their lives up a notch or salvage it from imminent disaster. Taking one's own life is an ugly subject to try and discuss with someone. It should be no secret to any American able to read that the suicide rate for veterans, any veteran who has witnessed grotesque death in a war is a problem that is not going away very soon. Multiply the trauma for someone who is forced to watch a buddy wasted, and you are helpless to do anything about it. It is not uncommon for some veterans to take their own lives because they suffer a guilt complex in that they survived and their buddies did not. The medical community actually refers to this condition as Survivor's Guilt.

The ways in which *Condemned Property?* has impacted so many who have read it might be the "second" most gratifying feeling of my entire life. The first most gratifying feeling is…knowing I helped save lives in life-threatening combat in Vietnam. I will never forget that indescribable feeling. What a flush of adrenalin it is. Writing *Condemned Property?* was a three and a half year journey I often thought about taking on since I came home from Vietnam. I will keep going for as long as the Lord above allows me to and nourishes me with the energy and right messages for our veteran buddies.

Payback Time! can have a similar impact on someone's life as my first book did. I am counting on it to turn someone around who was near the bottom in his or her daily struggle to carry on. I've been down that lonely and terrifying road and no doubt, I am acquainted with several others who have as well. Some of them did not make it. If I can put out one book that reaches a few thousand people and it impacts a dozen of them…enough to lift their spirits to carry on the fight, then I need to write more books I hope to reach a lot more than a few thousand. **The stories in the first and second book needed to be told and there remain many more that need to be told.**

CHAPTER 14

CHAMPIONS FOR VETERANS!

Freedom is never more than one generation away from extinction. It is never passed on genetically to our children. It must be fought for, protected, earned, and then handed over to them to do it all over again, or one day Americans will spend our sunset years telling the next generation's children what it was once like in the USA when men and women were free.

- Ronald Reagan
President of the United States

I had to position this very important chapter near the end of my book, as some of the heroes' stories kept making headlines as I was trying to finish *Payback Time!* That is what makes writing and "organizing" a book like this so difficult. As you have surmised long before this, my books are not typical, and they do not have plots. Actually, there could be several books within each of my first two books, which provides me with ammunition to consider for future books... God willing.

Veterans of all wars still hanging in there should appreciate this chapter as my tribute to Champions for Veterans may surprise, disappoint, enlighten and might make you do something you have not done in awhile...smile. My Champion for Veterans chapter just had to start with someone who has made millions of people around the world smile. We lost him in 2014, and that was a horrible loss for all who loved him...Robin Williams.

How will we remember Robin Williams? His shocking death by his own doing? Let's not do that, please. I even regret mentioning it. *People* Magazine featured him on the cover of their December 29, 2014 with this headline, "A Legacy of Love". That was fitting. The one celebrity comedian, actor and great American that Robin Williams should make many veterans relate with is an icon who has been referred to as...entertainer of the "century", Leslie Towns Hope, known to the world as Bob Hope. The great white Hope was not a perfect human being by any stretch of the imagination, but veterans of World War II, Korea and Vietnam would defend him with their lives. In fact, Mr. Hope had to be defended during a couple of his tours in Vietnam. It seems the Viet Cong had little respect for his inspirational antics. In *Condemned Property?* (Yes, I mentioned that book again.), pretty much an entire chapter is dedicated to Mr. Hope and...a little known hero, Chris Noel.

Robin Williams—come on, give me a break. No one should be allowed to be that entertaining and funny. Some nights, I could not get to sleep because I would suddenly burst out laughing from a TV performance I had viewed that day. This did not bode well for two family members, my lovely wife, Ginny and our terrific BIG dog, Bella. You see, they cannot distinguish whether I am having a nightmare, experiencing a hallucination or something else when I just blurt out loud laughter from my bed.

Robin McLaurin Williams, born July 21, 1951, deceased on August 11, 2014... seems like yesterday, doesn't it? He was known for *Mork & Mindy*, *Popeye*, *The World According to Garp*, *Good Morning Vietnam*, *Dead Poets Society*, *Awakenings*, *The Fisher King*, *Aladdin*, *Good Will Hunting*, *One Hour Photo*, *Mrs. Doubtfire*, *Jumanji*, *The Birdcage*, and *Night at the Museum*. Oh, for Pete's sake, this man was barely into his sixties, and we have lost him. What a bummer. Most of us "older people" might remember him from his early stand-up comic days, especially his *Saturday Night Live* appearances. I remember those. How was he able to talk so fast and think so fast while performing live on-stage in front of thousands or millions? It might be that he was comfortable with who he was during those performances, and he thoroughly enjoyed what he was doing rather than being afraid of it.

Robin Williams performed on USO tours from 2002 to 2013. Where did he find the time and energy? He brought nothing but smiles and laughter. Once he was reportedly seen turning himself loose during a 2007 USO Chairman's Holiday Tour where he jumped over a barrier and a fence, ran through a field (it was a war zone) to simply...shake hands, thank and hug some military guys who waved to him during one of his performances.

As I gather from my research into his life, he seemed to take an extra liking to his USO tours to entertain and mingle with America's military. In fact, he took it very personally. I read where a USO entertainment team estimated that Robin performed for or visited personally with nearly 100,000 service members during his twelve plus years of volunteering for the USO. Many of today's veterans (and some older ones) now refer to Robin Williams as the...modern day Bob Hope.

There has never been anything I have enjoyed more than traveling with the USO and giving back to our troops in whatever way I can.

- Robin Williams, 2007

Good morning, Vietnam!

Pat Sajak (Wheel of Fortune)

I was compelled to mention this great American Vietnam Veteran in this section. During my exhaustive and costly marketing campaign to celebrities, mostly known to be conservatives, only Pat Sajak responded back to me. It was a simple, but heartfelt personal note to me, which read:

July 17, 2014

Dear Dusty—
Congratulations on your most recent timely book. I hope things are going well and that we can all continue to speak out on this important topic!
Best,
Pat

In 2009, Pat Sajak was selected as one of the recipients of the Vietnam Veterans of America (VVA) Excellence in the Arts Award. Sajak went to Vietnam at the worst time, in 1968 during multiple Tet Offensives. Almost immediately, he became the disc jockey at Armed Forces Radio very popular morning show called "Good Morning Vietnam!" He remained there for one and a half years until his discharge in 1970. His heart is still with those who served in the Vietnam War and he has proven this many times. Thank you, Pat.

Colonel David H. Hackworth (U.S. Army, Deceased)

If he were alive today, the Department of Veterans Affairs would never be able to handle or comprehend what had hit them. I am referring to a man who has been called the "Patton of the Vietnam War," and he didn't even have a tank. Dear readers, this man is none other than…Colonel David H. Hackworth. "Hack", as those close to him affectionately called him, was not only the Vietnam War's most highly decorated hero by some accounts, but also America's second most highly decorated warrior behind the legendary General Douglas MacArthur. Not bad, finishing second to MacArthur, especially for a "mere" Vietnam War veteran. This real American hero was honored with more decorations and awards than this section can print. To give you an idea:

253

- Eight Purple Hearts
- Ten Silver Stars
- Two Distinguished Service Crosses
- Four Legion of Merits
- Eight Bronze Stars
- Four Army Commendation Medals – Valor

Tons more, not to mention being nominated for the Medal of Honor...more than once. But politics and jealousy among his peers has put a long stall on getting the approval. Hack has said often that the single award or medal that he treasured most was the award that only a grunt in the trenches could qualify for, the Combat Infantryman Badge. To qualify:

- **Serve in a front-line combat infantry unit for ninety days under constant fire and...live through it!**

Having the distinguished opportunity to meet Hack at one of Kokomo, Indiana's welcome home events for Vietnam veterans, I was able to get a fairly good understanding of what he was about, where he had been and where he wanted to go next. Hack did not ever have the opportunity to get to where he wanted to go next as he left us much too early. And it was the Vietnam War and Agent Orange that brought him down in 2005.

Very few officers in America's wars made the rank of Colonel and kept it if they were openly critical of the decisions of people above him. Then again, I guess that is why he never made General. Hack constantly challenged the strategy of his superior officers during the Vietnam War. In fact, he viewed many of them as "perfumed princes" in that they were far more concerned with their next promotion than the safety and welfare of the troops that fought in front, alongside and behind them...keeping them alive for that next promotion. Hack battled with President Bush and his administration for their strategy in Iraq and Afghanistan. After all, he did fight in combat in two wars for seven years in the trenches with his men.

Few things would set Hack off quicker than seeing the grunts get the short end of the stick. In the latter years of his life, he became more devoted to making sure soldiers got what they needed, what they deserved. He hesitated not in calling out the phonies after a promotion who sent the combat grunts off on dubious missions. Hackworth was buried with full military honors in Arlington National Cemetery on May 31, 2005. That does not seem that long ago, as I remember when and how he died...from his Agent Orange and Agent Blue caused illness. Thanks, Hack, you were truly the "real deal". We are truly in need of a reincarnation of your kind.

Hack, one of my personal favorite champions, fought in and survived three wars only to be killed by the last one, the Vietnam War…thirty-four years after it allegedly ended. He died of cancers caused by his exposure to a weapon that was used by our own country…Agents Orange and Blue. Hack never lost a battle during his twenty-six year military career in those three wars until his final battle with cancer. One of Hack's famous quotes seems very appropriate today, so I will share it.

There are two groups of Americans who support the American troops…those who stick ribbon magnets on their SUVs and talk about backing them, while staying at a safe distance away from the troops. Then there are the Americans who work at it to make sure that our troops are felt appreciated. These are people unafraid to actually talk to them and utter these words—THANK YOU.

\- Col. David Hackworth
Veteran of WWII, Korea, Vietnam

I found this information in the April 2014 issue of *VFW Magazine*. The article was written by Robert Widener. I enjoyed it and I was quite surprised at the results. Excerpts of Widener's article follows:

Through the years, military historians and amateurs alike have touted different individuals as being the most highly decorated serviceman of all time. But their conclusions varied as much as the methods they used. It left the question more unanswered than ever. That is, until Erich Anderson took up the task.

"Often times you hear that this person or that person was the most highly decorated soldier of WWII or Vietnam, or whatever time period they are talking about," said Anderson, an Army and Air Force veteran and amateur military historian. "The only problem is that the way this is determined is never really explained."

Posted on Anderson's website, www.veterantributes.org is a comprehensive list of the top 50 highly decorated medals recipients from the Civil War to the present. The rankings are based on a point system Anderson developed that assigns a value to each award. It is loosely based on the military's promotion point system.

Anderson's effort substantiates once and for all, who is the most decorated serviceman. It also allows other heroes to be in the spotlight for their valor, as well as making interesting comparisons between wars.

AMERICA'S TOP 50 MOST DECORATED
REGARDLESS OF HIGHEST DECORATION

1.	Gen. Douglas MacArthur	USA	WWI, WWII, Korea, Cold War, Other
2.	Col. David H. Hackworth	USA	WWII, Korea, Vietnam
3.	Lt. Gen. James F. Hollingsworth	USA	WWII, Vietnam
4.	Col. Edward V. Rickenbacker	USAAS	WWI
5.	Lt. Gen. Thomas M. Tackaberry	USA	WWII, Korea, Cold War, Vietnam
6.	Brig. Gen. John T. Corley	USA	WWII, Korea, Cold War
7.	Vice Adm. John D. Bulkeley	USN	WWII, Korea, Cold War
8.	CDR Samuel D. Dealey	USN	WWII
9.	Sgt. Maj. Daniel J. Daly	USMC	WWI, Other
10.	Col. James H. Kasler	USAF	WWII, Korea, Cold War, Vietnam
11.	BG Charles E. Getz	USA	Cold War, Vietnam
12.	Lt. Gen. Lewis B. Puller	USA	WWI, WWII, Korea, Cold War, Other
13.	Gen. John C. Meyer	USAF	WWII, Korea, Cold War
14.	Col. David C. Schilling	USAF	WWII, Cold War
15.	Col. Robert L. Howard	USA	Vietnam
16.	Gen. James A. Van Fleet	USA	WWII, Cold War
17.	RADM Eugene B. Fluckey	USN	WWII, Cold War
18.	RADM Richard H. O'Kane	USN	WWII, Cold War
19.	Gen. William E. DePuy	USA	WWII, Vietnam, Other
20.	Col. Francis S. Gabreski	USAF	WWII, Korea, Cold War
21.	Maj. Thomas B. McGuire, Jr.	USAAF	WWII
22.	VADM James B. Stockdale	USN	Vietnam, Cold War
23.	Gen. Alexander M. Haig, Jr.,	USA	Korea, Cold War, Vietnam
24.	Col. James C. Harding	USAF	Cold War, Vietnam
25.	Maj. Gen. Smedley D. Butler	USMC	WWI, Other
26.	MG Patrick H. Brady	USA	Cold War, Vietnam
27.	VADM Joel T. Boone	USN	WWI, WWII, Korea, Cold War
28.	Maj. Gen Frank O. Hunter	USAAF	WWI, WWII, Cold War
29.	Brig. Gen. R. Stephen Ritchie	USAF	Cold War, Vietnam
30.	Col. Ralph S. Parr, Jr.	USAF	WWII, Korea, Cold War, Vietnam

31.	RADM Roy M. Davenport	USN	WWII, Korea
32.	Maj. Richard I. Bong	USAAF	WWII
33.	Col. Jack L. Treadwell	USA	WWII, Cold War, Vietnam
34.	Col. Chester J. Hirschfelder	USA	WWI, WWII
35.	RADM James B. Linder	USN	WWII, Korea, Cold War, Vietnam
36.	Gen. Barry R. McCaffrey	USA	Vietnam, Persian Gulf, Other
37.	Maj. Gen Robert M. White	USAF	WWII, Korea, Cold War, Vietnam
38.	Gen. Creighton W. Abrams, Jr.	USA	WWII, Korea, Vietnam
39.	LTG Edward M. Almond	USA	WWII, Korea, Cold War
40.	ADM Bernard A. Clarey	USN	WWII, Cold War, Vietnam, Other
41.	Col. George E. Day	USAF	Vietnam
42.	Lt. Col. George A. Davis, Jr.	USAF	WWII, Korea
43.	Col. William T. Whisner	USAF	WWII, Korea, Cold War, Vietnam
44.	Lt. Gen. John P. Flynn	USAF	WWII, Korea, Cold War, Vietnam, Other
45.	Brig. Gen. Robin Olds	USAF	WWII, Korea, Vietnam
46.	Gen. H. Norman Schwarzkopf	USA	Vietnam, Persian Gulf
47.	LTG Welborn G. Dolvin	USA	WWII, Korea, Cold War
48.	Col. Leo K. Thorsness	USAF	Cold War, Vietnam
49.	Col. Donald J.M. Blakeslee	USAF	WWII, Korea, Cold War
50.	Brig. Gen. Paul P. Douglas	USAF	WWII, Cold War, Vietnam

An interesting, if not very impressive, statistic or fact about this list of ultimate heroes and champions is that more than half of them (54%) served in that conflict, which was eventually, named the Vietnam War. How many Americans would know that?

Where do I go from here in discussing and paying deserved credit to today's champions? The list is too long to give them the space in my book that they deserve. So I will pay tribute to a small sample in no particular order of significance. All veterans from any war should be grateful for these champions of America's veterans of foreign wars. I hope you will enjoy this journey of mine to recognize these patriotic Americans who have been fighting for our future welfare.

Gary Sinise (Lieutenant Dan)

Too bad the Lt. Dan Band and Robin Williams didn't team up for some special performances for a military or veteran audience. Maybe they did, and I just missed it.

When I think about the life and sufferings of Christ, when I think about the stories of the extreme hardships and heavy burdens that our military men and women and their families were willing to and continue to bear, I can't help but think about this verse, "For greater love hath no man than this, that he lay down his life for his friends."

- Gary Sinise

Gary had been involved with supporting Vietnam veterans since he hosted a Vets' Night in the 1980s. But he has stated that the recognition he received at the 1994 Disabled Americans Veteran National Convention in Chicago is what really influenced his beginning of a lifelong endeavor to honor America's military and its veterans. On that evening in 1994, Gary was presented with the DAV National Commanders Award mainly for his role as Lt. Dan, a wounded, disabled soldier in the movie *Forrest Gump*. By the way, that movie was not negative toward Vietnam veterans like so many before; it honored us and showed some of the sacrifices we made to make sure we never left our own behind.

The 1970s and 1980s were filled with ghastly newspaper, television and radio reports of violent crimes by people who "just happened to be" veterans of the Vietnam War. Well, maybe the criminal was someone who was related to a Vietnam War veteran, or maybe the criminal knew a Vietnam War veteran…good enough for the media to sign off on convicting the alleged offender. Of course, it usually made the evening news as to how another Vietnam War veteran went… berserk in public.

Guess what, folks? While most Vietnam War veterans were attempting to find ways to get over that war and lead a somewhat normal life, there were those Vietnam veterans who were not dealing well with the society that America handed to them when they came home. And the inflated or over-exaggerated news reports about one Vietnam veteran after another turning himself loose on society hit home with those Nam vets who were "human time bombs" and required little stimulation to cut loose, which many did. The Vietnam Syndrome continued to grow from coast to coast throughout the 1980s and 1990s.

What about NOW? Certainly the Vietnam Syndrome had faded out by the 2010s, right? I mean, who the hell gives a rat's ass about a war and its "victims" that took place back in 1960 to 1970? When half of today's Americans had not been born yet! What about NOW? How about accurate history? How about a fair and respectful **legacy?** From heartbreak to hope, even at our age because…**IT IS NEVER TOO LATE!**

Our aging warriors need and deserve unprecedented attention, TLC and support from Americans…who will answer the call? We are all getting older. What is scaring me is the thought that many of my aging veteran buddies will need to be cared for in their homes…including this author. I am prepared to chip in. I have been chipping in, and I will continue to chip in. Will you?

Here is a guy who is still "chipping in" and he is a couple years older than all of you…he is one hundred eight year old former POW, U.S. Army veteran Richard Overton who is the state of Texas' oldest living World War II veteran. Rumors say that Overton walks around without a cane, let alone a walker. He smokes cigars and still drinks whiskey (God bless brother Overton). He was contained in a small tiger cage during the Vietnam War for ten months in Cambodia. Overton has certainly answered the call as he remains vocally active in support of all veterans. I will leave you and move onto the next chapter from an interview with Overton on November 11, 2014:

Most veterans are just looking to have someone reaffirm that what they did was an honorable thing to do.

– Richard Overton
Veteran, World War II, Vietnam War

There I go again, unleashing my emotions, passion and anger as I have done throughout both of my books. How the hell can I prevent it? I wander off often in my daily thoughts, wondering if I could have done more to help expose the VA's crimes. What if I had written *Condemned Property?* ten years ago—what if? Would Americans have cared about our story then in the 1990s before 9/11 happened? I'll never know. So at the tender age of seventy years old, with one ischemic stroke behind me and other sporadic eruptions of Agent Orange influenced illnesses to contend with on a daily basis, I have elected to…march off to do battle using the most powerful weapon available to me called…**the freedom of speech and expression.**

Today's Bravehearts! I have mentioned an assortment of champions in this chapter from past eras and a few who are still battling for us. Recently, two super champion bravehearts have exploded onto the battlefield. What battlefield? The battlefield to…SAVE AMERICA…the battlefield to…TAKE BACK AMERICA.

I am going to finish this chapter by mentioning just two more of America's up-and-coming bravehearts who have shown no fear in speaking their minds in profound ways that get people's attention...Trey Gowdy and Pete Hegseth. I mentioned earlier that many of today's politicians are wimpy. They just go with the flow, which is not how the United States of America became the greatest country in the history of the world (yes, I believe that). America's endless generosity continues to substantiate this, although some fanatical idiots would have you believe that America is just a big-time "bully", always imposing its will on weaker countries. Of course, that is often a liberal's viewpoint.

Many of our country's past presidents became great leaders—more of them than we can give credit. If I were to name them from my point of view, my list would contain a balanced representation from either political party. I doubt if many of the "die-hards" from those parties would agree with me, but that is how I see it. One thing is certain in my mind—the man that so many Americans elected into the White House for the last two terms...for the list of great American leaders, Obama is not one of those we like to refer to as a braveheart.

Trey Gowdy just destroyed the Obama administration and Democrats with one short speech. On January 16, 2015, I watched the video of House Representative Trey Gowdy doing the thing he has become highly famous for simply by using his brain, his mouth and his right to exercise his freedom of expression. Oh, I have listened to this rising great American several times before this brief speech and I do not know how anyone could not be impressed by him, regardless of his or her political brainwashing. Anyone can research Gowdy's performances online, and if he continues his outspoken, patriotic, straight-talking fact supported by Constitutional law, his name could be on every American's mind, of those who care. Trey Gowdy should be every Vietnam veteran's champion. He should be on every veteran's champion list, regardless of what war he or she participated in.

Here is a partial blurb from Gowdy's speech that I listened to on January 16, 2015, taken from his website:

Representative Trey Gowdy (R-South Carolina) today voted for H.R. 240, legislation to fund the Department of Homeland Security and stop President Obama's overreaching executive action on immigration.

"Extra-constitutional acts, regardless of motive, warrant the full breadth of constitutional response. Otherwise, there is a precedent for the executive branch to ignore the process and acquire by fiat what the legislative branch rejects," Gowdy said. "The fact that previous administrations may have also acted in an extra-constitutional way does not mitigate the act. Rather the legislative branch should collectively reassert the equilibrium upon which this country was founded and defended.

"As Senator, Obama rallied against executive overreach. As President, he asserted more than 20 times that he lacked the legal standing to do what he did. His position may have changed, but the text of the constitution has not. In this country, the end does not justify the means. Process matters. As a prosecutor, I saw confessions thrown out of court on technical violations. When a President fails to follow the constitutional process, the remedy should be just as certain."

We are blessed with so many; I cannot begin to name them all. This is why I have dedicated this special chapter for you and me to discuss our Veterans' Champions. These heroes are finishing up so many of the projects that you bravely pioneered. I was compelled to add this chapter.

Who is my next Veteran's Champion? Come on—I have only a couple hundred pages to work with here. Heck, I could have reached my limit on Robin Williams alone. Here are some more of my personal contemporary favorite Champions for Veterans:

Oliver North	Jeff Miller
Ann Margret	Allen West
Denzel Washington	Michael Gallagher
Charlie Daniels	Sean Hannity
American Legion	Laura Ingraham
Michael Medved	Megyn Kelly
Fox News	Glenn Beck
The U.S. Congress	Dennis Praeger
Montel Williams	Ann Coulter
Concerned Veterans for America	Rand Paul
House Committee on Veteran Affairs	

To culminate this chapter, one of my personal favorites for justifiable praise, and to whom I perceive as one of the ultimate Champions for Veterans is…Pete Hegseth. Never heard of Pete Hegseth? Wake up. Get out from underneath your shell. This guy has been everywhere for the past couple of years. I've seen him in person, met him, and watched him on Fox News dozens of times. I am not sure that he has any time left in his life for anything but being a Veterans' Champion. Please check this guy out. He is awesomely putting himself out there for us.

Pete Hegseth's accomplishments for veterans over the past few years has been utterly mind-boggling. This short testimonial won't do the justice he deserves, but I had to give it a try. Hegseth can be seen often on Fox News, rightfully so. His background is impressive—bachelor's degree from Princeton University and a master's degree from Harvard. He is the CEO of Concerned Veterans for America (CVA), with which I have had some interaction. Prior to this, he was the director of another company with similar goals, Veterans for Freedom. You can get an idea of where his heart is and where his mind is going. He is on our side for sure.

Hegseth is a U.S. Army veteran. He was an infantry platoon leader at Guantanamo Bay. He volunteered to serve in Afghanistan and Iraq and served as an infantry platoon leader again. Hegseth earned several awards for bravery and honor and attained the rank of a captain.

Since their earliest beginnings, Concerned Veterans for America has made its position clear—that they were formed to serve as a watchdog of the corrupt and beleaguered Department of Veterans Affairs. (VA has done more than their share in harassing, pressuring and in some cases, launching well-planned attacks on them.) In a nutshell, my dear war buddies, we would not have seen the havoc that was raised with VA in 2014 without Pete Hegseth's group of patriots. Please do not forget his name...Pete Hegseth, a true Champion for Veterans.

If someone or some organization is not user-friendly towards our country's veterans, rest assured that they or it will not be spared from receiving a call from CVA's strike team or a hotly worded written communication from Hegseth himself. Even if your name just happens to be...Barack Hussein Obama and you are the President of the United States, you will not be immune from Hegseth and his band of veteran advocates.

I would see Hegseth as a really good Secretary of Defense or Secretary of State someday...or higher. In the meantime, count on it that his organization will be out there for us with a task force, addressing existing problems, identifying solutions and proposing reforms that will continue to improve healthcare for America's veterans of all wars. Please support them or...join them. (www.concernedveteransforamerica.org)

Every morning I begin my day by checking Hegseth's newsletter, *The Morning FRAGO*, sponsored by Concerned Veterans for America. *The Morning FRAGO* is a daily aggregation of top stories, articles of interest, CVA media and happenings in D.C. Hegseth's highly dedicated staff is all about this—fixing veterans' health care. Here is a copy of one of his letters, which Hegseth endorses us to share:

Roland,

This morning, Military Times published an exclusive "first look" article on our Fixing Veterans Health Care Taskforce -- and the half-day Summit we are excited to announce next week.

As you can see, our reform efforts are gathering momentum. Take a look:

> When officials from Concerned Veterans for America hold their summit on veterans health care next month, lawmakers will be listening.
>
> **The event, scheduled for Feb. 26, will feature the unveiling of the group's almost five-month review into the Veterans Affairs Department's health care offerings**, designed to offer a blueprint for internal reforms and legislative action.
>
> The effort has been led by former Republican Senate Majority Leader Dr. Bill Frist, former Georgia Democratic congressman Jim Marshall, and former VA undersecretary for health Mike Kussman.
>
> And the work -- still incomplete -- has drawn interest from several Capitol Hill offices, where the issues of VA bureaucracy and veterans health care have gained extra attention in the wake of last year's scandals over patient wait times and records manipulation.
>
> House Majority Leader **Kevin McCarthy**, R-Calif., House Veterans' Affairs Committee Chairman **Jeff Miller**, R-Fla., and Sen. **Joe Manchin**, D-W.Va., have already announced plans to participate in the event. Other lawmakers are expected to follow in coming weeks.
>
> CVA officials say they're confident the report won't end up just another dusty, unread tome on congressional shelves.
>
> **"Our goal is to put the veteran at the center of all of these discussions,** not to undermine the current system," said Pete Hegseth, the group's CEO. "But we know there's no way you create something meaningful that isn't going to tick someone off."

You can read the whole piece here.

For our Veterans and our Country,

Pete Hegseth
CEO, *Concerned Veterans for America*
Army Veteran of Iraq, Afghanistan, and Guantanamo Bay
@PeteHegseth | @ConcernedVets

⟳ FORWARD TO
A FRIEND

Jeff Miller and the House Committee on Veterans Affairs

Those of you who are not familiar with them or just don't think they do much for veterans, shame on you. I have written to every member of this pro-American veterans group—everyone—at least three times or more just in 2013-2014. As I mentioned earlier, many of them have been quite responsive and seemingly appreciative that I wrote to them. Several of them have read my first book and I am confident that even more of them will read this one.

Chairman of the committee is Jeff Miller, a Florida Congressman who has been pleasantly sympathetic to our problems and surprisingly responsive to my letters. He encourages us to contact his office with our concerns and our horror stories. If the VA becomes indignant or resentful to you because you have brought Jeff Miller's committee into your situation, by all means, let Miller and his group know whatever details you can provide about that too. Retaliation, red-flagging or blackballing a veteran for seeking benefits will be viewed as a serious matter by the entire House Committee on Veterans Affairs. I personally know this for a fact.

Jeff Miller was sworn in as the Congressman of the First Congressional District in Florida in October of 2001. In 2010, the people of Northwest Florida sent Congressman Miller back to Washington for a sixth term. After taking the oath of office in 2001, Congressman Miller was appointed to the House Armed Services Committee and the Committee on Veterans Affairs. He has quickly established himself within Washington as a strong advocate for veterans' concerns and immediately supported and acted on policy changes such as a greater co-sharing between the military veterans and veterans' clinics. In 2011, Miller became the Chairman of the House Committee on Veterans Affairs. The Committee on Veterans Affairs is responsible for authorization and oversight of the Department of Veterans Affairs (VA), the second largest department in the federal government with over 300,000 employees and a budget of over $120 billion for 2016. Congressman Miller also serves on the North Atlantic Treaty Organization Parliamentary Assembly (NATO PA), where he serves as Vice Chairman of the subcommittee on Transatlantic Defense and Security Cooperation. Since coming to Congress, Miller has established himself as one of the staunchest conservatives in the White House. He has championed numerous tax relief and veterans' measures and fought for less government.

The House Committee on Veterans Affairs has, I believe at last count, twenty-two members, fourteen Republicans and eight Democrats. In case you do not know who they are, here is the list I have on file:

Republicans
Jeff Miller (FL), Chairman
Doug Lamborn (CO)
Gus M. Bilirakis (FL), Vice Chairman
David P. Roe (TN)
Dan Benishek (MI)
Tim Huelskamp (KS)
Mike Coffman (CO)
Brad Wenstrup (OH)
Jackie Walorski (IN)
Ralph Abraham (LA)
Lee Zeldin (NY)
Ryan Costello (PA)
Amata Radewagen (AS)
Mike Bost (IL)

Democrats
Corrine Brown (FL)
Mark Takano (CA)
Julia Brownley (CA)
Dina Titus (NV)
Raul Ruiz (CA)
Ann McLane Kuster (CA)
Beto O'Rourke (TX)
Kathleen Rice (NY)

Most of these fine representatives also believe that securing our border and *stopping* Obama's executive amnesty is a national security priority. They believe that we must stop Obama's damaging actions before he leaves office, before they magnify out of proportion.

Also in closing this chapter, please get to know every veteran in Congress. There are eighty veterans in the U.S. House of Representatives at this time. Please don't be a stranger to them. Okay, veterans—Korea, Vietnam, Gulf War, Iraq, Afghanistan veterans, let's...STRIKE BACK! Seek and pursue what we have earned and deserve...*Payback Time!* is here and from here on out. (Feel free to contact us anytime—we are all veterans.)

Veterans Strike Back LLC
Earl "Dusty" Trimmer, Managing Partner
John "Jack" Bellemy, Managing Partner
Daniel "Danny" McGinnis, Managing Partner
Richard Arceci, Managing Partner
Hans "Pete" Funk, Partner
J.R. Wager, Partner
Address: P.O. Box 500, Twinsburg, OH 44087
Email: dustytrimmer@yahoo.com

Veterans Strike Back LLC is not a 501(c)3 not for profit or charitable organization, but all contributions or investments help us to continue what we do.

VOTE "RIGHT" in 2016!

CHAPTER 15

STRESSFUL OR...THERAPEUTIC?

Throughout my second book, there are references to my first book, *Condemned Property?* and rightfully so, as one book is connected to the other. They complement each other. I thought that the best way to make the connection from my first book to my second book would be to share some of the comments from those who read *Condemned Property?* from cover to cover (at least once)—all 464 pages. So here they are, abbreviated versions quoted in their exact words. These are their stories, not mine.

In just a few hours I have spent with your book so far—holy shit, you really put together a fine book, 460 pages? Pix galore, a Table of Contents, Prologue, serious detailed, specific first person accounts of specific locations, actions, results and the images—wow—they will stay forever in the readers' minds. Dusty, you have honored all men who served in Nam with the persistence, dedication, the endurance, the stamina and yes, the valor of those who swore to defend our country. You and others like you are the strength and the goodness of America. We are honored to serve side by side with you. I am honored to know you. *Condemned Property?* tells the tale and that is in itself an honest book. Norman Mailer's *Naked and the Dead* was criticized for its stream of consciousness, and yet the book became a classic. I mean this; you should do something even more noble than the book like advocating for our brother and sister veterans against the VA. I am dead serious on this. I sense Americans are moving towards facing the broken VA system— your passionately written book influenced a few over to our side, like some in Congress. Bravo, Dusty! I bought a place in Montana with my son. Love to have you and your wife up sometime as guests. In the meantime, keep the heat on VA.

- Pacho (Polish Prince), Vietnam Veteran
U.S. Army – Stars & Stripes Reporter
Author, *Night Flares*

Once I began reading, it was hard to put it down. Your book, *Condemned Property?* brought out what I never want to forget about this country, those men and those times. Most importantly, I have never forgotten my friends and acquaintances who died in Vietnam and I think of them all the time. Some of them probably never even kissed a girl yet, or owned a souped up car yet or never lived even a small part of their dreams. Dusty, your book had a great impact on me, as I am sure it did on a lot of other Nam vets. More than I can tell you in this letter, I thank you for what you did back in those troubled 60s as a soldier and what you have volunteered to take on today for us. If it ever becomes the right time in a conversation with my Vietnam buddies, I'll most certainly mention *Condemned Property?* to them as well as to others who need to know the truth. We owe this to the living and to the dead…and the generations that follow.

- Joe Martanovic
Vietnam Veteran
Vice President, Ostendorf-Morris Company

I contacted the author of *Condemned Property?* sometime in August 2014. I needed to meet this Nam brother who in his gut wrenching book has moved me like no other Nam book has done before. My wife and I were calling it quits at this time and I was going to reinvent myself somewhere, someplace IF I came to a decision on whether I could continue living or not. The first reading of Dusty's moving book helped put a hold on my plans to evaporate from the planet. Dusty's story gave me a new dose of something I thought was gone for me…hope. I am actively into the second reading of his book and I suspect it will remain a reference tool and a motivational boost from time to time in the future. I do feel like there will be a future for me. At least for the time being, I plan to stay around awhile longer.

- C.K., Special Forces
Vietnam (1966-1967)

I found it difficult to believe that *Condemned Property?* was Dusty Trimmer's first attempt at the monumental task of writing a book, especially one with such a sensitive subject—for himself as well as his target audience. To his credit, he presented staggering descriptions that cut to the heart of the combat experience: the fear and the belligerence, the quiet insights and raging madness, the lasting friendships and sudden deaths. Yet the book is much, much more. The book differs from most Vietnam War tomes. It does not have a plot. However, what it does more importantly, is bear witness to the things men do in war and the things war does to men. To dramatize his points, Trimmer shares many of his own personal experiences, observations, concerns and sentimental feelings. This book moved me.

- Michael Christy
Army Vietnam Veteran
Editor, Togetherweserved.com

Dusty, I found your book disjointed structurally—hold on—I also found your book to be a parallel with the Vietnam War as it too was ever so disjointed. Accident or intentional, your book is much more credible than anything that would have originated from a seasoned writer. Honestly, Dusty, this is the beauty of your book; it is raw, unscripted, without plot and from your heart. Nobody else could have written this but you.

- B.W.
U.S. Marines
Vietnam (1970-1971)

Hello Brother Dusty,

When I came into Bravo Company 3rd 22nd, I was welcomed into my new platoon by several recovering wounded soldiers, telling me two completely different stories. One version—they told me when I go out to the bush (Michelin Rubbers) to take plenty of reading material because it can get real boring out there. They told me this as their wounds were oozing through their bandaged heads. Another bit of brotherly advice was to leave the reading material back at base camp and carry as much extra ammo as I could possibly carry, as I would surely need it. I took only one small book and several extra bandoleers of M-16 ammo with five grenades. That was all I could carry along with a poncho, c-rations, etc. Little did I know that this visit to the Nam boonies would not be anything like the weekend stays in the state-side boonies that was part of our training in basic and advanced training camps. You mention eighty-eight days out there. Well my first stay away from all the conveniences of home—that base camp offered—was only forty straight days and I hoped they would never do that to us again. I was ready to go home after those forty days. Take me, please take me, I thought.

I never got a chance to read that one book while I was out there for what seemed like a full year, but unfortunately, I would still have about 320 days left to endure on my tour. We had quite a few firefights with Charley during those forty days. It was just too much fun to sit down and read a boring and fictional book. Check out the Bravo Company website, www.bravoregulars.com. In the action pictures section, check out the ones I donated because I think you are in one of them in the top left photo. You have my permission to use any of those photos. Thanks for putting together such a good rendering of what we went through in Vietnam. I hope your book opens a lot of eyes. I plan on taking an extra copy to my VA doctor.

- Brother Steve
B Co 3/22nd 25th Infantry
U.S. Army, Vietnam (1968-1969)

Dear Dusty,

I was about one hundred pages into your book *Condemned Property?* and was compelled to contact you. I feel like I have been your shadow for the past forty-five years. I can relate so much to your story. I am Tom Petty of Yukon, Oklahoma. I served with the 11th Light Infantry Brigade of the Americal Division in I Corp in 1969-1970.

In 1975, I woke up on a cold stainless steel x-ray table in the hospital, having been transported to the hospital by ambulance from a car wreck. The hospital had called my wife and she had arrived before I came to. The hospital workers had brought her in to try to orient me to where I was. Evidently, I thought I had been wounded again and was in a hospital in Nam again. I had been asking the hospital workers who else had been wounded and if anybody had been killed. The hospital workers were all freaked out and hoping my wife could get me to the present, which she did. I too, went through about fifteen jobs in twenty years. I was also drinking heavily. I got sober on 8/28/88. Although I got sober, nothing else changed. I still had trouble sleeping, issues with anger and sorrow, and issues with authority. That prompted me to seek help. I got plugged in at the local Vet Center. They helped me file paperwork for disability for some nerve damage that had occurred when I was wounded in the neck in '69. They also steered me toward the post office to seek a job. I was hired as a letter carrier. Then in 1996, I started having discipline problems at work. My union steward suggested I go see a counselor at the employee assistance place. I did. The guy there started having sessions with me. He was all psychobabble, but to me it was job insurance. Then the guy discovered I was a VN combat vet. So in this one session, he did a rapid eye hypnosis to me. Suddenly, I was back in the jungle on April 19, 1969. JJ and Joe were dead, Nelson was all shot to shit and we were surrounded. I was begging the guy to get me out of there, but he just told me to go on through it. I did go on through it, but was in shock for the next two weeks. When I came out of that battle in the guy's office, his eyes were as big as a coffee mug. He had never been exposed to a real life gunfight in VN before. He told me I probably had PTSD and to go to the VA for help. I went to the Vet Center and they helped me file for PTSD.

Back to being your shadow all these years. I seem to have the same anger about the same issues as you. I too, am regularly saddened to be burying old and true friends because of Agent Orange. John Walker, Tommy Glass, Owen Harding, Sparky Conkrite, Smiley Ramirez, Freddy Davis, Ed Bausinger and others. Condemned property, you say. Sprayed and betrayed I say. My proudest award is that of the CIB.

- Tom Petty
11th Light Infantry Brigade, Americal Division I Corp
U.S. Army, Vietnam (1969-1970)

Dear Mr. Trimmer,

The Officers and Members of American Legion Post 383 of Chagrin Falls, Ohio would like to take this opportunity to commend your efforts to bring about awareness of the Vietnam War veteran's experience and related issues as presented in your recent book, *Condemned Property?* You have given voice for millions of veterans.

This may be one of the last great books written by an actual Vietnam combat war veteran. The author's recollections of events and combat operations of the war give readers invaluable information about the war that the TV news failed to provide.

We hope there is widespread distribution of your book so that current and future generations of American leaders will realize the long-term implications of instigating wars and the effect on its warriors.

I close with two relevant quotes, "God and a soldier all people adore; in time of war, but not before; and when war is over and all things are righted, God is neglected and an old soldier slighted." Anon.

And this from General George Washington, "The willingness with which our young people are likely to serve in any war, no matter how justified, shall be directly proportional to how they perceive the Veterans of earlier wars were treated and appreciated by their nation."

For God and Country,

Thomas Gretchko
Commander Legion Post #383
U.S. Army Ranger, Vietnam (1970)

Dusty,

My wife and I attended what we thought would be a Blossom concert over Blossom weekend. We did not know it would be a memorial and you would be the featured speaker discussing your book and Vietnam experience. I live in Chagrin Falls so we are almost neighbors. We really enjoyed your talk and were very moved by it.

We bought your book in the lobby and I am totally enjoying it. It certainly stimulates many memories that I have consciously laid dormant all these years. I am up to page 238 and will probably read it again when I finally finish it.

Some other very cogent points you made in your fine book:

1) The number of non-combatants—We were told at the time that it took ten men in non-combat roles to support one grunt in the field. I don't know if that was true. You could get a lot of MPCs by selling captured Chi-com pistols in Cu-Chi so I assume there were a lot of phonies. I didn't spend more than 4-5 days all year there, so I don't really know what went on back in Cu-Chi. I did read Tunnels of Cu-Chi, so I'm glad I was never there.

2) Red ants—ouch! We were in the middle of an on-line combat assault (two infantry platoons and one mechanized platoon) with the battalion S3 group observing and directing the action directly behind my platoon. The APC in front of my platoon tore through a hedgerow and I was immediately attacked by swarms of red ants from above. Right in front of the battalion command and in the middle of a firefight, I ripped off my gear and shirt and pants getting those bastards off me. I must have been some sight. They hurt like hell. I didn't care about getting shot at that point. I took a lot of ribbing later.

3) Swamp water and chlorine tablets to replenish canteens.

4) The same filthy, smelly uniform for days at a time—no personal hygiene, no showers, jungle rot, no clean, dry replacement socks.

5) Salt tablets and dry heaves from them after humping all day in the heat and humidity.

6) The most important and timely of all—your anger and criticism of the VA and how poorly they treated some of your friends and fellow warriors. I think this explosion in the news last week about the VA Hospital System is just the beginning of a massive criminal investigation (with jail sentences for many implicated in this system-wide cooking of patient records and appointments). They need a total overhaul of that system and every official in it. I visited a VA hospital once in Brooklyn to visit a friend back in the Vietnam era. I still remember the filth and smells at that place. It was depressing. I would never

go to a VA hospital myself for medical care. The idiots in VA hospital management never estimated how many patients they need to staff and budget for as our troops are coming back from Iraq and Afghanistan with real problems. From an article in the paper this morning, they under-estimated by over 70,000 patients this year alone.

7) Inferior weapon—the M16 sucked—much inferior to the gooks' AK47. Jams at the worst possible times. One of your pictures in the book shows a squeeze bottle of that white lubricant we constantly used attached to your steel pot— exactly the same as we did.

I've never discussed my experiences in Vietnam with my family or any friend or business associate. I have not joined or participated in any veteran's organizations or veteran's activities (parades, etc.) As you characterized it in your book, I have been an avoider all of these years. I too came home to the embarrassing and humiliating "baby-killer" greetings at the SF Airport and I was almost ashamed of my uniform at that moment. I couldn't believe what was happening and why we were the objects of so much hate after all we had gone through. Reading those chapters in your book on the protestors, Jane Fonda, John Kerry and Kent State brought back all those memories. I clearly remember Hanoi Jane, but I must have missed Kerry's histrionics except for his Swift Boat controversy during the presidential election a few years ago. After reading what you have to say about him, I don't think I'll ever be able to see John Kerry in the news again as Secretary of State and not want to vomit. On another note, I was plant manager for a number of years at Mactac on 91 in Stow, just down the road from you. Two of my production managers were in that National Guard Unit at Kent State in 1970 and our female QC manager was a student protestor. They surely didn't get along well years later.

I wanted nothing to do with remembering those experiences. I never kept in touch with anyone I served with, either in Nam or in the states, although a fellow graduate of the OCS company I graduated with recently tracked me down through my wife and now has me on his e-mail distribution list for their alumni group. They apparently have been a very active club and have a reunion scheduled in Las Vegas sometime this fall. They sent me a CD of their last reunion. I didn't recognize any of them on the CD and don't even remember the names listed, so I don't plan on getting involved anytime soon.

If nothing else, your presentation and reading your outstanding book brought back a lot of terrible, but a lot of good memories. I'm not likely to change my spots after all these years of avoidance, but it sure brought those memories back. If you plan on any future letter writing campaign, feel free to get in touch if financial support would help with the cost.

Wishing you best of success with your book and your continued friendship and support to your Vietnam brothers.

- Bob Simpson
Vietnam Veteran, III Corp (1967-1968)

Mr. Trimmer,

Read your book *Condemned Property?* It was great. I served with the 4th Infantry 2/8 Mech in 1970 and was an in-country transfer to the 23rd Inf. At Chu Lai later on after our unit was deactivated in August of that year. Getting back to your book, I didn't realize the 25th Infantry took a lot of casualties back then. I have always thought the Marines or 1st Cav had the most casualties of anybody. That's the media, I guess. But anyway, the book was a great read. I hope you will take the time to write another one and who knows, you might be another Ernest Hemingway. Hang in there. God bless you.

- Thomas Daniel
Vietnam Veteran

Hello Dusty,

I have read your book. It was very emotional and hard hitting. My uncle is Robert Wayne Best. He served with you with the Army in Vietnam. I love him very much. I also love you and every one of your brothers that put his life and emotional well-being on the line for us back home. What you have done with your book is a wonderful thing that will last forever and help many generations understand life on a far more personal level.

I just wanted to thank you for putting yourself out there with your book and thank you for making my life better. I now have a much better understanding of what my uncle went through over there.

- Val Best Cantrell
Niece of Vietnam Veteran

Dusty,

I just finished reading your book. Please allow me to share some thoughts.

1. First, let me thank you for your service to our country. I never served in the military, but I was called for a pre-induction physical as I was graduating from high school in 1964. I flunked the physical (overweight, flat feet and who knows what else) and, while I was in college, my birth date drew a relatively high number in the draft lottery. So, I was never called to serve. However, I will assure you that, if I had been drafted, I would have proudly served. Running off to Canada would have never crossed my mind.

Of course, a major point of your book is the lack of respect and even hostility that many people have exhibited toward Vietnam vets. Perhaps it was because I am from Kentucky and I lived in that state for virtually all my life until I moved to Ohio in 1973, I really didn't see much of that negative reaction. I had a cousin who served in Vietnam in 1967-68, and one of the fellows I went to high school with was killed over there soon after he arrived in country. The locals in Kentucky tended to be conservative politically and perhaps more patriotic than the average person back in those days. So, we tended to welcome the vets back home without making much of a big deal about it. Of course, those of us who were paying attention to the national news were aware of the protesters, of the actions of Jane Fonda (but not those of John Kerry, who most of us had never really heard of until he emerged as a presidential candidate a few years ago), and of the generally bad reputation of the VA in dealing with the Vietnam vets.

By the time the servicemen and women returned from the first Gulf War, the climate had changed somewhat, but it seems to me that the turning point in the public's appreciation of military veterans and those in active military service came as a result of the events of September 11, 2001. That was the day that so many "first responders" charged into the two towers to assist in the evacuation and, of course, many of them lost their lives because they were willing to put themselves in harm's way in the line of duty, just like the servicemen and women in every war this country has ever fought. I don't think some people had realized this until 9/11.

Although it has come too late for many Vietnam vets, I do now frequently see people thanking military personnel for their service to our country. This happens most often in airports, where servicemen and women are most likely to be in uniform, but it happens elsewhere also. I was at a convention in Jacksonville, Florida in November and two young Marines in dress uniforms came into the bar where I was sitting with several people. Two fellows at my table actually saluted them, and several people went over to speak with them. While things are getting better from the standpoint of showing appreciation to the military, we as a nation will probably never be able to make it up to the Vietnam vets for the injustice done to them. However, I hope that the government (especially the VA) and the public make an honest effort to do so.

2. Although you are not an experienced book writer, you were able to really establish your "voice" as a writer. It was always clear where you stood on each issue, and you were able to convey this in no uncertain terms. While the subject matter is obviously serious, you were also able to lighten things up from time to time with some humor. I actually laughed out loud at your description of how you met Jack Bellemy. I can just see Jack flying through the air like Mighty Dog going after some guy's throat. You were also able to convey your more sensitive side, especially when writing about your wife. She must be a remarkable woman, and she has obviously had a positive impact on your life. I know you described her as the "Italian Princess" who saved you, but it seems to me that maybe you actually saved each other.

While the organization of the book is a bit like stream of consciousness, each chapter had a definite focus. You were able to intermingle personal experience with historical background, and you certainly did your homework to find facts and figures to back up your arguments. Again, there was never any doubt about what point you were making.

3. As you seemed to anticipate, one of my favorite parts of the book was Chapter 18, which features letters from other military veterans, mostly Vietnam vets. There were many remarkable stories told in this section. I also enjoyed one of your points—while the combat personnel carried most of the load in battle, they could not have done their jobs without the support of the non-combat and "near-combat" personnel who were also there. And of course, occasionally these non-combat folks were themselves in harm's way.

As you know, it is hard for anyone who has not experienced hard combat to really understand what it is all about. I hope you get lots of media coverage.

- Edward G. Thomas
Professor, Cleveland State University

Dusty,

I have finally finished reading your book *Condemned Property?* (after many inter-ruptions), and wanted to say "thank you" for taking time to write this account of your life. It truly gives one a real picture of your experiences as an American soldier, both during and after you return home. I am now beginning to re-read parts of the book and find myself realizing there were many different aspects of the war for so many veterans.

It also made me realize how fortunate I was to be a Navy flight crew member instead of a ground soldier faced with so many perils, natural and human, which increased my chances of survival ten times plus what you experienced facing daily. Although our days were long and hard, faced with frequency of fire from the ground and occasional skirmishes with river sampans and junks, at least we were not faced head to head with the VC.

Unfortunately, my scars came in the form of health issues from Agent Orange, Type II diabetes and prostate cancer, skin disorder. I deal with the diabetes on a daily basis and the cancer was a greater problem, requiring major surgery and frequent (every three months) checking to ensure it is kept in check and has not resurfaced. The skin disorder had to be reported within one year of discharge. That of course didn't happen. It took me over 1.5 years to finally get the VA to determine that my exposure to Agent Orange was the cause. Countless months of filling out and re-filling out documents, all which were part of military records, to get this resolved. I finally had to write the VA and tell them that I had no more information to offer, that everything was part of military records, and get the Disabled American Veterans to assist in pushing the claim forward. These people were my saving grace and backup for getting this resolved.

You mentioned in your book an aircraft called "Puff the Magic Dragon." This was one of our aircraft from my squadron (VP-48), which we shared missions while there; most all our aircraft carried a name selected by its crew. It was good to know that our Squadron was able to assist any and all troops during this conflict. Our door mounted 50 CALs were terror and could pack a pretty big impact when needed. Of course, I had already left Nam by 1968.

I believe returning home was the most confusing and disappointing aspect of my involvement in Vietnam. To be hated by your own country, unable to talk about Vietnam for fear of being rejected by the American people was a hard thing for us all. Even today...this still continues. Perhaps veterans like you, sharing their story, has and will change American thoughts about Vietnam. Again, thank you!

- Ed Fontaine
U.S. Navy, Vietnam

Hi Trimmer,

I loved the book. Thanks for sending it...have you sold many? I talked to Jenner after I received it and we talked and talked and talked. He is the only person I have had contact with that was in the 3/22 since Vietnam...I really get pretty emotional thinking about the men in our platoon and the good men that died...I guess I would not be human if I forgot what happened over there...I am going through some counseling at the VA about Vietnam. It is helping but there is a lot to deal with. I live here in Indy with my wife of forty-eight years and have one son who lives about six houses from me. He is a patent attorney with two children. I garden, go to the gambling boat and try to stay busy. Your book really told it like it was. I can still say that I hate Jane Fonda--haha. I remember you out there at point. You wanted it. That must have taken a long time to compile all of the info in the book. What are you doing with yourself every day? Book tours, I hope...I will try to call you. It is so much easier on the phone... Thanks.

- John Maines
1st Platoon Sergeant
B Co 3/22nd Infantry
U.S. Army, Vietnam (1968)

Mr. Trimmer,

I read your book *Condemned Property?* with interest. I served in the Brown Water Navy stationed at the Phu Quoc Island, Vietnam near the Cambodian border from 1968-1969 on the USS Krishna (ARL-38). I was a seaman.

My second tour of duty was 1969-1970 on the USS Taluga (A0-62) as a postal clerk serving ship in the 7th fleet from Yankee Station and somewhere in between.

I think those two books you wanted to write, you should do. 1970-1980 was not a blur for me. I went back to school; got my MPA. I worked for the Post Office from 1970-1974 and 1974-1979 at the VA as a claims adjustor, helping the VA in LA convert from a manual to a computerized system. 1980-1981 I worked at GAO.

I knew about Vietnam before I went there because I was a stamp collector. I was also older than the average vet at twenty-two and had completed college. I tried ROCS but walked out—too much BS and not strong enough at math. Ironically, Lt. Gustafson was my disbursory officer in the USS Taluga. He and I went to ROC school together.

I had twenty-five years in the federal government and retired. I went back to school and became a certified paralegal. I've more awards from the federal government than I can keep track of. I worked for an immigration attorney and INS so I have experience in VA and INS law.

Since 2004, I have worked as a veterans service officer for AMVETS, MOPH and VVA. I have worked for the VA in Los Angeles Regional office and VA Hospital Westwood. I have seen all aspects of the VA. It took me eleven years to win my claim. I tell veterans to be patient. I had to do the case myself because my service organization was incompetent and inept. Also, the regional offices are slow with their decisions. Another problem is the quality of adjudications at the regional offices. How competent are they?

I look at Vietnam this way. You can define yourself by Vietnam, or like me, accept it as a part of my life, but I am more than Vietnam. I am not going to let it destroy my life. Have I had problems with Vietnam? Yes. I don't blame all my problems from Vietnam. I would have had these problems regardless of whether I served there or not. Will I get over it? No. It is impossible. Do I think about Vietnam? Yes. It made me a better person. I was in the unusual position of being a reservist reactivated to Vietnam, a distant minority in the war.

Each veteran has to process Vietnam in their own way because of their unique experiences. I had two years of therapy because I felt I needed this. Your book was one of the best about Vietnam and necessary reading, and I have read many others.

- Richard B. Stoudt
Proud Vietnam Veteran
U.S. Navy, Vietnam (1968-1970)

Dear Dusty,

I am a U.S. Army veteran (1968-1969) of the Vietnam War. I make it a personal mission of mine these days to express my gratitude every time I pass a veteran on the street—regardless the war in which they served, such as the 97 year-old WWII vet I passed in my neighborhood just a few days ago.

WWII was obviously the really big war of this past century and were it not for our participation we probably all would be speaking the German language at this time in our country.

A few days ago, a request for a $35.00 donation to the National World War II Museum in New Orleans came with my mail. The outside envelope was stamped "Ticket Enclosed-Please RSVP." Both actor Tom Hanks and retired NBC newsman Tom Brokaw's names appeared inside in the way of personal endorsements.

Let me be perfectly clear. I have the greatest respect for both the living and deceased WWII vets and their surviving family members. My issue is with how Vietnam vets have been treated by many of the press and citizens of our country both during and after the war.

I spent a good hour of my time in nearby Chagrin Falls in the Cleveland area with my family on Memorial Day. As always, I proudly wore my Vietnam Vets cap. Not a single passerby—young or old—stopped me that day to express their gratitude for my time in service. Not a single "Thank You." Not a single smile directed to my attention.

Wake up America! It may be true that in some aspects Vietnam may have been a black eye in the history of our country. But certainly not owing to the actions of the vast majority of those who answered the call to duty. Don't judge us all by the actions of a few (i.e. Lt. William Calley). The reality of the matter is that the media should shoulder much of the blame for the many distortions and misfacts that were directed at our citizens.

Better to blame the politicians and elected officials in this country — both back then and now — who, had they done their jobs in Washington D.C. there might never be a need for this nation to sacrifice the lives of so many good young men and women of our country.

When you pass a Vietnam veteran on the street today or tomorrow or next week, try to remember SFC Edwin Byron Ryder, 31, from Greenville Junction, Maine with wife, Melanie and their five children; or Sgt. Michael Preslipski, 21, who lived in Pennsylvania; he had extended for a second year of duty to serve his country. And two others who served with the U.S. Army 59th Land Clearing Company. Four soldiers who met their untimely deaths on August 31, 1969. A "friendly" but "forgotten" land mine snuffed out their lives in just the blink of an eye.

Someday I may be too old to remember my birthday, but the date of their tragic deaths will never be forgotten.

- Glen A. Weinberger
Specialist 5th Class
59th Land Clearing Company
U.S. Army, Vietnam (1968-1969)

Dusty,

First I would like to say God bless you for trying to help so many Veterans by writing this book. It took me a while to finish it. I had to stop so many times to regroup. I felt every emotion that a person can possibly have. It had to be very hard to you to relive the memories of the battles and the death and the destruction, but I understand why you did! I felt your anger and your compassion and the brotherhood with every paragraph. I also felt the constant struggle of the last forty years. You said that some people would rather leave some things unsaid and I can understand. I think you were destined to write this book and if this book can put pressure on the VA to make a better effort to help all the boys coming home process their claims. You have done a great service! It's evident that you have scars because of what you endured but I also think your actions have glorified the term "We were soldiers."

- Carl Finocchi
U.S. Navy, Vietnam (1970)

Dear Dusty,

I did buy your book, I did read it and I could not have said it better myself. I'm even more bitter than you. My Armored Personnel Carrier took a direct hit by a rocket on a morning mine sweep ambush near the I Corp II Corp border on Highway 1 on Veterans Day, November 11, 1969, the day after I extended for 15 days. I ended up in Walter Reed from 1969-1971 during the war protests in Washington D.C. where they carted protesters away by bus loads. I was Medically Retired from the Army under Chapter 31 from Walter Reed. Reed was in a ghetto and people were killed in the middle of the hospital.

My family suffered dearly in trying to be with me at Walter Reed. They were treated like second-class citizens while they were there just like many other families. They treat the new vets and families a hell of a lot better today. The irony is my birthday is September 11 (9/11) and we were overrun on Hill 4-11. That was not the only time we were overrun in the north to the I Corp II Corp border in the south to Laos in the west.

Your points on the WWII vets are right on. We suffered dearly because of their non-acceptance of our war. I have not even touched on how I was treated when I came home by my so-called friends and neighbors. That was real ugly.

I have been in this fight with VA since 1975 with the Dr. John Wilson's "Forgotten Warrior" project at Cleveland State. If it was not for him, his research and testimony in front of Congress there would have never been any recognition of disability for PTSD.

Unfortunately, I am at a point in my life and health I cannot fight anymore. It's up to the new Vets to take up the battle. They're getting a hell of a lot in comparison to what we got/get. I just read Social Security is going to speed up their disability claims. It took me three years and a lawyer at 62 to get Social Security Disability (after double hip replacements, diabetes, prostate cancer, etc.) because they said I could still work as a Vet Rep so therefore I wasn't disabled.

My bitterness runs deep and I just don't care about the people in this country that don't care about Nam vets or our families. I can't even talk about my father

281

who was on Iwo Jima and married to my mother at that time. He had 2 brothers in laws that were WWII DRAFT DODGERS. Yeah…the greatest generation.

I wish you the best of luck with your book and your effort to educate, but I doubt that most Americans will listen, other than Vietnam Vets themselves. I hope you will prove me wrong.

-Harry V
Disabled Colonel Vietnam Vet

Dear Dusty,

Congratulations on your book. I found it to be superb reading and very timely. The VA mess going public "after" *Condemned Property?* came out is giving you and your book a whole lot of credibility! All of America and especially the Veterans groups owe you many thanks. You make me proud.

- Ralph Storage
Twinsburg High School Principal (Retired)

Dear Dusty,

For your outstanding support to the Combat Infantrymens Association, please accept the enclosed Certificate of Appreciation as a small token of gratitude for the work you have done promoting the rights of past Vietnam U.S. Veterans with your fine book *Condemned Property?* It truly is an inspirational book, shedding light on a dark subject in our American history. It is Veterans like you that help us all gain what we rightfully deserve from the government that put us in the condition we are in.

- Chris D. Callen
Commander, State of Ohio
Combat Infantrymens Association

Dear Mr. Trimmer

This is to acknowledge that we have received a copy of your book entitled *Condemned Property?* Your book will make a fine addition to our archives. On behalf of the United States Army, The Center of Military History, Fort Benning and the National Infantry Museum, thanks.

I also want to thank you for your military service and for all you did to protect our country. Thanks to your service and that of all those who served during the Vietnam War, today's servicemen and women can come home to a nation that appreciates their service. So welcome home. I am proud of you and what you did. May we always have men like you to stand up for our republic. You are the greatest generation to me!

- Zachary Frank Hanner
Military Staff – Director
National Infantry Museum

Dear Mr. Trimmer,

Your book *Condemned Property?* was transferred to the Archival Library of the U.S. Army Heritage and Education Center (USAHEC) where it will be made available to future researchers.

Your work contributes to our understanding of the Vietnam War and the experiences of American Soldiers, both on the battlefield and their return to civilian life. *Condemned Property?* is a welcome addition to USAHEC's already unrivaled collection of historical materials.

Again, I thank you. You've demonstrated a firm belief in our mission and personally helped to preserve and illuminate the contributions of the U.S. Army and its Soldiers to our nation's history.

- Mike Perry
Executive Director
Army Heritage Center Foundation

Mr. Trimmer,

I was very pleased to obtain a copy of your book *Condemned Property?*. It looks really good so far and once I have completed reading it, it will be sent to our History Research Center where it will be available to all researchers and visitors of Canada's War Museum and Military History Center.

- James Whitham
Director, Canadian War Museum

January 25, 2015

Brother Trimmer,

I just finished reading *Condemned Property?* I found the book to be well written and very informative. Although I was not infantry, I too, am a combat veteran. I quit high school and signed my enlistment papers in April of 1968. I had been a student at Chanel High School in Bedford, Ohio. I lived in Cleveland on Miles Avenue. I entered the Army in June of 1968 right after my seventeenth birthday. Fort Knox, Kentucky was where my basic training occurred. Then on to Fort Rucker, Alabama for A.J.T. in aviation-related matters. I had enlistment guarantees that I would be a helicopter crew chief / gunner. As I was too young to go to Vietnam, I was sent to Germany to the 42 Transportation C. I spent approximately 11 months before requesting duty assignment to Viet Nam.

On December 9, 1969, I arrived in Viet Nam. After a week of training I was sent to Camp Eagle in the I Corp region of V.N. After 2 weeks I became a gunner on a huey. My first Sergeant honored my enlistment rights. As soon as the next crew chief rotated, I became crew chief of LOH6 #628. We flew every day from sun-up till sundown. We flew missions as forward observers to adjust artillery, also search and destroy missions. Sometimes we flew eyes of the snake with cobra gunships. We flew at tree top level trying to visualize targets or to get the enemy to fire on us, exposing themselves. I would mark their position with W.P. grenade and the cobras would work then back down low to assess damage. Somebody always wanted a body count.

We also worked with your guys, the infantry units as a reactionary group. Also, there were times we transported snipers somewhere and later extract people we had dropped off. On July 4, 1970, communication was lost to firebase Ripcord. One of our pilots, W.O.2 Giles volunteered to fly radios to Ripcord. At approximately 9:00 p.m. he came to me and asked if I would go to Ripcord with him. I asked him, who me? He told me he felt safe with me. I thought he was nuts, but together we left. Upon arriving at Ripcord, we did not know what we would find. As you know, Viet Nam is extra dark. We landed and I started offloading radios. A few guys that called that firebase home came forward to retrieve those radios and in a few minutes, communication was restored. Me and Giles were gone as soon as the radios were received. We took hostile fire. The last man extracted from Ripcord was taken off the hill by CW2 Leslie Rush from A/377th FA in a LO6 as documented in the book, *Ripcord Screaming Eagle Under Siege* V.N. 1970 written by Keith W. Nolan.

You are right that I rarely talk about the war. I will talk to other V.N. veterans because non-veterans cannot comprehend what we did. I also can spot the so-called V.N. wannabes by the conversation.

Each year for the last 10 years, brothers from my unit hold a reunion. I have attended all but one. It is great to be with my brothers again. As I write this, tears are coming to my eyes. It is a shame that in over forty years those reunions seem to be the only time I feel respected for who I am and what I did over there. You know the bond we shared and the brotherhood we have.

I am now 63 and have many demons and battles but as you said, "my country could still count on me again if I was needed."

I am honored to have read your book.

Mel A. Oberlin (Breeze)
Viet Nam Combat Crew Chief
A/BTT 377th F.A. (1969-1970)
101 Airborne
100% PTSD
Camp Eagle I Corp

CHAPTER 16

WHO TAKES CARE OF...THEM?

I received the news from my great friend of fifty years on a very icy, cold Saturday morning on January 10...his wife passed away at the very young age of sixty-eight. Cause of death will be officially credited to a heart attack. Another Vietnam War veteran has died prematurely. No, Kathy Bellemy did not serve in-country physically with her husband, Jack. But she has had to live and re-live that war for forty-seven years, day after day, night after night. This sudden and tragic loss of a life won't be registered on the Vietnam Memorial (The Wall) but as I mentioned earlier in this book...there should be a memorial for Vietnam War veterans who have died prematurely after Nam. There should be a memorial for the wives of Vietnam veterans who have also passed away...prematurely because of Vietnam.

Many marriages fell apart after Vietnam vets came home. Those sad stories also go untold and they also dissolve after the veteran and/or the veteran's wife has gone. How sad. How heartbreaking.

I cannot tell you what went on in the Bellemy household since Jack went to Vietnam in 1967 and what events transpired for the nearly five decades after Jack survived the Vietnam War experience. I just know firsthand how that war has haunted him and his wife ever since he came home...a very changed man. And unlike many other Vietnam veterans' wives who separated from their veteran husbands, she stood by her husband till her last day.

Most of the horror stories that you may have heard about or read about pertaining to that stinking war and the almost unbelievable stories that have been shared by Vietnam vets or other victims—their families—Jack and I have lived them all together. They are not fabricated or exaggerated. After the war, our adventures and our escapades continued, and we tried our best to top them with another challenging event up until recent years well into our sixties. Peter Pan Syndrome, I guess. Maybe we had not grown up. Maybe guys like us who have experienced the ultimate adrenalin rush of fighting for our lives and the lives of others in combat will never be able to refrain from our daredevil, thrill-seeking ways. Frown on us if you will and many do, referring to us as childish, immature and selfish men who care only about satisfying our own egos. Maybe they are right. But as we Nam vets say universally to someone when they ask this extremely stupid question..."What was it like over there?" Our answer... **YOU HAD TO BE THERE!** Both of my books, *Condemned Property?* and *Payback Time!* are attempts to bring the Vietnam War experience into your living rooms.

Until the morning of January 10, 2015, I had never seen or heard my great friend and war brother, Jack Bellemy cry...as he wept over the telephone, attempting to deliver the news of Kathy's ending battle. The Bellemys are not your typical Vietnam War husband and wife team. Unlike so many others who suffered from ugly divorces, suicides and incarcerations, Kathy and Jack Bellemy have stood by each other's side since they were high school sweethearts at Solon High school in Solon, Ohio. They were always meant for each other and nothing, NOTHING could ever pry them apart. In 2014, they celebrated their forty-eighth wedding anniversary together.

One of the ironies about the relationship between Jack and Kathy Bellemy, their entire family and me is...our bonding relationship had its roots planted in the sand, dust, mud, and swamps of South Vietnam, yet we did not know it at that time...during the Tet Offensives of 1968. He was a combat infantry engineer. I was a combat infantry pointman. We participated in some of the same operations and fought in some of the same battles and ambushes together...we did not discover this until we hooked up at a New Year's Eve party at our friend, Ron Krzewinski's house on December 31, 1969. I describe this part in more detail in my first book. Although we had known of each other since 1962 or 1963, we really did know each other, but our lasting and inseparable friendship began that night and into the next morning. I don't think we even slept that night, but Jack and I were used to that in Vietnam. A good night's sleep of three hours over there was about as rare as having a "nice day" over there—they never happened.

Our conversation that night probably went something like this from what both of us can remember:

Jack: Holy shit, Trimmer, you were a grunt with the 25th Infantry's 3/22? Man, did they ever get into it with Charley (Viet Cong) big time and often. I was assigned to you guys on several missions. Do you remember the ambushes at Trang Bang and Hoc Mon? I was at a couple of those with you guys. We really kicked Charley's asses, didn't we?

Dusty: Damn, brother, you were there! I remember your guys blowing up the gooks' bunkers with C-4 and bandoleer torpedoes after we had wiped out their inhabitants. You engineers were awesome—holy shit, we were there together on those days in May and June of 1968…Wow!

Then we hugged and proceeded to completely annihilate Ron Krzewinski's entire bar inventory. My head still hurts thinking about that party over forty-five years ago.

"Yeah, this really happened, didn't it," we kept telling each other at that party. This was a rather large party and the entire audience was completely captivated as we told one story after another, bringing the Vietnam War's Tet Offensive right into the living room by two living participants. It was some night. Kathy Bellemy was there, of course. My date was a lady named Madge, from Twinsburg where I grew up. We too, were high school sweethearts, but our lives would take us into different directions, unlike Kathy and Jack. However, Madge Beck Epstein and I remain friends today, and she says she has kept some of my "letters to her from Vietnam". I have not asked to see them.

"Phu Cong! Jack, were you at Phu Cong?" I remember yelling to Jack. "You son of a bitch, I sure the hell was. My group of engineers built that bridge and rebuilt it after the gooks blew it up. You were there too?" Jack said. "Yup, we were." We pulled bridge security on that bridge for a while. It was a breather for us until our units got back to strength as our casualties had devastated our ranks. We also pulled shotgun for the Navy's Riverine Patrol at that time and that was scary, scary shit looking head in at those tracers coming at us in a little motor boat, defenseless in the middle of the Saigon River or whatever it was at the time.

"How about Go Dau Ha?" "Yup, there, too," we chanted. We leveled that VC stronghold—both of us were there that same night. And the stories continued, as they continue to this day.

My first trip to The Wall was with Kathy and Jack and my new wife, Ginny Brancato Trimmer in 1989, I think. Two of my own platoon brothers were with us on that visit—Jack "Bud" Gainey, his wife, Marty (both deceased), Robert "Smokey Ryan (deceased), his wife, Betty and two great friends, Lenny Piazza (Vietnam veteran) and his wife Chris. When we arrived at the statue of three Vietnam War brothers, I froze, unable to advance another step forward. In fact, I tried to step backward, but I could barely move and my heart was beating at hummingbird speed. No one had seen me freeze up back there as they were all walking towards The Wall. Jack turned around first, then Kathy. They both came to my aid and comforted me until I snapped out of it and was able to walk forward, not backward. I thought I was experiencing a heart attack, but fortunately, that was not the case. That weekend was a sobering, heart-throbbing, emotional roller coaster ride for us. We played together like kids. Even though Bud was wheelchair-bound at the time, he was game to racing in the park with us. We must have been something to behold to the onlookers in Washington, D.C., especially our friendly police. Heck, some of them had to be Vietnam vets, so they left us alone and actually, we think they may have been watching over us as our personal guards.

Jack attended Bud Gainey's funeral with me. Jack and Kathy attended Marty Gainey's funeral with Ginny and me. In more ways than one, Vietnam killed both Gaineys. In more ways than one, Vietnam had a hand in Kathy Bellemy's premature death. I don't just believe this...I know it. Stories like this could continue, but too few of them will be told and they should be told. Kathy Bellemy (50) and Ginny Brancato Trimmer (30) marked their combined eightieth anniversary this past year. Good grief, did we ever put those fine ladies through hell or what. I don't know if I'll ever be able to pay Ginny back for what she has done for my life, for sticking with me through trials and tribulations that have come close to ending my life several times, frightening her beyond levels she had ever imagined—but she has hung in there. I have little doubt that Kathy experienced many of the same horrible, near-death episodes with Jack as we were usually together or in on it together when we would attempt to pull off some of our very challenging follies.

Kathy Bellemy should have lived longer—of course, she should have. If our government had taken better care of Jack, she might still be here today. Just my opinion here, based on my close real-life experiences with this family.

So, I wonder who would have taken care of Kathy had Jack passed before her? That is a question that could be asked about thousands of tragic, premature deaths of Vietnam War veterans, and it is a question that should be asked of our government over and over. In fact, this will become one of my top priorities of 2015 as I bombard Congress and the Senate with letters.

Vietnam veterans' wives? If our government abandoned and betrayed most Vietnam War veterans, what kind of support would their wives and other family members receive? The best I can tell is that the wives of Vietnam veterans have pretty much taken care of themselves or each other. There are or have been some organizations formed by the brave and forgotten ladies. They have worked hard to console and consult with other wives and families. Just like Vietnam War veterans, the wives have gone out of their way to comfort other wives of veterans. Again, this proved in my opinion that the Vietnam War generation was as great as any generation.

Vietnam veterans' wives, as well as today's war veterans' wives, can and often do suffer from their warrior husbands' PTSD problems. Why wouldn't they? Kathy Bellemy had to stay behind in a helpless state and wait, wait, wait while her husband was living in constant danger every day. The wives did that, watching the war on their living room TVs and watching the protesters of the war at the same time. At least we veterans could face our enemies. The veterans' wives had to remain brave and loyal and just wait…wait…wait. How painful. I would prefer to seek out and confront our enemy or demons rather than idly sit back with a false sense of security around me. Then, by the time the veteran returns home, (IF) and IF he returns intact, the wife is at her wit's end.

Post-Traumatic Stress Disorder (PTSD) is fully and completely recognized by today's medical profession. Very few combat veterans are able to avoid it. How does this affect the person(s) living with a veteran with PTSD?

Basically, when you're living with a veteran who has Post-Traumatic Stress Disorder, you become his (or her) caretaker. You slip into a role without even realizing it, constantly watching for people or circumstances that might "set him off." You try to make sure everything stays in line—that nothing aggravates or upsets your vet—that everything is "perfect." Despite your best efforts, you still get screamed at and berated by the person you are trying to help on a much too frequent basis.

Your vet is not emotionally "there" for you. When you are upset or happy, angry or sad, you have to deal with your emotions on your own. You begin to feel ignored and unloved and start "protecting" yourself by treating others—especially your vet—the same way.
(Source: familyofavet.com ENewsletter)

This really is hard to explain unless you have lived it. As Vietnam veterans say when asked what it was like over there…**you had to be there.**

Secondary PTSD is not a disorder that is recognized by the *Diagnostic and Statistical Manual of Mental Disorders*. However, many wives and family members of combat stressed veterans can begin to behave similarly to the veterans with PTSD. The symptoms and effects of Secondary PTSD are just as varied, just as trying as the symptoms of the veterans with…Primary PTSD. Unfortunately, we combat veterans with primary PTSD are usually the last ones to notice or even acknowledge that we have it, let alone that we have infected our loved ones with secondary PTSD. After all, they did not go through what WE went through, did they—so we selfishly thought. WE have real PTSD, so how could

WE possibly be expected to recognize and understand our loved one's problems, which WE caused?

It is pretty well known by many Americans that when Vietnam veterans returned home and underwent "out processing", most received little or no knowledge of what was available to them in benefits, health care, counseling, etc. There just weren't any programs in place for guidance in helping us find out..."Where do we go from here?"

Guess what? The VA, aka the American government, left the wives and families of Vietnam vets well behind when it came to services available to them. They flat-out did not exist then and from what I hear and have experienced, adequate care remains "inadequate" to non-existent. For veterans of any war, having people shoot at you or trying to blow you up on a daily basis is not fun (though for some it is an adrenaline rush). It can have a long-term negative effect on your mental health. The long-term mental damage...Post-Traumatic Stress Disorder is possible for your entire life.

Is PTSD a contagious illness? Before I provide my opinion, listen to this—while there are loads of opinions available to all who care about whether or not PTSD is "curable", almost everyone I have even been in contact with who has been affected or associated with this topic agrees that the effects can only be lessened **IF** treatment is received early.

Regarding early treatment of PTSD for Vietnam veterans, it almost never was administered early. Who even knew what PTSD was when we came home? The term had not been created yet.

If you are living with a Vietnam War veteran who has PTSD, you will either become his (or her) caretaker or...you will bag out of the relationship. If you hang in there and stand by your Nam vet, you may wake up twenty or forty years later find yourself with Secondary PTSD. HEY! You don't have to just take the word from an amateur psychologist like me—if you know a present or former (lots of those) Nam vet's wife—ask her. Of course, the level of pain suffered will depend on the level of PTSD a Nam vet harbors, which could be determined by the level or frequency of combat horrors to which the Vietnam vet was exposed. Unfortunately, the medical profession still does not seem to get it on Secondary PTSD, but it only took them about three decades after the Vietnam War ended to figure out there were a few hundred thousand Nam vets who were trying to deal with it...IF they were still around.

Other casualties of the Nam vet's illness could be the children living with the PTSD veteran, but I am not going to dwell on that sad problem. You can find enough information on it yourselves if you choose to research it.

Secondary PTSD can and does cause depression and exhaustion. Many Nam vet wives have found themselves tiptoeing around their vets on a daily basis with no one to go to for help.

One might be thinking that today's Vietnam veterans are well into their sixties or early seventies—shouldn't they have their PTSD under control by now? That is one of the unfortunate misunderstandings about a combat vet's PTSD...it has no expiration date. For many, it sets in twenty-five to forty years after his or her war ended. Obviously, this makes life for all around very uneasy and unstable.

I have known a few Vietnam vets who have made it through their original marriage since the end of the Vietnam War, very few. Most Vietnam vets who suffer from varying degrees of PTSD and other illnesses related to that war will get married more than once. In fact, I recall reading the results of one research study in which it was estimated that ninety percent of all PTSD-infected Vietnam vets will have at least one divorce in their lifetime. I know of some Vietnam vets who have been married five or six times. Imagine the after-trauma in each of those relationships if children were involved!

PTSD sufferers from combat experiences have been known to experience fits of rage, extreme irritability, hyper-vigilance, paranoia, high anxiety, hypertension and suicidal thoughts. What a burden this has put on our Vietnam vets' wives to be the caretakers of their families—without much support or understanding from the PTSD-infected veterans.

I have only begun to realize and understand what I have put my lovely wife through since the day she married me on my fortieth birthday on August 29, 1984. I ask myself...how can I ever make it up to my Ginny? I appreciate her more now than ever, and she remains very supportive of me. I often wish that I could have realized this much sooner than I did, but she knows that my Vietnam War buddies and I have suffered huge amounts of trauma from being in that war and from the after-effects of Vietnam. The after-effects? Yes, they do continue and the memories don't get any less sorrowful. Despite all those years, the memories remain in place for so many of us.

Our wives did not cause our problems. Combat trauma and the horrors of a war like Vietnam did. Our wives are not psychologists (unless you were lucky enough to have married one) and they cannot make us better. They can only try to love us better...IF we allow them.

How many times have I seen Kathy Bellemy, my wife Ginny, and the wives of other Nam brothers weep as we told our stories? Sometimes we shed our own tears, but mostly we show anger. So the $64,000 question (remember that show on TV) remains unanswered—**Why can't we get over a war that ended so long ago?** Whoever comes up with the answer to that one should be enshrined or given their own kingdom in a far-off paradise and waited on by hand and foot for the remainder of their lives.

There were programs available at some VA hospitals that offered assistance to wives of disabled veterans who were one hundred percent service-connected. Those programs were spotty and difficult to locate.

My parting advice on this critically touchy subject is directed to the veterans themselves. I, too, have experienced your pain, your grief. I, too, have moments of anger—sometimes desire to seek revenge, but instead, I found that "writing" is good therapy for my emotional problems. Please don't blame your loved ones for what the Vietnam War (or any war) did to you. It wasn't their fault. Please don't try to make others as miserable as you might be. And...DON'T GIVE UP!

I never set out to be a writer. I still don't consider myself an "author", but I am convinced that sitting down and writing about my own personal experiences and the personal experiences of others has helped bring some healing to my body and soul. At first, it was not easy, and I had to take a "time-out" from writing my first book. But I was compelled to resume and finish it...all 464 pages. Writing helps to dig up some of those deep feelings that I never realized were hiding in the back of my self-conscience. Writing helped bring me to the realization that I was infecting others with my own PTSD and trust me, my war buddies, that should be the last thing for what you want to be remembered.

There have been a few books written by Vietnam vet wives, but they seem to have been well-kept secrets—what a shame. Kathy Bellemy and her husband, Jack made their marriage survive for fifty years before her passing in January 2015. What a testimonial that marriage is to both of them—they made it happen, and to be sure, they had their Vietnam War-caused problems. Hats off to the Bellemys and a salute to a great wife of a real Vietnam veteran.

I have not mentioned the names of the Vietnam veterans' wives' organizations because I have not had any experiences with them. I have not recommended any titles of books on this subject because I have not read them, but I plan to because I want my marriage with Ginny to make it for as long as the Bellemy's. If this short section in this book pertains to your own situation, I hope it motivates you to at least become more educated on dealing with it rather than avoiding it or running away from it.

Since psychology is not my forte, I may have overstepped my bounds with my statements in this chapter. If so, I would welcome comments from a professional mental health provider. (Please do—dustytrimmer@yahoo.com.)

The Veterans Administration is currently operating 207 "Vet Centers" throughout the United States, Guam, Puerto Rico, and the Virgin Islands. These centers are designed to provide counseling and support for combat veterans. The description

of the centers on the VA website, which says, "Services are also available for their family members for military related issues. Veterans have earned these benefits through their service and all are provided at no cost to the veteran or family" is a little misleading though. Availability of counseling for spouses depends on the resources at an individual Vet Center. Some Vet Centers offer individual counseling, some offer only marriage or family counseling, some offer both. But the centers are a great FREE resource.
(Source: familyofavet.com ENewsletter)

The Vet Center that I have been using, located in Ravenna, Ohio, has been an excellent source, and it is free. The staff is warm, knowledgeable, compassionate and very accommodating to each veteran's needs. Secretary Bob ought to visit this facility to try to find out what is wrong with these people. They just don't act like VA workers at most other facilities...they seem to get it!

CHAPTER 17

BEGINNING A NEW CAREER...
AT SEVENTY?

F ind something that allows you to help other people. Having just about finished my second book made me suddenly realize something very profound—I
was starting all over with a new career at age seventy—wow! Not a small task
to tackle at retirement age and just coming off a pretty serious ischemic stroke
barely one year ago. Am I crazy? Well, of course, I am. I am a Vietnam War veteran—we are all crazy—as most of America was brainwashed into believing for
decades after the Vietnam War ended. Crazy or not, I am on it, my new writing
hobby. Hopefully, it will last long enough to put food on the table for Ginny, Bella
and me. Yes, Bella eats with us.

I was born near the end of World War II into a sub-middle-class family that
could only afford a five hundred dollar down payment when they purchased their
first house for the price of $8,900. It was a bold move for them and the entire
family shared their enthusiasm. We were Republicans all the way. I still remember
when WWII hero, General Eisenhower was in a parade in Cleveland, as he was
in the beginning stages of running for President. I remember the thousands of
small button pins that virtually everyone was wearing that day. The message on
those buttons was "I LIKE IKE".

On the other side was the Democratic Party and many of the Republicans
thought the Democrats were actually members of the Communist Party, so there
was a lot of mistrust in the air back then. That Democratic Party occupies the
White House today in the person of one Barack Hussein Obama and his top advisors. Obama was raised and trained in the Communist left as well as the radical
new left, the so-called liberals and he has remained heart and soul a part of it.
Today, instead of calling themselves communists or socialists, they call themselves liberals or progressives. In the end, they are usually…registered Democrats.

I think most Americans from both parties were just waking up from a state
of shock since Obama was elected, when the mid-term elections rolled around.

It appears to many that Obama had been on a mission to systematically bankrupt America.

Hold that thought because I think enough patriotic Americans, mostly conservatives, have been shocked into reality—putting genuine fear into their bones at what Obama's administration has accomplished towards their socialistic goals for America. Most military and veteran families should feel more relieved since the Republican victories at the mid-term election. Why? I should not have to address that question, but here is why:

- Liberals are very radical with their anti-military thinking. Maybe if their sons and daughters served in the military, making the parents more vested, they would not be so historically condemning of our country's warriors who do the fighting.
- Those who protested during the Vietnam War and those who financed them, were devoted to the socialist left, just like today's liberals.
- Every time Obama cuts the Defense budget or acts in a disrespectful manner towards our military, he insults you, me, and our country.

The answer, the solution? Serving in the military should probably be a prerequisite to running for Congress. The good news for our future is that the gloomy Obama years, which we have survived so far, helped to rouse a sleeping giant among young Americans and those in the military who never imagined what Obama's crowd was doing. All of a sudden, people are speaking openly with their neighbors and family about addressing them by their correct name, and they are...**SOCIALISTS!**

Patriotic Americans, mostly conservatives, are once again organizing at the grass roots level to defend the freedom for which our veterans fought. And that is what my starting over at age seventy is all about. I have become more involved with people and with groups that are serious about preserving this great country so that it has a bright future for generations to come.

I am one of those Americans who is still disgusted over the Benghazi disaster. Regardless of what your political leaning is, if you care about America and its people—especially the military—you should harbor deep resentment for what our President and Commander-in-Chief did *not* do around the Benghazi episode. Those three Americans were fighting for their lives that terrible night and their Commander-in-Chief did not come to their rescue. Just a reminder.

The Most Powerful Military on Earth…Downsized?

Listen up, war buddies, in case you have not been privy to this alarming information. We are all fully aware of the massive reduction of America's military force under the Obama administration. It has been decimated down to pre-World War II levels and this is very dangerous. Our military morale has also depleted from the high it was under both Bush administrations. This is real, not just my opinion. Anyone can access the sources to substantiate what I am saying is true. So we have a downsized military in strength and attitude. How safe does this have you feeling? The morale of our present military is so bad, read the following:

Tens of Thousands of Troops Deserting. Prosecutions are Rare.

I found this news in several media outlets just after Christmas 2014. One source reported that a few hundred cases of desertion have been prosecuted in the past decade, while tens of thousands have fled in the face of combat, long and repeated deployments in Iraq and Afghanistan.

Desertion is not difficult to prove. But the rise of PTSD and increased family problems have complicated the process. The maximum punishment for desertion during a time of war is death. However, only one desertion has been executed since the Civil War. Private Eddie Slovik was shot by a firing squad at age twenty-four in January 1945. His execution was approved by General Dwight D. Eisenhower.

The military's problem of desertion is not a new one. But this is supposed to be an "all volunteer" military, right? In the Vietnam War, which included a large force of drafters, desertion was not a major concern, not until the war was nearing its final years. Then nearly everyone wanted out of a war that was given up only by the American government. Any military veteran will vouch that the morale of the troops is dictated or affected from the top. In this case, our military's leader is…Barack Hussein Obama.

Obama does not appear to have an allegiance to this country's welfare. He does not identify with it, so why should he have any affection for those who have chosen to defend it…our military? Barack Hussein Obama is by far the most shameless President I have ever seen. But hey folks, Obama is not stupid as I've heard so many people shout out in front of a TV when he is giving a speech. He knows what he can say and get away with and what he can't.

There is someone else out there who can match our current President with one lie after another. She is also a minority. Beware, my fellow Americans because Hillary has all the potential possible to continue with Obama's plan for the destruction of America. If any of you want to see America continue its power decline...remain a bystander in world events...our enemies continue to gain strength...and worst of all...**diminish our military strength,** I am sorry you have read this far.

If there is anyone like that reading *Payback Time!*, then by all means, your vote for the next President of the United States of America has already been cast... HILLARY. Beware, as you might be voting for another Obama...in a pantsuit.

Hey out there to my black brothers. You think I am picking on Obama because he is half-black? The truth is--Obama has escaped being criticized for so long because he is partly black. He has received more than his fair share of free passes from the media. By the way, as I grew up always with or near a black influence, I distinctly remember the type of spoiled white kids who looked down on blacks. Those were generally members of families with financial advantages and they were not what would be considered conservatives today. They were the so-called elite left liberals. I saw it that way in the Vietnam War as well. The left-wing slanted troops clashed more with the blacks than the guys I hung around with.

NEWSFLASH: Most conservative Americans are not the defenders of the rich; they are defenders of policies that favor minorities and the poor. I know this to be true.

My dear war buddies and fellow Americans, even some of Obama's opponents have been hesitant to tell it like it is. When they debate him or in their next day's follow-up, they pat him on the back by referring to him as a "good man". How about—he is a liar and is without moral conscience?

The Tale of Two Well Known Black Americans

"We'll tear this g*dd*mn country up!" So said the self-ordained leader of the American Nation of Islam as he was speaking at Morgan State University to a largely African-American audience this past November 2014. Louis Farrakhan also told the captive listeners that violence was not only justified; it was required to deal with situations like the ones in Ferguson, Missouri. These statements of his appeared in several media sources in 2014.

The majority of Farrakhan's speech was directed in his usual tirade manner against "white America" as well as constant calls to violence from minority communities. To his credit (somewhat), he also issued strong complaints about his good old buddy, Barack Hussein Obama for his lack of action to support black America. Right. For those of you who are not very familiar with Louis Farrakhan's stand, he has long been a hate-mongering, violence promoter, and this speech continued to write his legacy. He is not likely to appear in any books for…great black American "role models." Just my opinion.

I love my black brothers. I really do. I also understand and sympathize with the pain and suffering they have endured. But I am completely confused by what some of their leaders have done to their own. Our black brothers and sisters have an abundance of inspirational role models to proudly emulate. The Farrakhan types are not among them.

As I read several reports on the not-so-honorable Reverend Farrakhan, probably the most uneasy part of this speech was the enthusiastic applause that was lavished on the speaker. One media source noted, "There should be calls to the Department of Justice to arrest and charge Louis Farrakhan with inciting insurrection with his comments. However, we all know what that would bring from this administration…nothing. They are in bed together."
(Source: *Freedom Outpost*, December 5, 2014)

I would strongly but respectfully urge our black brothers and sisters to separate themselves from the so-called black leaders such as this. In fact, I would use even stronger words for my request: **Don't fall into the plan to create race wars. They who instigate this, to fight each other in the streets do not have motives that will advance your standing in life, but it might…bring in martial law!**

How about a real…"breath of fresh air" that comes from Detroit Michigan? Dr. Benjamin Solomon Carson, Sr. He is one of my role models today. I could care less about his skin color. In fact, when I look at him, I do not even think of skin color. If we could put this genuine and caring man into the White House today, and extract the person running the show — Obama, of course — I would go for that in a heartbeat.

Dr. Carson used to be one of those on the left of the political world. Something made him change his political views. There has been much discussion about Dr. Carson as a presidential candidate…as a Republican. The rumors abound on that one. Unfortunately, I will have closed this book before we know his status on running for President.

Actually, I'm thinking that Dr. Carson might be one of the best candidates to start up and lead…a third political party. Just a thought. Anyway, this man has had my attention for a long time, and I would look forward to having an opportunity to vote for him in whatever capacity he decides. He sure would bring a breath of fresh air to the White House or anyone's house. By the way, not only was he a renowned neurosurgeon, but he has also received more awards and honors than I would be able to list in this entire book. Incidentally, one of the reasons I have pushed myself to try to get this book out by mid-2015 was so that my personal endorsement of Dr. Ben Carson would be out there with more than a year to go until November 2016. **GO BEN, GO...ALL THE WAY TO THE WHITE HOUSE!**

Two things I know will improve under a Ben Carson regime. Number one—poor blacks will do better than they are doing under the Obama reign. Yep, he lied to them too. Number two—Israel would once again know for sure that the good old USA is Israel's friend. Dr. Ben has been referred to as...the Anti-Obama. How could the Anti-Obama heal and unite our country? Simple straight up front answer...just do the opposite of everything Obama has done. Simple. Wouldn't that be a breath of fresh air?

Dr. Ben might scare the meek, mild people with his forthright ways. How can a man be this honest and have an interest in politics? There has to be something terribly wrong with him—something that he has been carefully hiding from America—there has to be. After all, he has been quoted already this year (2015) with such bold statements that few other politicians would only whisper in the safety of their homes. Did you know that Dr. Ben has been quoted with these statements about our friends at the Internal Revenue Service—yes, the IRS. "We need to do something about taxes. There is no question about that. We have a horrendous tax structure. It is too complex. Nobody can comply with it and it is unfair. We need something that is equally fair across the spectrum for everybody and that means either a flat tax or a fair tax. The important thing is that whatever we come up with, it needs to be...eliminating the IRS!" So said Dr. Ben Carson at a speech at the South Carolina Tea Party Convention. Do you have a problem with eliminating the IRS?

Unfortunately, most Americans have little or no faith and trust left within them to believe anyone would challenge the establishment, or allow the establishment to eliminate the IRS. Has something slipped your mind? The Republicans own the House and the Senate and Dr. Ben is surely not a Democrat! Obviously, if the next President decides to take on the age-old IRS monster, whatever would be put into place would also be a tall undertaking, and no doubt a costly one in the initial restructuring stages. Then there will be more Americans out of a job as our friendly IRS agents will be looking for a new career. Imagine having to put on your job application or your resume that you were an IRS agent for the last dozen years of your proud career? That might be worse than telling your prospective employer that you were one of those dreaded things called a...Vietnam War veteran.

Oh, how I wish Dr. Ben had some military background, but many of our past Presidents did not have military experience. What the hey, I am talking as though Dr. Ben has already been elected, and at this writing, he has not even committed to being an official candidate.

My dear active military and veteran brothers and sisters, think about this—we have lost our military to sodomy, our freedom of speech to homosexuals' human rights campaigners. Dr. Ben has been heard to say something like this about gay marriages…"Recall any justice who votes for gay marriage."

Why does it seem that racism talk has reached new heights in our country when actually, just the opposite is happening in our neighborhoods? I grew up in a small suburb halfway between Akron and Cleveland, Ohio. In the 1950s and 1960s, Twinsburg, Ohio was pretty much the only integrated of those two cities. I don't mind telling you that we paid the price with our high school sports teams because we were the only school in a thirty-mile radius with athletic teams that were black dominated. How did we pay the price? We usually got a raw deal from the white officials and referees in our sporting events, except of course, in track and field where we were nearly unbeatable during all of the 1960s.

Today, every suburb between Akron and Cleveland has black representation in their towns and racial tension is practically non-existent. The brothers I ran track with in the 1960s and the brothers I fought side by side with in Vietnam, also in the 1960s--where are they today in regards to my life? They are still my brothers. We still hang together—always will, I hope. So why do people like Al Sharpton (Obama's close buddy) spew racism out of their mouths on a daily basis, it seems? And why would the president of the United States include such a troublemaker among his close circles of chums? Sharpton was all over the Ferguson, Missouri protest with one goal in mind—to stir up a hornet's nest between races. Even Bill Clinton considered Sharpton a pure troublemaker and politically poisonous, as did George W. Bush, naturally. But Sharpton and Obama have embraced each other with Sharpton having visited the White House with alarming regularity. In fact, *Politico* has described Sharpton as Obama's "go-to-guy on race." If Sharpton is currently our President's "go-to-guy" on race, no wonder racism is making headlines in America again like it did way back in the 1960s and 1970s. No wonder. Why doesn't Sharpton and others like him spend more time with the African nations where black-on-black and black Muslim-on-black Christian ethnic cleansing continues? Spread your love with them, Al.

Okay, this white boy will get off this subject. I am not the most qualified person to speak about it, so I will turn things over to a couple of very qualified black men. To paraphrase former Florida representative and U.S. Army

Lt. Colonel Allen West when he was a guest in 2014 on *Fox and Friends* with guest host, **Charles Payne:**

For President Obama, when you look at it from his perspective, as a progressive socialist community organizer, he believes race relations are fine because of the impact they are having on social justice. So when you have this divide among us because that is the goal of collectivism, which is what the President believes in, then everything is fine for him. When you have somebody like Al Sharpton visiting the White House and providing him counsel eighty-two times and standing and putting pressure on Sony and other individuals, and this mob atmosphere that is going on, this is really what the president would like to have. This vomiting of dissension. But that is not what the inner city needs right now. We need economic growth, we need better education opportunities, but that is not the focus...

This quote from the December 30, 2014 edition of *Freedom Outpost* continued with this profound comment:

"If we are to win this fight over racism and racial division that the liberals in our nation seem to be so desperately spoiling for, we will need men like Col. West (and Charles Payne) to lead us. Their honesty, integrity and insight will be crucial to moving our country forward in a productive manner—something very different than what we've seen over the last six years. Hopefully, the upcoming GOP Presidential nomination race will show the nation that the GOP is the real Party of diversity. We hold the best answers to the problems faced by our minority communities and we won't pander or fudge the truth simply because it's convenient. We'll stick to our guns because we actually care..."

(December 11, 2014) – *The National Review:* "Al Sharpton at the White House, it seems as if he spends more time there than anywhere else. Why?"

I would think that Martin Luther King, Jr. would roll over in his grave if he could hear Al Sharpton's race-baiting publicity stunts. Dr. King put his life on the line fighting for an America in which all people would be judged by their character rather than their skin color. Sharpton has displayed none of the leadership or character of Dr. King. I wonder how Dr. King would have embraced Sharpton today. Then again, would he have embraced Obama? Last I read, Obama still had refused to relate terrorist attacks like the Kosher deli attack in France with Islam. More and more, people are leery of where Obama's allegiance leans. One media source, *Freedom Outpost* asked that question in this manner, "Where is his allegiance? Either Obama is not so secretly a jihad sympathizer, or he is a believer. It's one and the same."

Representative Michele Bachmann, outspoken in her own right, stated in an interview as reported by *Freedom Outpost* on September 30, 2014:

"[Seeking] amnesty for illegal aliens is the number one achievement of the president's second term," Bachmann said on an interview that aired on Breitbart News Saturday on Sirius XM Patriot Channel 125. "He's planning to get it, and he's planning to jam it down the throats of the American people. It's a plate of dog food to do this," Bachmann said. "It's not what the American people want— they're going to react—which is why the president is taking the coward's way out, and he's waiting until after the election."
(Source: *Freedom Outpost*, September 30, 2014)

Louisiana State Senator Elbert Guillory stated in an interview on January 6, 2015, "I never use the terms Sharpton and King in the same sentence or in the same paragraph. I believe that those of us who have some grey hair, as Sharpton does, have a responsibility to move the American community forward in a non-divisive and peaceful fashion. If there are problems, those problems can be addressed, they should be. But to throw gasoline on fire is not a positive or valuable solution to society. It's not valuable at all. These professional race-baiters, it is so unfortunate they exist. They need to be stamped out."

Amen, I say. Martin Luther King, Jr. was a great man, Christian and American. Obama, Sharpton and Farrakhan are neither. Martin Luther King, Jr. could have been, and should have been the first black president of the United States, not what is presently occupying the White House. WAKE UP, BLACK AMERICA! Our Commander in Chief is setting another pathetic record or standard that presidents to follow will be hard pressed to live "down to." He has set a new record. This time he has set an all time low of a fifteen percent approval rating from the very military that he allegedly commands. Now keep in mind that the military is not committed to either political party, but they do hate military decisions that are made for political reasons to better one party over another. In a 2014 survey by *Military Times*, it was found:

- Obama's popularity has plummeted, falling from thirty-five percent in 2009 to fifteen percent this past year.
- Obama's disapproval ratings have increased from forty to fifty-five percent in the same time frame.

Oh, by the way, Hillary's closest advisor, Huma Abedin is a Muslim.

Good news, patriots! Over the years, the President that Americans elect is often a significant contrast to the President in office. Carter replaced Nixon… Reagan replaced Carter…Bush replaced Clinton…Obama?

If this somewhat accurate pattern holds true, our next President could be the savior of which our country is so desperately in need. The significant contrast to Obama would be someone with many or all of the following qualities, which Obama does not possess—honest, direct, strong on national security, tough on foreign policy and very supportive of the military and military veterans. Ask yourself—does the party on the left—the Democrats—have a person with most or all of these…outstanding qualities?

I think there are at least nine quality Americans who have already indicated that they are a possible presidential candidate, and each would deserve your vote rather than a vote for Hillary or whatever comes out from her cult-like group. We have the power in November 2016. Damn it; use it wisely. (This is not a paid political endorsement. It comes from the heart of a patriotic, combat-wounded Vietnam veteran who is trying to fight back.)

Well, my fellow Americans, it was quite a year for America's veterans in 2014—and some of the news turned into good news by the year's end, thanks to those who stepped up and emphatically, specifically told Congress about the atrocious treatment of veterans at VAs across America. By the end of 2014, I could see it on the news, read it in the newspapers, and I heard it on the street, that America's veterans must never be forgotten again, that every one of them deserves the respect of a nation that should be a grateful nation.

Putting "my money where my mouth is" during the writing of this book… *Payback Time!, Veterans Unite To Challenge VA For Overdue Benefits*, I have formed a new company to support the book and from which to launch future books. In my new "dream career" at age seventy, as one of the managing partners of VETERANS STRIKE BACK LLC and speaking for all of the veterans who have joined me, our mission is simply this:

Mission Statement of
VETERANS STRIKE BACK LLC

Veterans Strike Back LLC (VSB) is not just another start-up company looking for an instant profit at the expense of investors. **Veterans Strike Back** is a "pact" so to speak among a group of bona fide American veterans who have joined forces together for a common cause. This alliance of American veterans from several eras is a coalition of patriots with shared interests and goals in preserving our way of life.

"Help Them to Seek and Receive What They Earned and Deserved"

Our collaborative means-oriented arrangement will be open to other people or organizational entities to pool resources and combine efforts in order to affect changes that will impact the lives of America's veterans and their loved ones in the most beneficial way possible.

- We will continue to gain political influence or intervention with our efforts for the benefit of our patriotic veterans who served honorably.

Veterans Strike Back will conduct an organized program to achieve its goals. However, the organization will exist as a flexible, non-structured, unified group that can respond to problems, situations or threats to the quality of life for our country's veterans and their loved ones.

Veterans Strike Back is not a charitable 501(c)3 organization. We need to generate revenue in order to achieve the goals that have been set by the company's membership and volunteers. Mutual trust is paramount between our members, volunteers, investors and contributors, who are intensely dedicated.

Revenue sources could come from, but are not limited to the following:

4) Book sales

5) Contributions

6) Investments and grants

Other causes that VSB will address in its first year of operation will be, but are not limited to:

1) Why is our government helping illegal aliens before veterans who have fought for this country? Our stand is clear on this...VETERANS BEFORE ILLEGALS.
2) The 2016 Presidential election and influencing the prolific American veteran voters to support the best candidate for our country, regardless

of which political party he/she comes from. WE NEED A **STRONG** LEADER, ONE WHO LOVES AND RESPECTS THE USA…NOT DESPISES IT!

Combined results of several polls that I saw in late 2014 showed these as strong candidates for President in 2016:

Democrats	Republicans
1. Hillary Clinton	1. Rand Paul
2. Hillary Clinton	2. Ted Cruz
3. Hillary Clinton	3. Dr. Ben Carson & Marco Rubio

3) Ensure America is aware of its threats to our way of life, such as the Muslim brotherhood—because they hate us and they must be controlled.
4) We will continue to gain political influence with our efforts for the benefit of patriotic Americans whether they served in our military or not.
5) Watchdog of the Department of Veterans Affairs and to keep pressure on them to save veterans…not kill them.
6) Provide support for all veterans willing to stand up for themselves and who are being mistreated by the VA…we will get into the face of VA.
7) Help Vietnam veterans receive a better legacy in history…They **EARNED** it.

The main inspiration for forming **VSB** was the surprising, unexpected, profound way my first book, *Condemned Property?* impacted so many Vietnam veterans as well as non-veterans. This made me sit back and wonder to myself…if someone could write one book with overwhelming passion and impact people enough to keep them alive (from suicide), "Holy Batman," one can only imagine or dream how many people we could impact if a team of us got together and contributed great American "come from behind" stories about down and out veterans into a series of books, IF we had the funds and means to reach tens of thousands or hundreds of thousands rather than just a couple thousand!

We have an intense burning desire to …help them, our veteran buddies seek and receive what they earned and deserve…their rightful legacy in history, the opportunity to enjoy a better quality of life now, and to live a while longer.

I have never been more serious or dedicated about any endeavor in my life, except for my will to survive during the Vietnam War itself. I am recruiting dozens of volunteers, mostly veterans, to contribute time, energy, ideas and even some of their hard-earned dollars to this dream of mine to make a difference in the lives of America's heroes from all wars, for as long as we are able.

One terrific thing about the USA has always been possible for all Americans, that being:

- A small group of dedicated thoughtful, patriotic Americans can change the course of history. I believe this with all my heart and I believe Veterans Strike Back LLC can do just that...only the future will know. But the best thing about the future is that it only comes one day at a time, then the future will result from what we do this day and the next.

Nearly everyone I talk to lately expresses his or her concern for our country's future. Most of them do nothing about it. VSB will not sit back and do nothing, not while our warriors are still falling very prematurely at the hands of their own government.

The week of December 14, 2014 will be remembered as one of my most surprising...most stressful, most sleepless, most gratifying, most exhilarating, most forgetful, most memorable weeks I have experienced in a couple of decades. Looking back at those days, each one of them was chock full of meaningful happenings that would have been enough excitement or disappointment for most individuals to deal with in one full year. Then again, some of us seek out and thrive on the suspense of not knowing what is going to happen next in our lives. I have always been one of those people. However, it may be time to look for other excitement.

The week of December 14 was an extremely emotional week for me and my feelings about it right now remain optimistically guarded. This week began and ended with calls from Vietnam War brothers that I became acquainted with during and after their reading of *Condemned Property?* Four of these Nam vets were serious suicide candidates when they first started reading my book. All four of them reached out to me before they had finished reading the book to share their comments, critiques or compliments on the book. The critiques were minimal, and what I expected about the shortcomings of the book, which I was already aware of, such as:

- Too much anger—you have to let it go...(I can't)
- Disorganization—I jumped around....(could not help it)

On the other side, most of the Nam vets who communicated back to me had these comments or opinions about the book, which they willingly shared with me:

- It was not an enjoyable book to read, but it was one that opened their eyes and they were glad to have read it.
- Some said it was difficult to put down and that they often refer back to it. Some began reading it again.
- Several told me how the book inspired them to resume getting on with their lives and they are once again, looking forward to living on.
- Many were motivated to return to the battlefield to challenge the Department of Veterans Affairs again, to renew their long battle…**to seek and receive the health-care benefits they earned and deserve.**

As for those guys I spoke with during the week of December 14, five of seven were doing quite well and that was a relief for me and their family members and close friends. All were receiving care, therapy and/or financial benefits from the VA, and they were extremely happy about that. Two of the seven were not doing so well. One suffered an ischemic stroke similar to mine, and he was going to enter into a post-stroke rehab program shortly after Christmas. I referred some other Nam vets to check on his progress and they have done that, as I have.

Another told me of his experiences with group therapy for his severe PTSD with other veterans held at a VA facility. He was not satisfied with his classes, mostly because he felt some of the other "so-called combat vets" as I named them, were telling stories of their battle experiences that did not seem very believable. He was certain that some of these vets were "wannabes" and were guilty of…"stolen valor." Two of the guys and I decided to hook up before the holidays were over, and we have set tentative dates to do that. I would love to expand on this part of the story and I know my new Nam brothers would not mind me sharing more details about their situations, but I decided to save that endeavor for another time — maybe another book or two.

In the past, veterans could not dare to complain about the VA so they just died with their frustrations and anger. I feel that today this has changed and I would not be hesitant to take any and every measure to challenge anyone at VA at any level of responsibility. Unfortunately, very few of the vets I talk to, mostly Vietnam vets, have become confident enough to step forward and this just ain't right. This is too bad because getting the truth out into the public is our best hope for change but VA still presents itself as a very intimidating and vengeful organization. Who of us can afford to lose the benefits that we have fought so hard for and who our war buddies before us fought so hard for and in many cases died fighting the VA. If we could ALL dare — if we could be sure that some idiotic VA official could not flag us as a "troublemaker", there would be an uprising of hundreds of thousands of voices that would be heard.

I am no more brave than the next veteran, and I have just as much to lose as any of you by speaking up as I have done in both of my books. I tread water every day, wondering if some hateful VA official is taking notes from my books, "red flagging" them and sending them on to others to review for possible action to be taken. I have been privy to several of these "red flagging" instances as shared with me by several VA officials in mid-level authoritative positions.

One by one, we would not be very effective in challenging the VA for any retaliatory measures against us. This is another reason I have formed **Veterans Strike Back LLC** and have recruited dozens of volunteers and partners to join me so that we have a stronger voice. Make no mistake my fellow war buddies, the days of a VA official who has unjustly wronged us and remains exempt from prosecution…are over.

CHAPTER 18

VIETNAM WARRIORS' LEGACY?

How will the Vietnam War's heroes and victims be thought of and remembered in years and decades to come? Will they be thought of or remembered...at all? I am working on this with my books though my newly founded company. This is one of the purposes of **Veterans Strike Back LLC**.

Students and adults alike will have little or incorrect knowledge about what happened (really happened) over there. Most history books remain very inaccurate and far incomplete on the topic of the Vietnam War. What was going on in the Indonesian peninsula from 1954 to 1973 with America's involvement deserves to be represented, deserves to be taught and deserves to be remembered. I am not advocating for a class on the Vietnam War's history to be mandated in our high schools, although that would be nice. I am just saying that the truth should be more readily available.

There have been many books published about the Vietnam War. Very few of them offer historical data of much significance, and unfortunately, too many of them are fictional, which confuses people about what really happened over there. Not to mention these books contribute to the distortion of Vietnam.

I guarantee that none of my books will ever be classified into the category of fiction. *Condemned Property?* and *Payback Time!* as well as any future books I am associated with will always contain factual, historical information about Vietnam, told and researched by me or some of my Vietnam War buddies. This is my sworn promise. Knowledge of Vietnam needs to be part of future learning. Think about it. If we are asked questions like this: What exactly happened at Gettysburg...at the Alamo...Bunker Hill...Iwo Jima...or D-Day? Many of us would be capable of delivering an accurate and detailed explanation. At least, I hope so, and that is good. But ask random Americans basic questions about something like: What was the Tet Offensive and who was the victor? Where did Khe Sanh take place and what happened there? I do not have much confidence that a majority of those random Americans quizzed would provide a credible answer about Tet or Khe Sanh. I hope to live long enough to be proven wrong.

The Vietnam War is an integral part of American history as well as world history, just as Korea and the World Wars were. How could our own media disrespect the participants in Vietnam (and their families) by referring to it as a regional conflict? The Mexican-American War was a regional conflict. The Indian-American Wars were regional conflicts. Our own War Between the States was a regional conflict. The War in Vietnam was *not* a regional conflict. I know that I have covered this scenario earlier in this book, but it is pertinent to this section to mention again with historical and factual back up. These figures will undoubtedly shock some.

American Total Casualties – America's Conflicts vs. the Vietnam War
1775 - 2013
(Smallest to Largest)

Conflict	Duration	Total KIA/WIA
Haiti (Operation Uphold Democracy)	1994 – 1995	3
Islamic State of Iraq & Levant (ISIL) (Operation Inherent Resolve)	2014 -	8
Waziristan War (North Pakistan)	2004 -	10
2nd Barbary Coast War	1815	14
Panama (Operation Just Cause)	Dec 1989 – Jan 1990	23
Cherokee-American War	1776 – 1777	39
Yemen (Al-Qaeda Insurgency)	1998 -	56
Seminole Indian War	1855 - 1858	53
1st Barbary Coast War	1801 – 1805	99
Grenada (Operation Urgent Fury)	Oct 1983 – Dec 1983	135
Nicaragua Occupation	1912 – 1933	159
Utah War	1857 – 1858	U.S. Military 38 Mormons 126

Somalia (Operation Restore Hope)	1992 – 1993	196
Creek Indian War	1813 – 1814	584
Gulf War	1990 - 1991	1,231
Northwest Indian Wars	1817 - 1818	
Western Indian Wars (Black Hawk, Dakota, Modoc, Sioux, Ute)	1862 - 1898	2,665
Spanish-American War	1898	4,068
Philippine – American War	1898-1913	7,126
Afghanistan	2001-Present	12,135
Mexican-American War	1846-1848	17,435
War of 1812	1812-1815	25,000
Iraq War	2003-2011	36,395
Revolutionary War	1775-1783	50,000
Korea War	1950-1953	128,650
TOTAL:		**286,248**
Vietnam War	**1955-1975**	**362,924**

(Source: Department of Defense, 2012)

Even World War I realized fewer American casualties than Vietnam at 320,518. But of course, WWI lasted from just 1917 to 1918 while the Vietnam War is documented to have lasted different lengths: 1955 to 1975…1959 to 1973*…1962 to 1973*. (*America's duration of participation.) I do not intend to diminish anyone else's wars. I am just trying to point out the significance of our war.

Again, I feel it is important to mention that nearly thirty percent of all American casualties in Vietnam were registered in just one single year, 1968, the year of The Tet Offensives when the total casualties recorded were astronomical…104,387!

Arguably, the battles fought by Americans in that one year, which included multiple phases of the Tet Offensive could and should be described in the history books as some of the most intense, emotional, in your face and psychologically terrifying combat ever fought in American history. Warriors who survive such brutal life-threatening encounters repeatedly, are almost guaranteed to carry the memories of those minutes, hours, days or months for their entire lives.

Medical professionals continue to research and study the effects of combat fatigue or post-traumatic stress from different levels of combat. Fortunately, the mental sciences have gradually progressed to a level where today's returning combat veterans have a better chance of returning to a society that does have some capacity to understand them. The importance of a vastly improved Veterans Affairs is way overdue and its functionality as a first class medical provider can never receive a high enough priority in America.

VA is keeping me alive today. I feel that the health care I am receiving from the VA may be the finest of my life—finally. However, just seven to ten years ago, I used to dread my VA appointments. This is what a VA appointment process used to be like back then:

- Initiate contact with VA for an appointment IF you could make contact with a VA live person. Eventually, because of the veteran's persistence, the call is completed and an appointment is confirmed.
- Your appointment, regardless of the seriousness of the patient's problem, is scheduled a few months down the road.
- At your appointment, depending on your ailment and the department you are there to visit, you wait in the lobby for at least an hour or two. One misdiagnosis after another and another, which you have no way of being aware of at the time because you are not a doctor.

If any of you are math wizards, you should be very impressed because you have already done the addition. America has been engaged in 'at least' twenty-eight conflicts or wars since 1775. That sure seems like a lot, doesn't it? Aside from the fact that we have taken control over *none* of our adversaries' homelands, the other glaring fact that SHOUTS OUT is that the Tet Offensive will always be a major part of the Vietnam War legacy. Most of us who fought in it are proud of it as many of us continue to relive those battles in our minds to this day. Our legacy? Are we going to be remembered from the newspaper stories that have continued to plague us, depress us, and put us into graves so disgustingly premature? Newspaper stories such as these:

"Vietnam vet generation fading as death rates rises."
"Vietnam veteran in his final battle."
"Half of all homeless veterans are from Vietnam era."
"Tens of thousands of Vietnam veterans continue to die of their own hand."
"Vietnam vets continue coping with thoughts of suicide."
"Vietnam veterans are the majority of VA claims backlog."
"Vietnam veterans at greater risk of dying from violent death."
"Post service mortality rate of Australian Vietnam veterans five times higher than other Australian veterans."

"Five years after returning home, Vietnam combat veterans had an overall death rate of forty-five percent higher than non-Vietnam War veterans."
"Vietnam vets troubled by early deaths."
"Suicide rate spikes in Vietnam vets who won't seek help."
"Vietnam veteran goes on rampage."

These are but a few of many national news headlines that Vietnam veterans have made for themselves over the last forty years, even recently. ENOUGH!

Everyone who prays should pray for those victims of that unfortunate war. Pray that those of us who remain will not soon become a part of the horrendous statistics of our former war buddies. By all means, also include our more recent veterans, as many of them have also fallen prematurely after coming back home.

I, too, am dealing with the cursed memories of Vietnam. The major difference between me of today and me of ten years ago is that I am talking about it, writing about it and so should every other Vietnam War veteran who is able to do so.

Hanoi Jane apologizes again...almost!

There are so many important issues at stake in our lives right now, and Jane isn't one of them. But I just would not be able to live with myself if I did not exercise my American right to express myself about the daughter of the late, great Henry Fonda. Most of my Vietnam War buddies would expect nothing less of me and I never want to let them down...never. And after all, "Hanoi Jane" has affected our legacy in many ways. We should not ever forget her.

Sometime in mid January 2015, Hanoi Jane issued another feeble apology to make amends with survivors of the Vietnam War. Was it a genuine apology this time? Maybe. Maybe not. Here is an exact transcript of some of her comments at the Weinberg Center for the Arts. "Whenever possible, I try to sit down with Vietnam veterans and talk with them because I understand and it makes me sad. It hurts me and it will go to my grave—that I made a huge mistake that made a lot of people think I was against the soldiers."

For those of you who may have forgotten why the infamous actress was tabbed by Vietnam War veterans as "Hanoi Jane", here is the briefest recap I can afford to lend space to in this book.

In 1972, Fonda visited Hanoi, North Vietnam where she was documented to have criticized the American military for their attacks on North Vietnam. (We were still at war!) She was photographed wearing an NVA helmet while sitting on an NVA anti-aircraft battery, compliments of the Soviet

Union and from that moment, she became "Hanoi Jane" and was labeled as a traitor.

Fonda has been blamed, justifiably so, for encouraging North Vietnam to pull away from the peace treaty negotiation table. How many more Americans died from that move? And while she continued to express her regrets for her actions and that she understood why the veterans feel the way they do about her, she also said on this day, "I do not regret traveling to North Vietnam. It was an incredible experience."

Fonda was recorded on Radio Hanoi, condemning the war from America's standpoint. She issued harsh words against President Nixon for the bombings in 1972, which forced North Vietnam back to the peace negotiations. In my first book, *Condemned Property?* I have given Hanoi Jane more coverage. I don't have any more space or time to give to her anymore here. So did she really apologize? Probably not.

Wouldn't we do ourselves and our fallen war buddies much greater justice if we left this earth for the next life, if we left people behind that remembered us as true survivors who fought till the end rather than feeling sorry for ourselves? I would. Hanoi Jane can stop anytime now with her shallow apology attempts.

Loyal soldiers deserve to live their lives out naturally, but I know how the shadow of their war can intervene on that plan. Therefore, we can all use a little help from others. I am extremely fortunate to have a wonderful companion supporting me, my wife of thirty years, Ginny Brancato Trimmer. In fact, Ginny accepted me and married me on my fortieth birthday. She was my first wife and she will be my last—I swear this. Ginny met me and accepted me when I was in one of the most vulnerable and dangerous times of my life. I was very suicidal at the time. So really, she is the primary reason I am still here today, able to put this book together. Yes, plain and simple, if it wasn't for her, I would be dead by now.

My dear Nam brothers and sisters, writing my book has blessed me with another meaningful purpose in life. It has connected me with scores of other Nam brothers, drawn to me from my first book, *Condemned Property*? There are way too many of us out there, living like "lost souls" and I strongly believe we can and should be helping each other.

Here is a disappointing discovery I made as I was writing my first book. Since I wanted and felt I needed other Nam veterans to be a part of my first book, I reached out to about ninety of them, asking them to share a story of their Vietnam War experience with would-be readers of my book, most of whom I figure would be Vietnam War veterans, which has been the case. I was almost shocked and certainly disappointed at the response to my quest for willing Nam vets to share with others. Approximately eight out of every ten vets I approached had little or no interest to share anything about Vietnam, not in my book or with anyone. This is why I had to try to make close to one hundred attempts. That was sad, but in reality, I should not have been surprised.

Fortunately, I was able to gather thirteen very powerful stories and some readers have referred to that chapter in *Condemned Property?* as one of the most impressive parts of that book. Lo and behold, I have received over one hundred responses from Nam vets, expressing their pleasure with the book and this has inspired me to write this book and to form the company I mentioned in a previous chapter…**Veterans Strike Back LLC.**

My dear war buddies (of any war), doesn't it sound much better to you if someone said this about us…"He was a fighter. He never gave up," rather than if they thought or said this about us…"He quit. He gave up, etc."? Hey, if you feel like talking, you can always reach me anytime at my email address, dustytrimmer@yahoo.com.

Unfortunately, our brothers and sisters from the present wars are also battling to escape their personal wars, and it is very difficult for them as well. Nam vets are experts at having to deal with their war that has continued for decades. Couldn't we offer comfort to some of these new and young wounded warriors? After all, we pretty much know what lies ahead for many of them and it will continue to happen for decades. Regardless of the age difference, I believe we can help each other in winning our battles with our demons.

Try it, Nam vets. Open up. Speak to an Afghan or Iraq vet tomorrow and then do it again. You may find that this will be good therapy for both of you and you may have made a new friend.

Maybe, just maybe, the legacy of Vietnam War veterans may eventually be something like this:

Despite what happened to Vietnam veterans when they returned home, the returning vets from the Gulf, Afghanistan and Iraq Wars were welcomed with open arms and kind words by Vietnam veterans.

Vietnam veterans truly are one of America's greatest generations. That would be a nice legacy to appear in the history books, wouldn't it? I know that most of us have been extending our comfort to the veterans coming home from today's wars and they are aware of it. **BRAVO, VIETNAM VETERANS!**

There are no words available to me in any language that would allow me to explain and properly describe now much pain these men have been forced to live with since they came home from Vietnam. As we often say to people who ask us from time to time, "What was it like over there?" Our response is common among us…**you had to be there**.

Again, I remind you—I am not a degreed psychologist or even a somewhat trained therapist. My only qualifications to listen and to talk to our war brothers about their life's stresses is that I have lived most of their experiences and that I am beyond harboring everything inside me. The latter has become very important for me in the last several years. Trouble is, always has been--finding someone "trustworthy" to share your experiences with and to find someone like that…who actually cares about your painful experiences. This is one of the main reasons why veterans (especially Vietnam veterans) are drawn together and may often save their stories to be shared only with someone else who they know will genuinely care.

The tragedy of Vietnam continues. Its aftermath continues. With so many Vietnam War veterans still unable or unwilling to share their stories, going to the grave with them, I am constantly saddened by this, but also motivated by this tragedy. Motivated to try and submit factual stories about Vietnam and its warriors who died there and continue to die after coming home to their beloved USA. I am motivated to continue with this battle, a battle to prevent an endangered species of humans from premature and complete…extinction.

Vietnam's veterans have been the pillars in many communities nationally, and have had to overcome many life threatening and life altering challenges, yet they may still face difficult life events such as retirement, a life of disability and loss of loved ones. No matter how long it has been since a veteran of any war has served, they can always improve their lives. Veterans Strike Back LLC is dedicated to this end.

At the time this book was submitted to Liberty Hill Publishing, multiple sources had estimated that of the 2.8 million plus who served IN the country of Vietnam during the war… approximately 1.8 million have perished.

I am fully aware that the long-term marketability of this book could be shortened by the amount of attention I have dedicated to my thoughts and facts about the all-important November 2016 election. If the "good guys" lose, I lose, and so will our great country lose. I pray that there are enough smart Americans out there who can see past the liberal slanted media, who can get past their family heritage in that their parents and their grandparents all voted for the left. Please America…get past that and place a vote next November that will go a long way towards resurrecting the United States of America.

Our Legacy, Our Future...Rests on November 2016 Elections

It is no secret that the course of American history was dramatically altered by the Vietnam War. In 1966, President Johnson lied about actions in Vietnam and because of this, he lost his trust and support from the American public. As we know, he would not seek reelection. Until Johnson's great deception, most Americans had great trust in their leaders and their government in general. I believe that it was at this point in time that the media turned into a watchdog of politicians. Hatred for the Vietnam War turned to extreme hatred and unfortunately, the American warriors who lived the horrors of Vietnam would also be punished yet again when they returned home to the coldest unwelcome home greeting an American military had ever faced. This unexpected reception would only add to the burden that Vietnam's returning warriors carried from the war itself. The American people wanted nothing else to do with the Vietnam War, especially since so many of them had witnessed through their own TVs what the media would allow them to see. In most cases, the American military was shown as violent and heartless killers of civilians and farmers who were fighting like revolutionaries for their country's ultimate freedom. Hogwash!

More than ten million people died, were casualties or were permanently displaced. The Vietnam War had more bombs dropped than all of World War II and vast amounts of Vietnam's forests were wiped from the earth by America's Agent Orange. Hundreds of thousands of American military were sent home, carrying poisons in their bodies from the Agent Orange Dioxins, which would eventually begin to kill them off from five to fifty years after the war had ended.

No American war had ever divided this country the way Vietnam did, not even the Civil War. One can trace today's lack of trust and skepticism of America's public toward their President and the government back to those Vietnam War years. Americans simply have never respected or trusted their own government after the Vietnam War.

How can we change this? How can the survivors of Vietnam and its lingering after-effects ever be given their just due...a legacy that future generations will look at with respect and admiration? I have a theory. I have hope that it can happen. Just like Johnson's regime shattered the faith and patriotic attitude of America, could it be possible that our next leader, our next President and Commander in Chief would begin a return to glory for Americans? Of course it cannot happen if we do not elect the right person from the right party, the Republican party, where most true-blue conservatives reside. A conservative Republican President with a Republican dominant House and Senate is our best shot, folks. I believe this with all my heart.

The VA pressure on the Veterans Administration did not erupt until 2014. It continued to escalate as the Senate lost its control to the Republicans. There is a heavy representation of veterans in Congress today. Most of the probable candidates for the Presidency are very sympathetic to veterans and yes, even or especially Vietnam War veterans. The right man from the right party with the right dominated Congress is the only chance to save America, to turn it around, to stop the insanity of legalizing "illegal immigrants", the utter stupidity of making our country more vulnerable to enemy attack because of an ungodly dismantling of our once proud and powerful military. This is the belief of one common American, a patriot, a combat Vietnam veteran American.

I want a safe America. That doesn't mean an America that is constantly fighting wars in far-off and unfriendly lands. We need to close and guard our own borders as a top priority. We need to deal with those who arrived here illegally and don't deserve to be here because they do not even want to be called Americans.

What is being called *The Tragedy of the American Military* under the Obama regime can be salvaged from ruination. I believe that once again, our military can be admired at the level it once was — before the Obama plan to humble it, weaken it and humiliate it. I believe this is going to happen. The beginning or starting point will be when you decide who our next President will be. Will you elect…an American son or something else? The legacy of the Vietnam War warrior depends on it. The legacy of today's military is going to depend on it. The future of our country will depend on it.

He was one of the greatest military leaders of all time…Giap! While papa Ho Chi Minh was the figurehead of North Vietnam, General Vo Nguyen Giap was the captain of Ho's army. Giap had a phenomenal military career, second to very few. His many victories included repelling China and defeating France.

General Giap was a brilliant, highly respected of the North Vietnam military. The following quote is from his memoirs currently found in the Vietnam War Memorial in Hanoi:

**"What we still don't understand is why you Americans stopped the
bombing of Hanoi. You had us on the ropes.
If you had pressed us a little harder, just for another day or two,
we were ready to surrender.
It was the same at the battle of TET. You defeated us!
We knew it and we thought you knew it.
But we were elated to notice your media was helping us.
They were causing more disruption in America
than we could handle in the battlefields.
We were ready to surrender.
You had won!"**

General Giap has published his memoirs and confirmed what most Americans knew. The Vietnam War was not lost in Vietnam—it was lost at home. The same slippery slope, sponsored by the U.S. media is currently underway. It exposes the enormous power of a biased media to cut out the heart and will of the American public.

**A truism worthy of note...Do not fear the enemy,
for they can take only your life.
Fear the Media
for they will destroy your honor.**

One of the saddest things about the Vietnam War is...it continues to kill so many who have struggled to survive it after they came home!

- Author Unknown

EPILOGUE – FINAL WORDS

I believe the Presidential election of 2016 is the most important one of my lifetime. For the first time since the election of Ronald Reagan, we have a number of quality candidates who would make excellent Presidents.

It is clear that if veterans and the military are ever going to regain the lost status suffered under Obama, a decisive vote against Hillary is a must. I like these three Republican candidates the best:

Rand Paul

Marco Rubio

Ben Carson

Please vote with your heart. Vote for a rebirth of America. There is only one option we have to save this country. Please vote against the Democratic nominee.

My love for our country runs deep. My love for Americans runs deeper because they are America. But my love runs deepest for my Vietnam "war buddies." My first book, *Condemned Property?* was dedicated to them, but I am so afraid that they are quickly on the brink of becoming an…"endangered species."

I fully appreciate that some people show their soft kindness and dedication to rescuing abused pets or saving and preserving natural wildlife or putting themselves out for other worthy causes. That is great, and right in the same neighborhood that I live in. Hey, I am Dusty Trimmer, a strong advocate for the underdogs, and I will continue to be. But there is this group of living human beings who put their lives on the line for all of us. This group has been dishonored…abandoned…abused…betrayed for decades. Our goal is to prevent this group from premature…

EXTINCTION!

Vietnam veterans have been the pillars in many communities nationally and have had to overcome many life-threatening and life-altering challenges, yet they may still face difficult life events such as retirement, disability and loss of loved ones. No matter how long it has been since a veteran of any war has served, they can always improve their lives. Veterans Strike Back LLC is dedicated to this purpose.

We used to be the lost kids of the 1960s and 1970s, but today, I am proud to say…**WE ARE AMERICA'S VIETNAM WAR ERA VETERANS…ONE OF AMERICA'S GREATEST GENERATIONS.**

INDEX

NOTES ON SOURCES

The material for *Payback Time!* was compiled from many sources—mainly from my own personal experiences and observations and those from other veterans, mostly Vietnam War veterans who I personally interviewed by telephone, in person, by email or written letters. In most cases, I have made a diligent effort to credit people by name for their contribution with their permission. Most images in this book that were not my personal property have been credited to the owner or where I discovered them. There were very few that did not belong to other veterans or myself. Some images can be found on numerous media venues, therefore it is impossible to give credit to its origin.

Here are some of the major websites or media vehicles in which I found much of the facts that support my book's statements:

www.25thida.org
www.besthistorysites.net
www.pbs.org/battlefieldvietnam
www.wikipedia.org
www.starsandstripes.com
www.concernedveteransforamerica.com
www.togetherweserved.com
www.newsmax.com
www.oathkeepers.com
www.patriotupdate.com
www.vfw.org/VAwatch
www.grassfirehq.com
www.freedomoutpost.com
www.armytimes.com
www.militarytimes.com
www.minutemannews.com
www.giveanhour.org

Brother Dusty, I ordered your book through Borders and I was unable to put it down until finished. So many things you wrote about brought back memories of VN, good and not so good. When I came into the company, I was greeted by three recovering wounded soldiers, telling me when I go out to the boonies, to take a book because it can get boring. Others said, carry all the ammo you can because you'll need it. So I did both and never got a chance to read that book. I needed more ammo. Check out the B Co. website, bravoregulars.com. In the Pictures section, you are in the top left photo. **You have my permission to use any of my photos.** Thanks for such a terrific rendering of Vietnam for us. I feel like giving a copy to my VA doctor.

- Brother Steve
Bravo Regulars 3/22nd 25th Infantry Division
U.S. Army, Vietnam (1968-1969)

'NAM TALK' GLOSSARY

ABN	Airborne
Agent Orange	Chemicals used as a defoliant in recent years found to cause medical problems in Vietnam Veterans
AIT	Advanced Infantry Training
AK-47	A Russian assault rifle
Alpha Bravo	Slang for ambush
Ameri-Cong	Term used in *Comrades in Arms* by author, Roger Canfield, PhD
Angel Flight	Aircraft used to transport soldiers' remains back to the United States, usually a C-130
APC	Armored Personnel Carrier used by mechanized infantry units, carries machine guns and an infantry squad
Article 15	Minor offense under code of military justice
ARVN	Army Republic Vietnam
AWOL	Absent without official leave
Ba muoi ba	33. Vietnamese beer, also called panther or "tiger piss
Bee hive round	Artillery round that releases thousands of steel darts
Big Red One	First Infantry Division
Boat people	Immigrants for Vietnam, Cambodia, Laos
Body Bags	Plastic zipper bags for corpses
Boom Boom	Sex
Boonies	Out in the field, jungles, swamps, etc.
Bu-coo	Much or many
Bush, The	Hostile jungle
Butter Bar	Freshly arrived Second Lieutenant
Cao Dai	Religious sect in Tay Ninh area
CAP	Combined Action Platoon
Charlie	Viet Cong
Chieu Hoi	Vietnamese government surrender program

Chinook	Army (CH46 Marine) A large, twin bladed helicopter used for transporting men, materials and used in Medevacs
Cholon	Chinese sector of Saigon
Choppers	Helicopters
Chu Hoi	I surrender
CH-47	Helicopter (Chinook)
CIB	Combat Infantry Badge
Claymores	Mine packed with plastique and rigged to spray hundreds of steel pellets
Click	One kilometer
Cobra	Helicopter gunships heavily armed with rocket launchers and machine guns
Combat Assault	Choppers picking up combat troops to drop into a hot LZ
Concertina Wire	Coiled barbed wire, strung around a perimeter
Corpsman	Navy equivalent to medic in the Army
CP	Command Post
C-Rations	Combat food in cans
C-4	Plastic explosive
C-127	Transport Plane
C-130	Cargo plane used to transport men and supplies
Deuce and a half	Two and one half-ton truck
Di Di Mau	Vietnamese for "Get out of here"
Dinky Dau	To be crazy
Division HQ	Command Headquarters
DAV	Disabled American Veteran
DEROS	Date of estimated returns from overseas
DMZ	Demilitarized Zone
Dong	Vietnamese currency
Dung lai	Halt or stop
Dust Off	Evacuating wounded by helicopter
Early Out	An early ETS (estimated time of terminating service)
Egg beater	Helicopter
Electric Strawberry	25th ID patch with red/yellow taro legs
EM	Enlisted man
Eagle Flight	Combat assault

ETS	Estimated time of terminating service
Fire Base	Reinforced bases established to provide artillery fire support for ground units operating in the bush
Firefight	Gunfire
Fire mission	Artillery mission exchange with the enemy
FNG	F-ing new guy
FO	Forward Observer
Fragging	Killing an American officer by own troops
Freedom Bird	Jet aircraft taking you from Vietnam to the U.S.A.
Free Fire Zone	Area where everyone is deemed hostile
F-4's, F-100's	Jet fighter aircraft
GI	Government issue
Gooks	Slang for the enemy
Greased	Killed
Grunt	Slang for a combat infantry soldier
Gung Ho	Military enthusiastic
Gunship	Armed helicopter
G-2	Division intelligence
G-3	Division operations
Hamlet	Cluster of homes; several make a village
Hanoi Hannah	Tokyo rose of Vietnam
Heads	Those who were potheads
Hoi Chanh	Returnees under Chieu Hoi program
Hooch/Hootch	Slang for any form of dwelling place (living quarters)
Hot LZ	Landing zone under fire
Howitzers	Large cannon
Huey	Helicopter used for transporting troops; Med-evacs
Humping	Slang for marching with a heavy load through the bush.
HQ	Headquarters
Incoming	Receiving enemy mortar or rocket fire
In-Country	In Vietnam
Iron Triangle	Viet Cong dominated area near Cu Chi
Jody	Guy back home who had your girl while you were in Nam
KIA	Killed in action

Klick, Click	One kilometer (0.62137 mile)
Koonza	Marijuana
Lai day	Come here
La Vay	Beer
LAW	Light Antitank Weapon
LBJ	Long Binh Jail
Lifer	Career man in the military for life
Lock & Load	Chambering a sound invasion
LP	Listening Post
LRRP	Long Range Reconnaissance Patrol
LT	Lieutenant
LZ	Landing Zone
MACV	Military assistance Command, Vietnam
MAYDAY	Distress signal
Medic	Field doctor
Medi/Medivac	Medically evacuating the wounded by chopper or plane
MIA	Missing in action
Million Dollar Wound	Just bad enough to get out of the bush, but not serious
Mona	Rain
Monday pills	Anti-Malaria pills
Monsoon	The rainy season in Nam
MOS	Military occupational specialty
MP	Military Police
MPC	Military Payment Certificate
MRE	C-rations
M-14	Rifle used before M-16
M-16	Standard automatic weapon used by American ground forces
M60	A machine gun used by American combat units
M-79	Grenade launcher used by infantry
NAM	Vietnam
Napalm	Jelly like substance in bombs – burns everything it contacts
NCO	Noncommissioned officers E5 to E9
NDP	Night Defensive Position
NLF	Regulars National Liberation Front – Communists

Num bah-one G.I.	Big spending soldier
Num bah-ten G.I.	Not a big spender
Num bah-ten thou G.I.	The worst spender
NVA	North Vietnamese Army
OCS	Officers Candidate School
Ordinance	Bombs or rockets
Over the Fence	Crossing into Cambodia
Papa Sierra	Slang for platoon sergeant
PAVN	Peoples Army of Vietnam
PBR	Patrol Boat Riverine
Phantom	A jet fighter (F-4)
Piastres	Vietnamese currency
Pointman	The lead man on a patrol through the bush
Pop Smoke	Mark a position with smoke grenade
PRC25 / PRICK25	Portable radio for ground troops
Puff	A C-47gunship armed with mini-machine guns: "Puff the Magic Dragon"
Punji Stick	Booby trap with pointed bamboo stakes pointing up
P-38	Can opener worn with dog tag
PX	Post exchange
RA	Regular army
Ranger	Specially trained airborne soldier
REAL LIFE	Civilian life
Recon	Reconnaissance
Reconnaissance-In Force	Replaced the former term of Search and Destroy in the 1967-1968 timeframe
Red LZ	Landing zone under attack
Rock N' Roll	Full automatic on an M-16
ROK	Republic of Korea ground troops
RPM	Resolutions per minute
RPG	Rocket propelled grenade
R&R	Rest and relaxation
RRF	Ready Reaction Force
RSVN	Republic of South Vietnam

RTO	Radio-telephone operator
Rucks	Backpacks
Ruff Puff	Regional/popular forces of South Vietnamese militia. Usually poorly trained and equipped, not effective in severe combat situations
Saddle Up	Load up, get ready to march
Saigon Cowboys	Officers and non coms working in base camps or large cities
Sampan	Vietnamese peasant boat
Sappers	Viet Cong infiltrators with explosive charges attached to their bodies
Satchel Charges	Explosive packs carried by VC sappers
Search & Destroy	Search for enemy and kill them
Sgt.	Abbreviation for Sergeant
Short	You were close to the end of your tour in Vietnam
Sin loi minoi	Sorry about that, honey
Sitrep	Situation report by radio
SK's	A Russian carbine
Slick	Huey chopper
SOP	Standard Operating Procedure
Spider Hole	Hole used by enemy for main entrance to tunnel complex
Spooky	Plane with electric mini-guns
Swift boat	Navy patrol boat used for coastal rivers
TDY	Temporary duty
TET	Southeast Asia Lunar New Year
The World	Home – U.S.A.
Ti ti	Small, insignificant
TOC	Tactical Office Command Post
TOP	Company first sergeant
Tracer	A bullet with a phosphorus coating designed to burn and provide a visual indication of the bullet's trajectory
TRAKS	Tanks or armored personnel carrier (APC)
VC	Viet Cong
Viet Cong	The local militias fighting Americans in South Vietnam
VFW	Veterans of Foreign War
Wart Hog	Air Force A10 fighter/bomber
WIA	Wounded in action

Your Six	I have your back
XO	Executive Officer
105mm	Howitzer cannon size
81mm	Mortar shell
50 Cal	Heavy duty machine gun
51 Caliber	Comparable to 50 caliber, used by enemy forces

CPSIA information can be obtained at www.ICGtesting.com
Printed in the USA
BVOW09s1546120715

408385BV00003B/43/P

9 781498 429764